JONAH HEX:
NO WAY BACK

JONAH HEX

NO WAY BACK

Writers:
Justin Gray
and
Jimmy Palmiotti

Penciller:
Tony DeZuniga

Inkers:
Tony DeZuniga
and
John Stanisci

Colorist:
Rob Schwager

Letterer:
Rob Leigh

Special thanks to
Rodney Ramos

Elisabeth V. Gehrlein Editor
Robbin Brosterman Design Director – Books
Louis Prandi Art Director

DC COMICS
Diane Nelson President
Dan DiDio and **Jim Lee** Co-Publishers
Geoff Johns Chief Creative Officer
Patrick Caldon EVP-Finance and Administration
John Rood EVP-Sales, Marketing and Business Development
Karen Berger SVP-Executive Editor, Vertigo
Mark Chiarello Art Director
Amy Genkins SVP-Business and Legal Affairs
Steve Rotterdam SVP-Sales and Marketing
John Cunningham VP-Marketing
Terri Cunningham VP-Managing Editor
Alison Gill VP-Manufacturing
David Hyde VP-Publicity
Sue Pohja VP-Book Trade Sales
Alysse Soll VP-Advertising and Custom Publishing
Bob Wayne VP-Sales

DC Comics, 1700 Broadway, New York, NY 10019
A Warner Bros. Entertainment Company. First Printing.
Printed in the USA.
HC ISBN: 978-1-4012-2550-6
SC ISBN: 978-1-4012-2551-3

SUSTAINABLE
FORESTRY
INITIATIVE
Certified Chain of Custody
Promoting Sustainable
Forest Management
www.sfiprogram.org

Fiber used in this product line meets the
sourcing requirements of the SFI program
www.sfiprogram.org NFS-SPICOC-C0001801

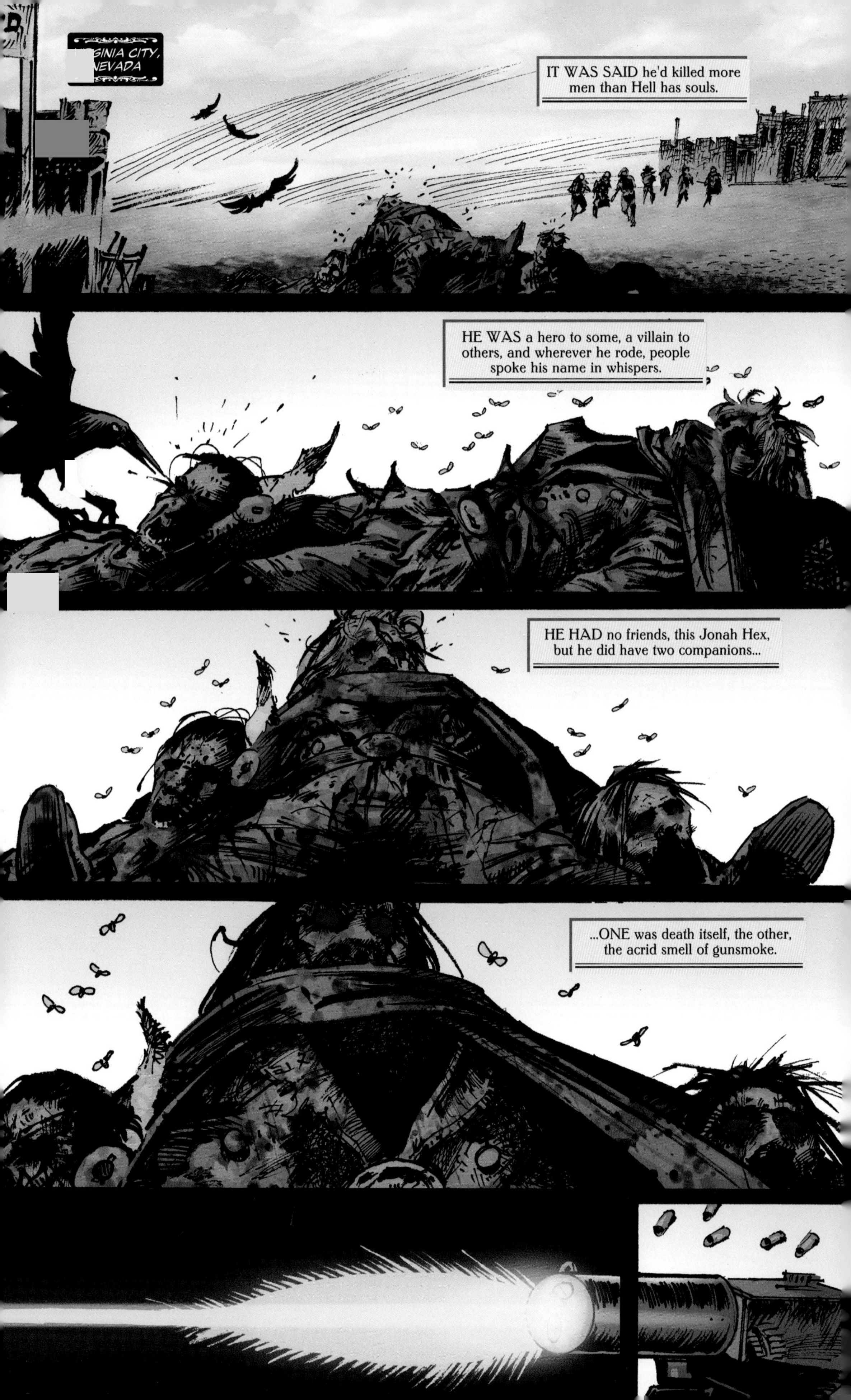
GINIA CITY,
EVADA
IT WAS SAID he'd killed more men than Hell has souls.
HE WAS a hero to some, a villain to others, and wherever he rode, people spoke his name in whispers.
HE HAD no friends, this Jonah Hex, but he did have two companions...
...ONE was death itself, the other, the acrid smell of gunsmoke.

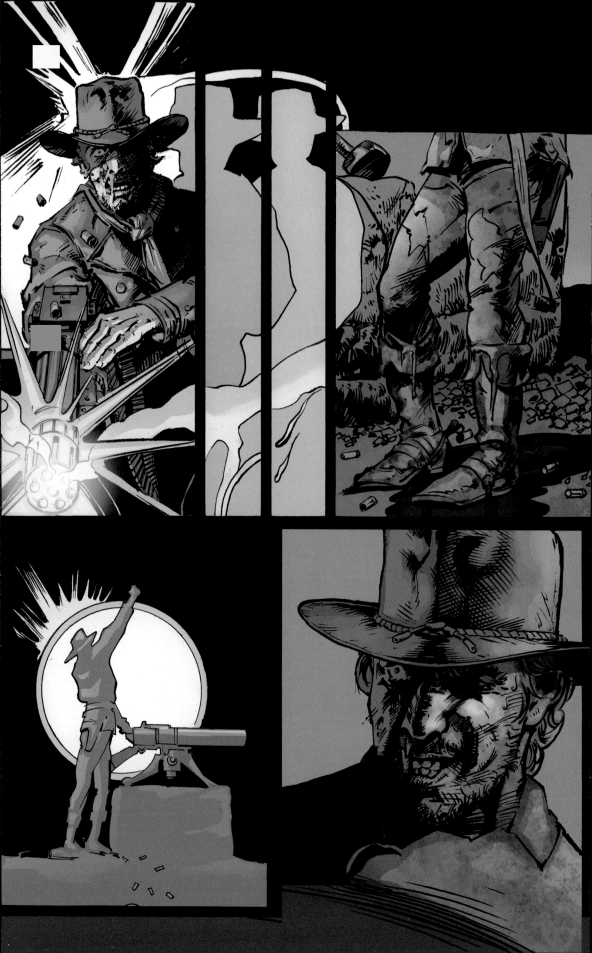

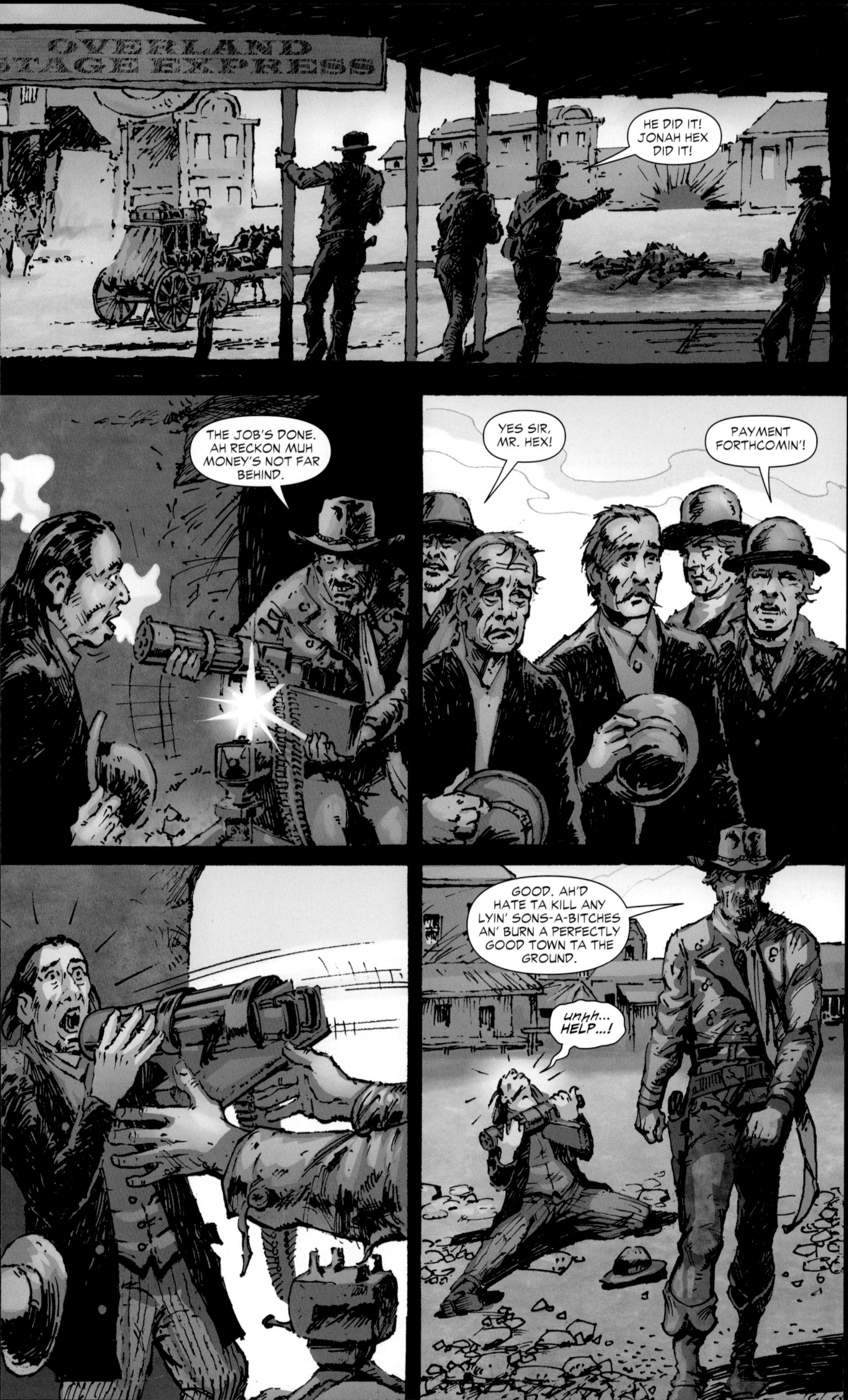
OVERLAND
STAGE EXPRESS
HE DID IT! JONAH HEX DID IT!
THE JOB'S DONE. AH RECKON MUH MONEY'S NOT FAR BEHIND.
YES SIR, MR. HEX!
PAYMENT FORTHCOMIN'!
GOOD. AH'D HATE TA KILL ANY LYIN' SONS-A-BITCHES AN' BURN A PERFECTLY GOOD TOWN TA THE GROUND.
unhh... HELP...!

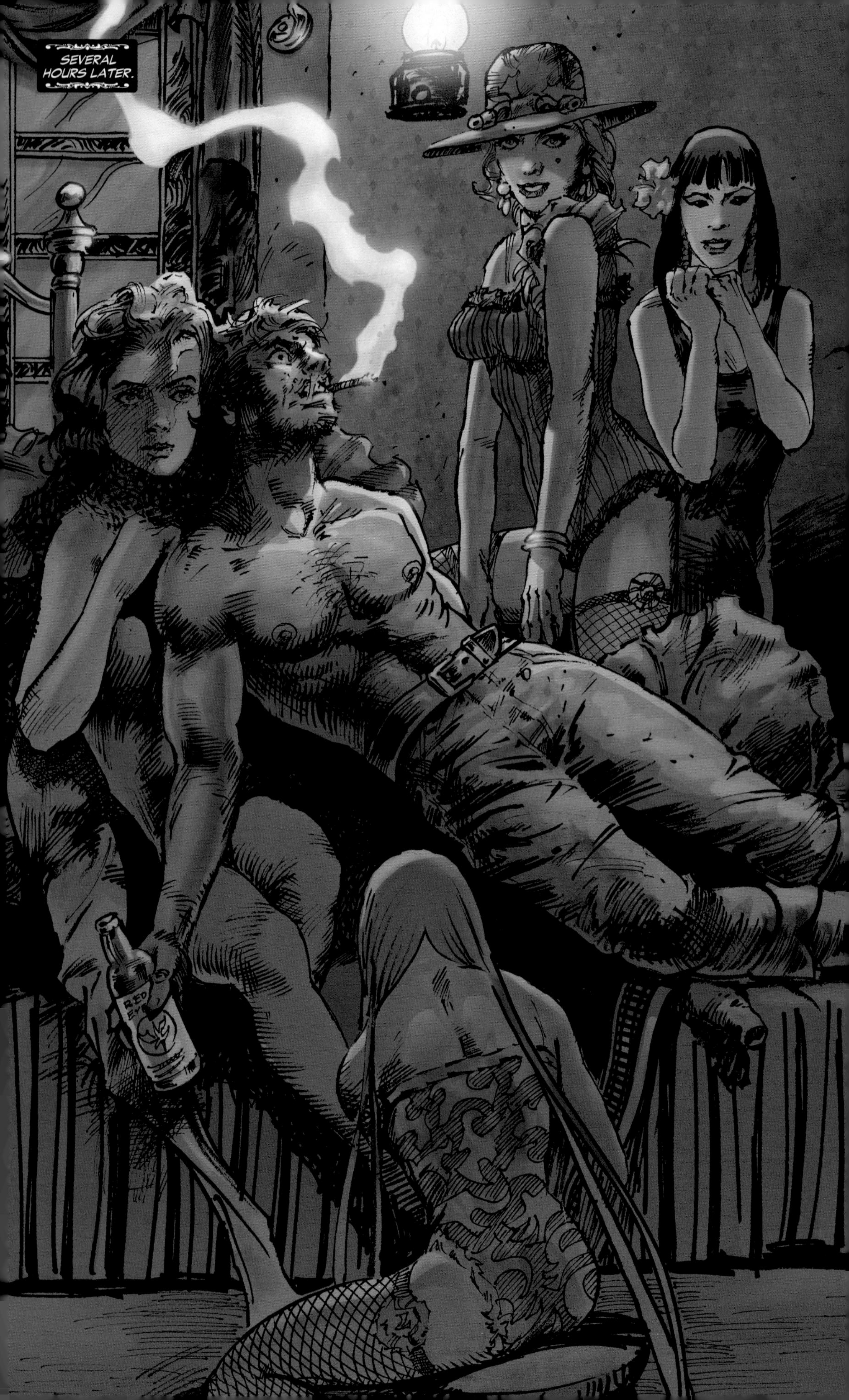
SEVERAL HOURS LATER.

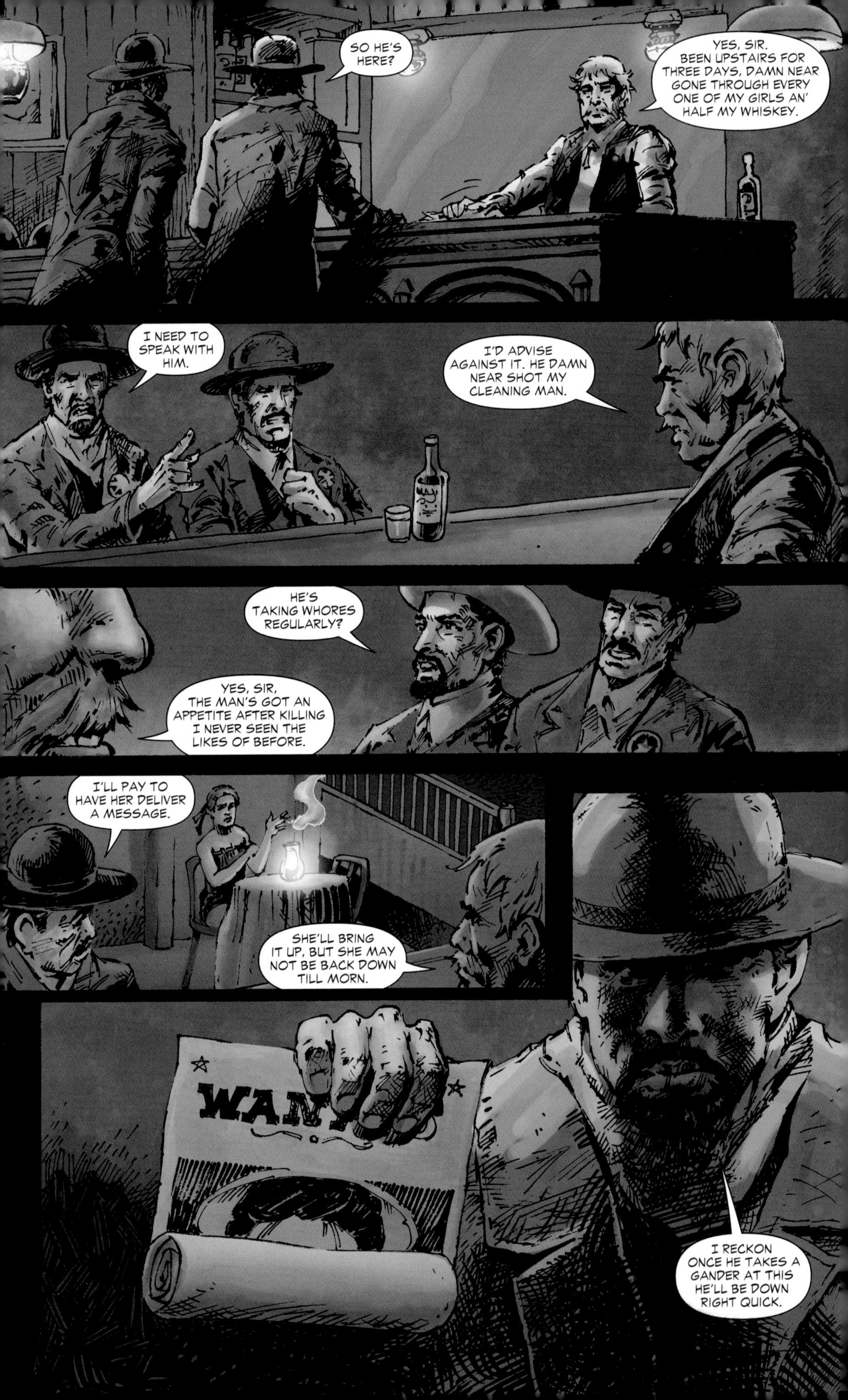
SO HE'S HERE?
YES, SIR. BEEN UPSTAIRS FOR THREE DAYS, DAMN NEAR GONE THROUGH EVERY ONE OF MY GIRLS AN' HALF MY WHISKEY.
I NEED TO SPEAK WITH HIM.
I'D ADVISE AGAINST IT. HE DAMN NEAR SHOT MY CLEANING MAN.
HE'S TAKING WHORES REGULARLY?
YES, SIR, THE MAN'S GOT AN APPETITE AFTER KILLING I NEVER SEEN THE LIKES OF BEFORE.
I'LL PAY TO HAVE HER DELIVER A MESSAGE.
SHE'LL BRING IT UP, BUT SHE MAY NOT BE BACK DOWN TILL MORN.
I RECKON ONCE HE TAKES A GANDER AT THIS HE'LL BE DOWN RIGHT QUICK.

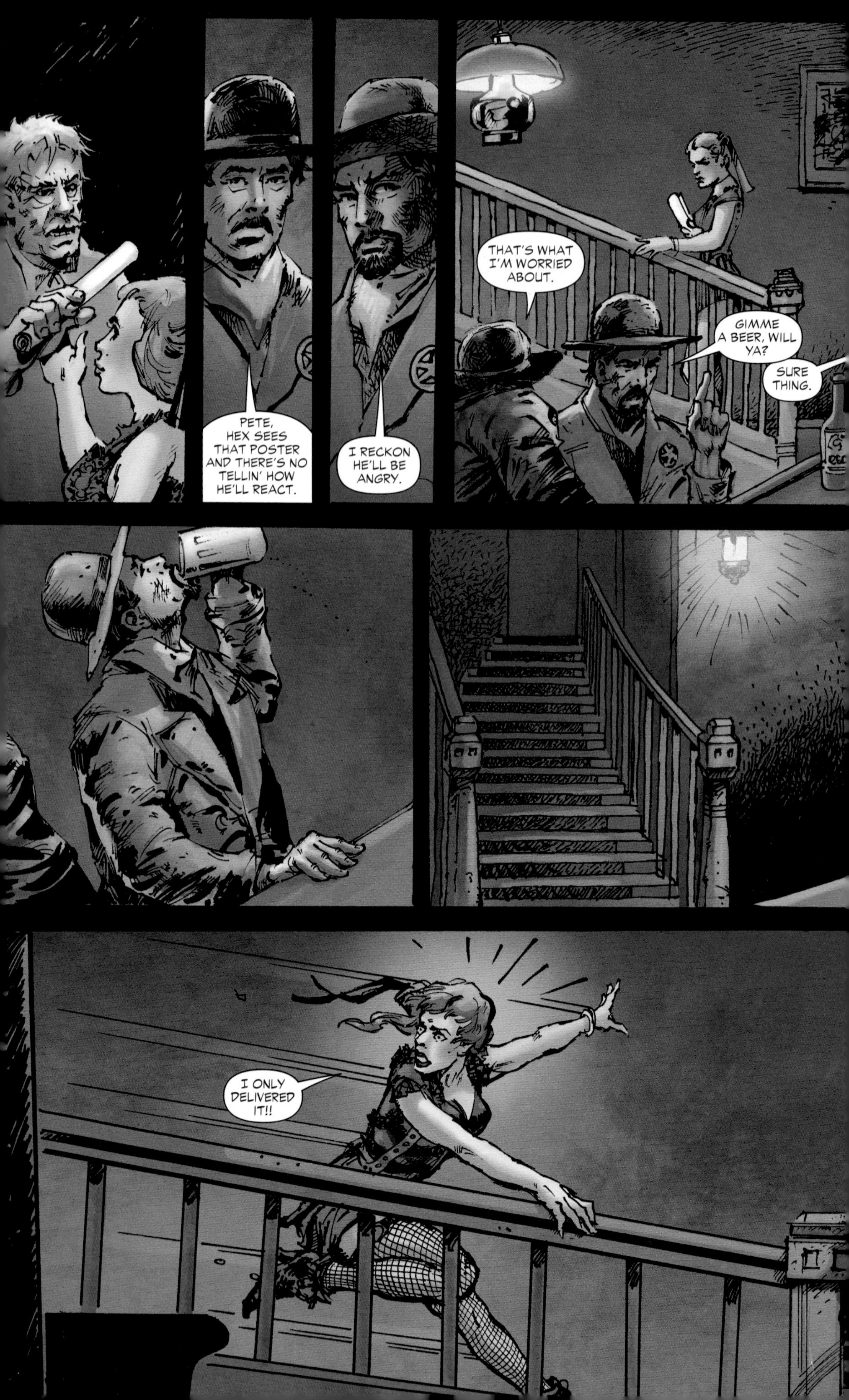
PETE, HEX SEES THAT POSTER AND THERE'S NO TELLIN' HOW HE'LL REACT.
I RECKON HE'LL BE ANGRY.
THAT'S WHAT I'M WORRIED ABOUT.
GIMME A BEER, WILL YA?
SURE THING.
I ONLY DELIVERED IT!!

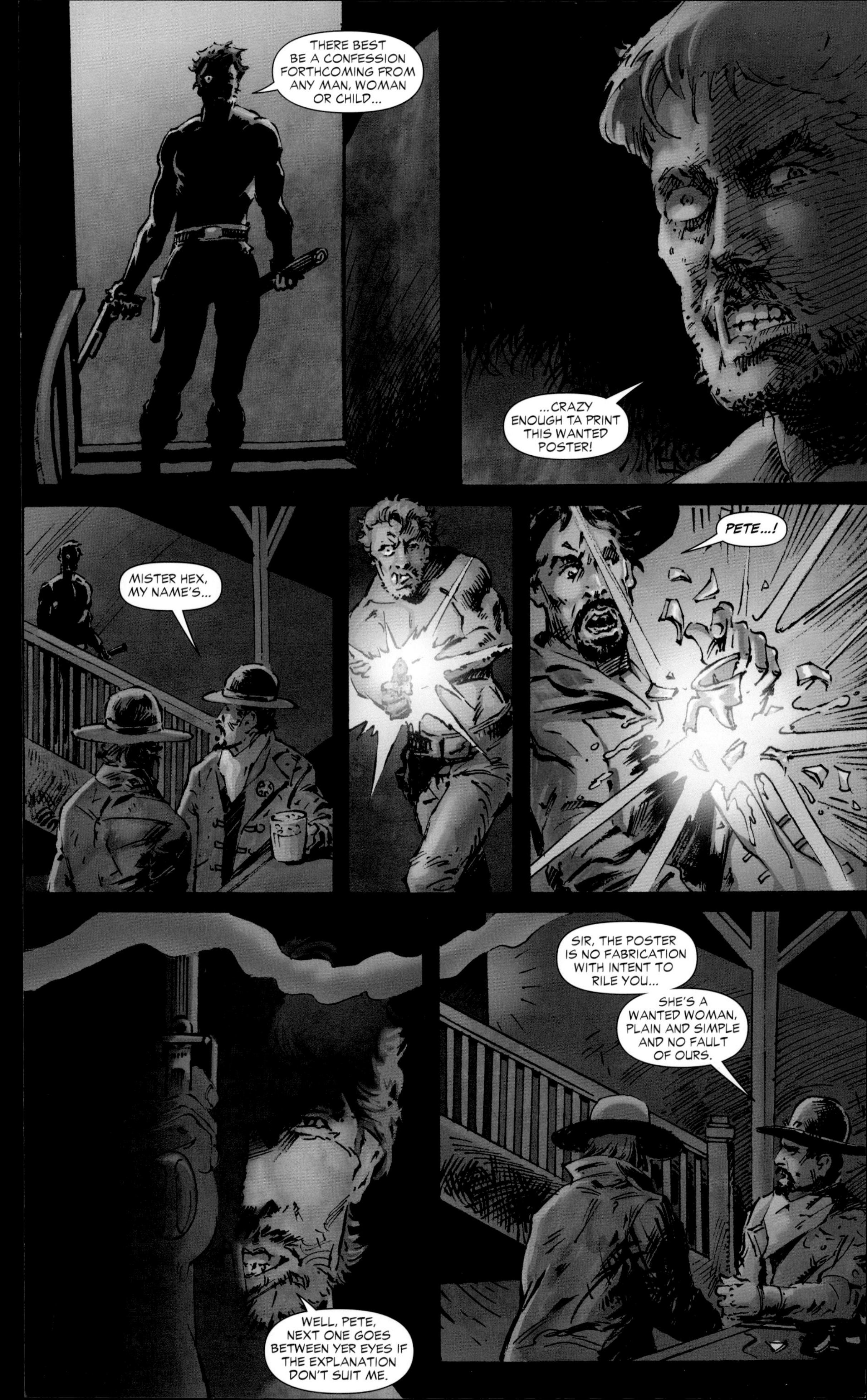
THERE BEST BE A CONFESSION FORTHCOMING FROM ANY MAN, WOMAN OR CHILD...
...CRAZY ENOUGH TA PRINT THIS WANTED POSTER!
MISTER HEX, MY NAME'S...
PETE...!
SIR, THE POSTER IS NO FABRICATION WITH INTENT TO RILE YOU...
SHE'S A WANTED WOMAN, PLAIN AND SIMPLE AND NO FAULT OF OURS.
WELL, PETE, NEXT ONE GOES BETWEEN YER EYES IF THE EXPLANATION DON'T SUIT ME.

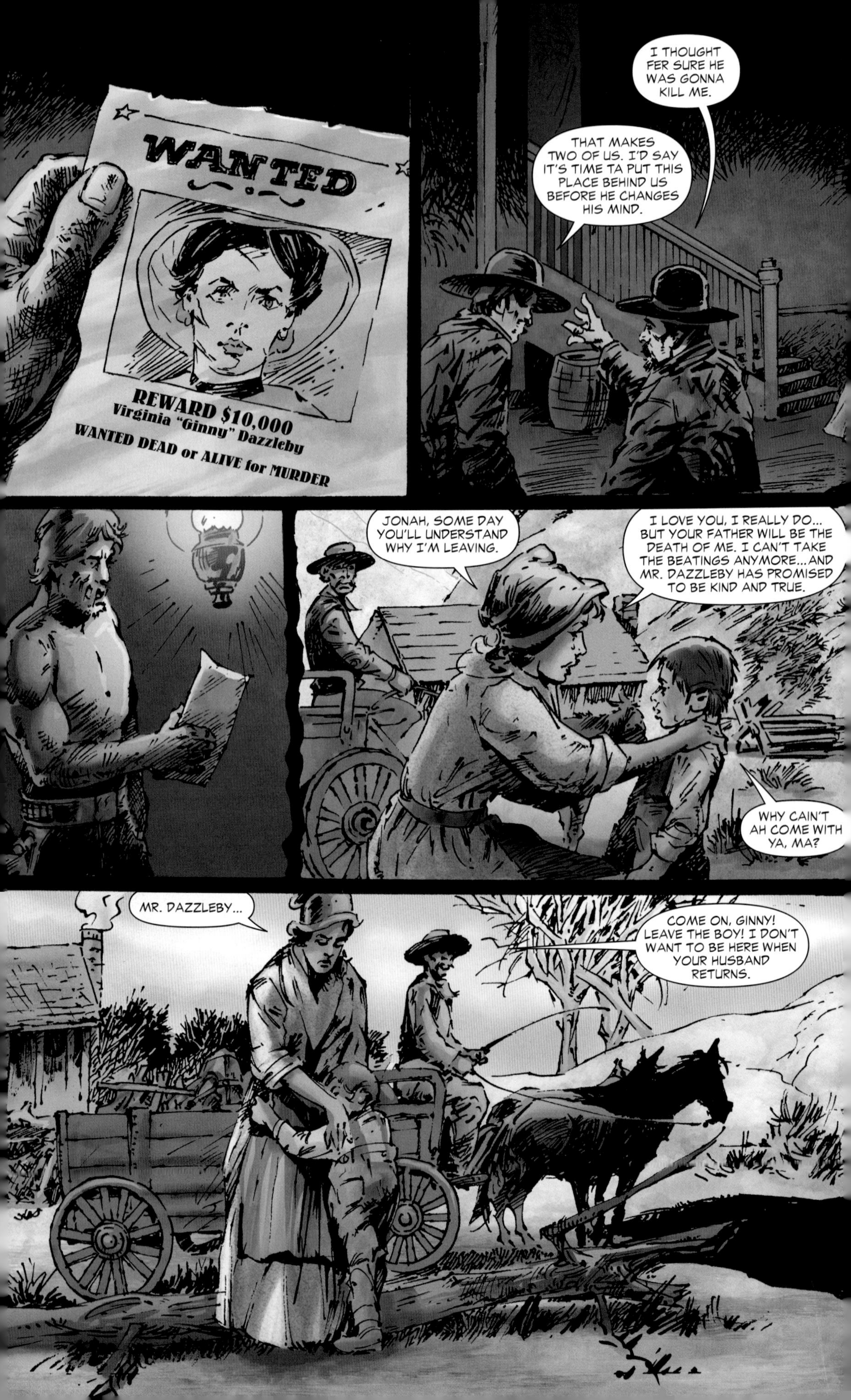
WANTED
REWARD $10,000
Virginia "Ginny" Dazzleby
WANTED DEAD or ALIVE for MURDER
I THOUGHT FER SURE HE WAS GONNA KILL ME.
THAT MAKES TWO OF US. I'D SAY IT'S TIME TA PUT THIS PLACE BEHIND US BEFORE HE CHANGES HIS MIND.
JONAH, SOME DAY YOU'LL UNDERSTAND WHY I'M LEAVING.
I LOVE YOU, I REALLY DO... BUT YOUR FATHER WILL BE THE DEATH OF ME. I CAN'T TAKE THE BEATINGS ANYMORE...AND MR. DAZZLEBY HAS PROMISED TO BE KIND AND TRUE.
WHY CAIN'T AH COME WITH YA, MA?
MR. DAZZLEBY...
COME ON, GINNY! LEAVE THE BOY! I DON'T WANT TO BE HERE WHEN YOUR HUSBAND RETURNS.

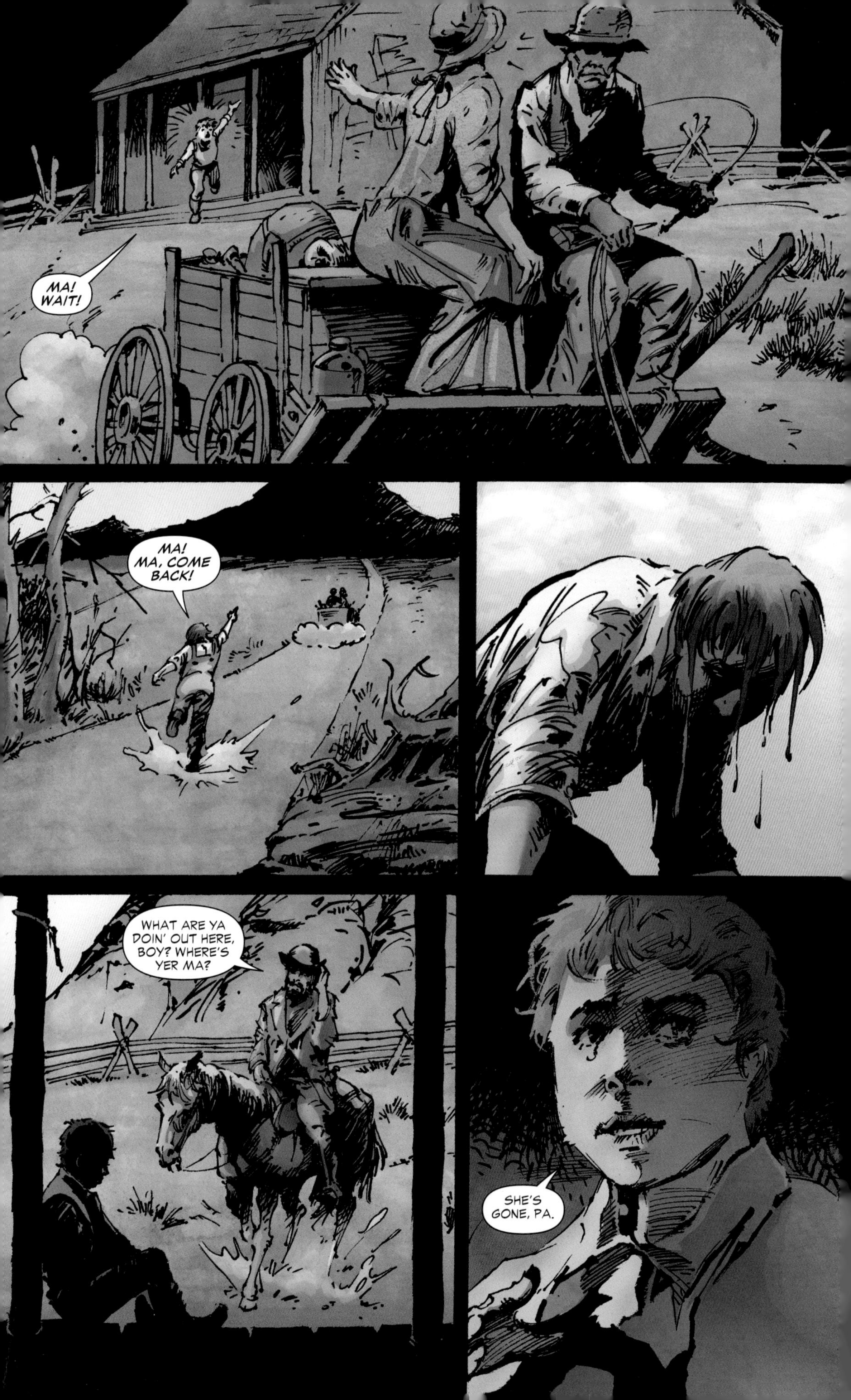
MA! WAIT!
MA! MA, COME BACK!
WHAT ARE YA DOIN' OUT HERE, BOY? WHERE'S YER MA?
SHE'S GONE, PA.

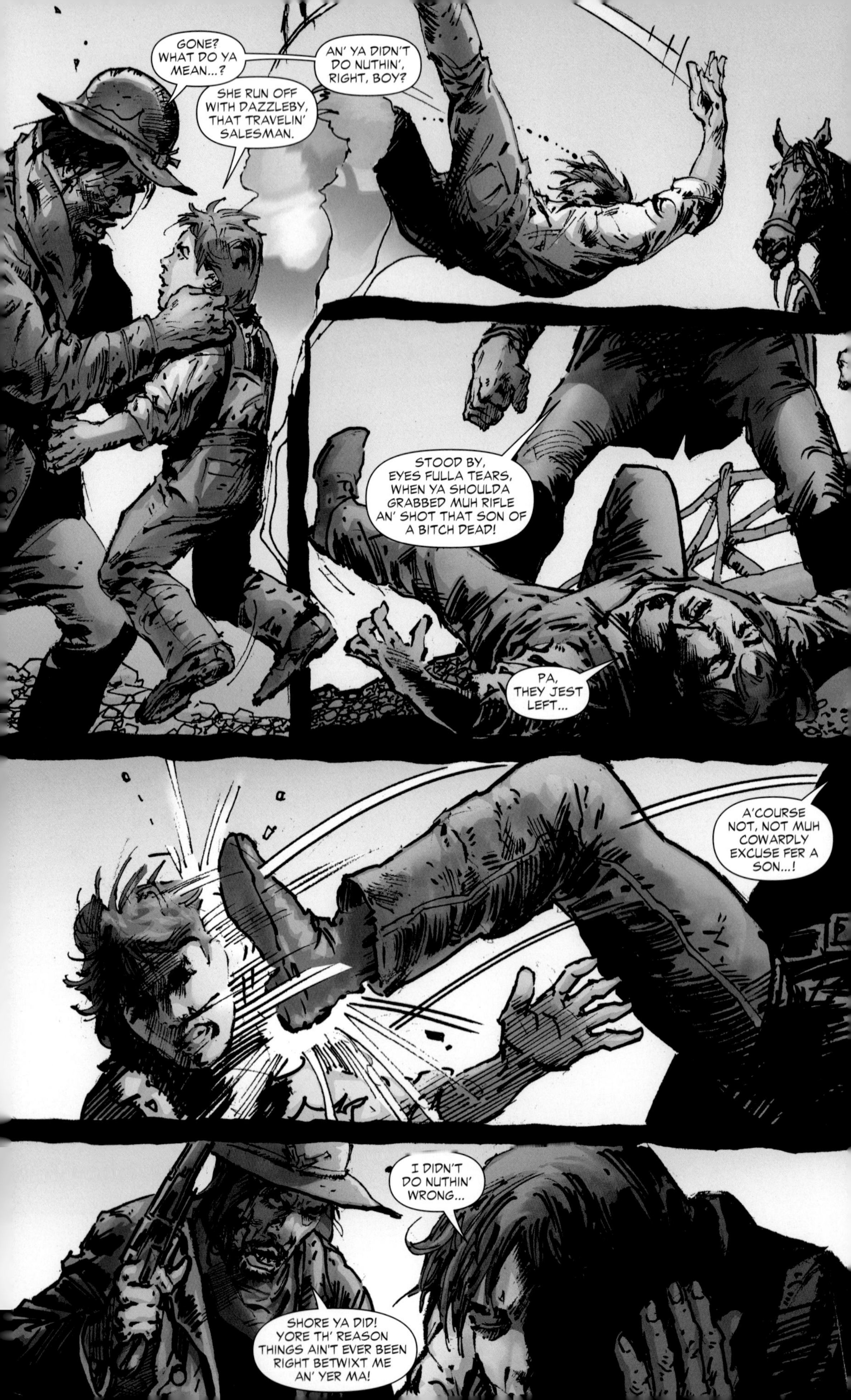
GONE? WHAT DO YA MEAN...?
SHE RUN OFF WITH DAZZLEBY, THAT TRAVELIN' SALESMAN.
AN' YA DIDN'T DO NUTHIN', RIGHT, BOY?
STOOD BY, EYES FULLA TEARS, WHEN YA SHOULDA GRABBED MUH RIFLE AN' SHOT THAT SON OF A BITCH DEAD!
PA, THEY JEST LEFT...
A'COURSE NOT, NOT MUH COWARDLY EXCUSE FER A SON...!
I DIDN'T DO NUTHIN' WRONG...
SHORE YA DID! YORE TH' REASON THINGS AIN'T EVER BEEN RIGHT BETWIXT ME AN' YER MA!

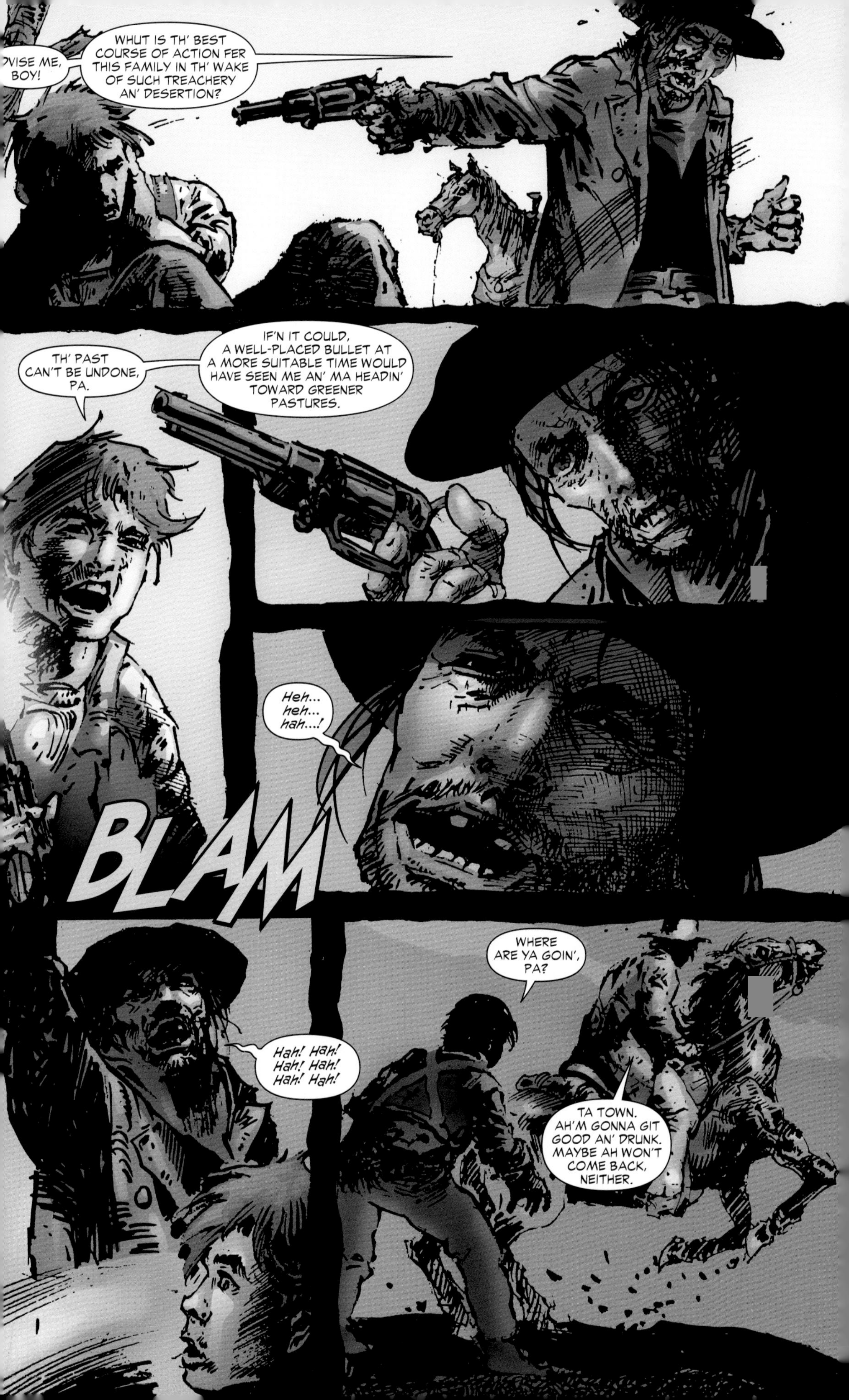

...VISE ME, BOY!
WHUT IS TH' BEST COURSE OF ACTION FER THIS FAMILY IN TH' WAKE OF SUCH TREACHERY AN' DESERTION?
TH' PAST CAN'T BE UNDONE, PA.
IF'N IT COULD, A WELL-PLACED BULLET AT A MORE SUITABLE TIME WOULD HAVE SEEN ME AN' MA HEADIN' TOWARD GREENER PASTURES.
Heh... heh... hah...!
BLAM
Hah! Hah! Hah! Hah! Hah! Hah!
WHERE ARE YA GOIN', PA?
TA TOWN. AH'M GONNA GIT GOOD AN' DRUNK. MAYBE AH WON'T COME BACK, NEITHER.

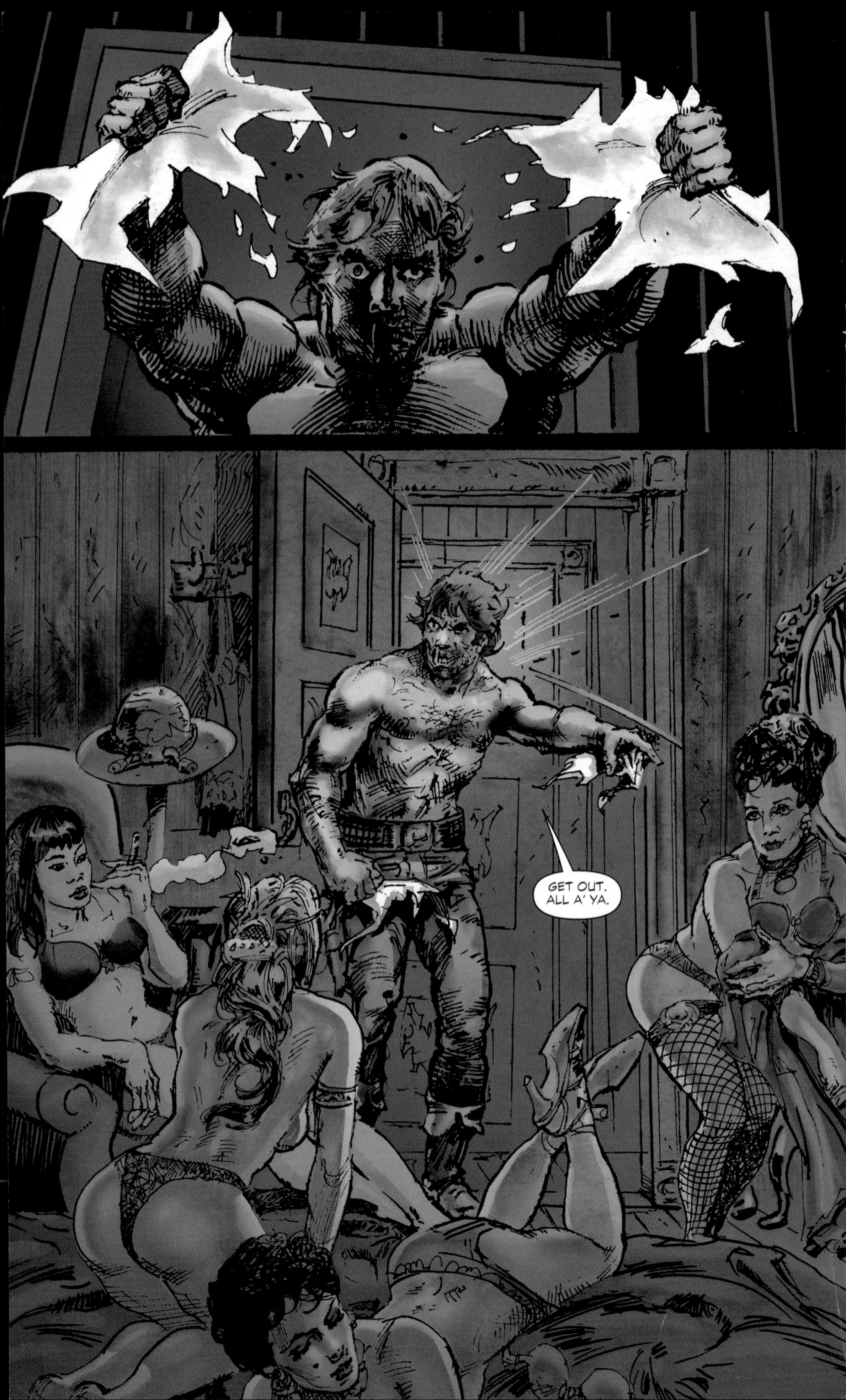
GET OUT. ALL A' YA.

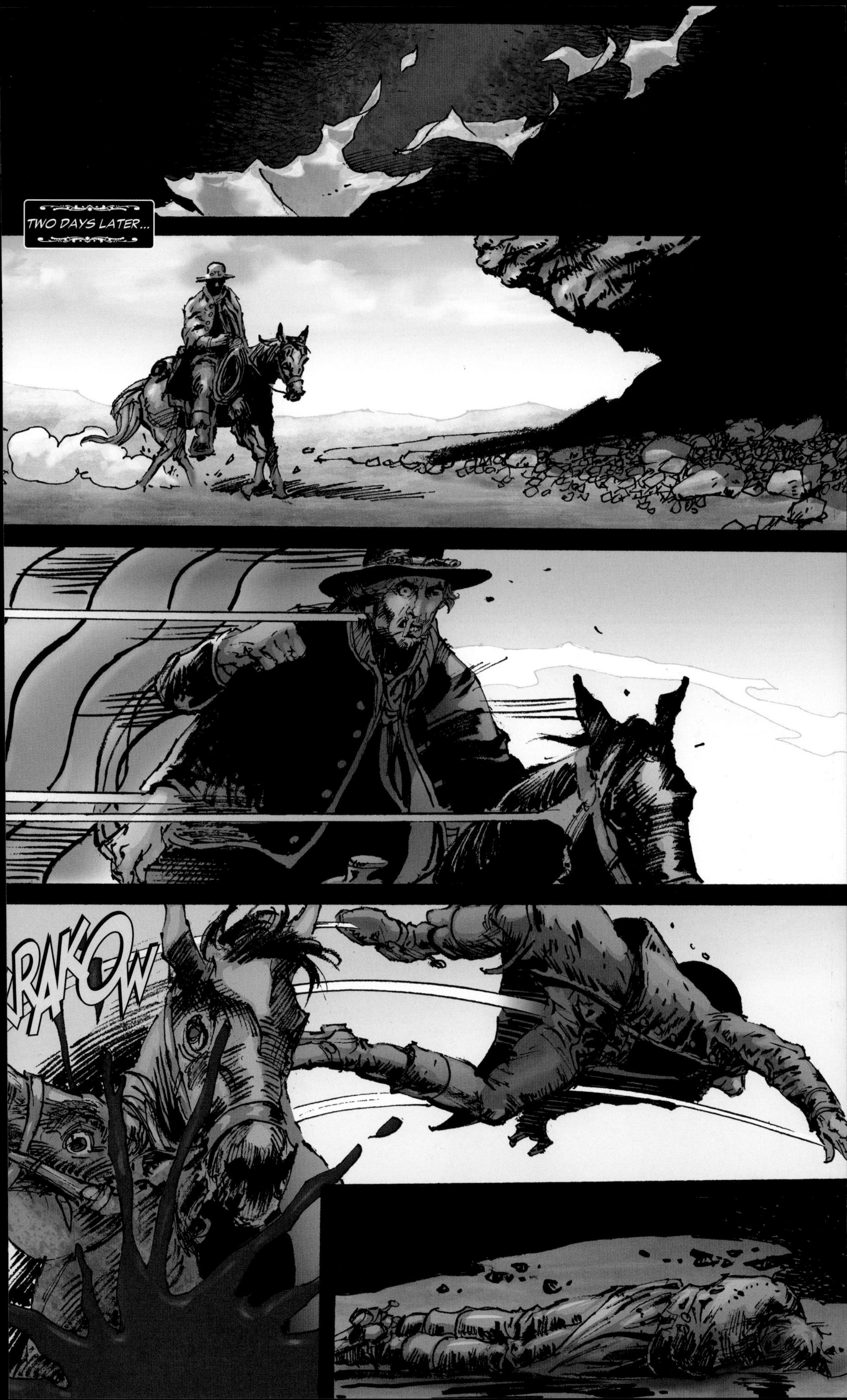
TWO DAYS LATER...
RAKOW

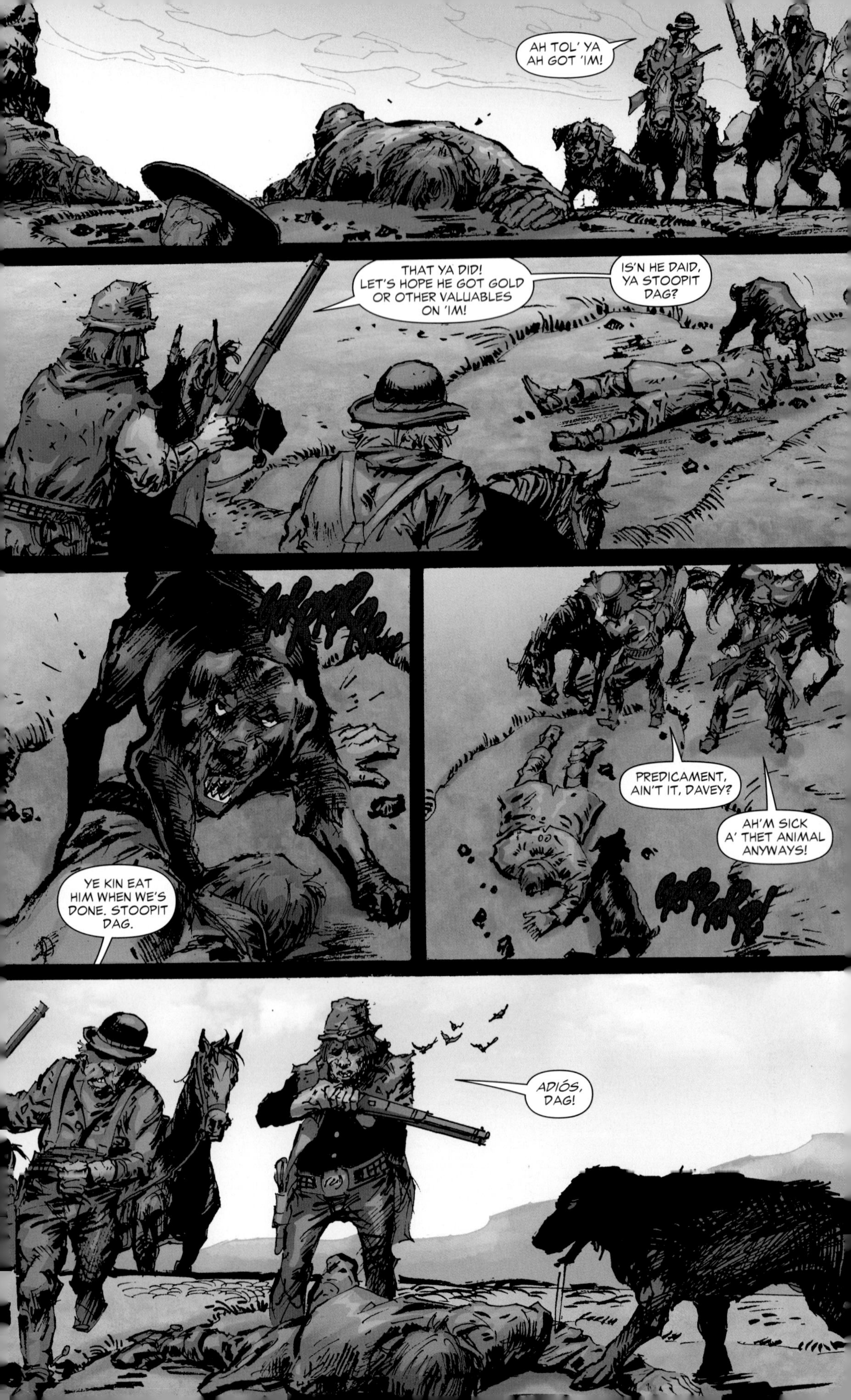
AH TOL' YA AH GOT 'IM!
THAT YA DID! LET'S HOPE HE GOT GOLD OR OTHER VALUABLES ON 'IM!
IS'N HE DAID, YA STOOPIT DAG?
YE KIN EAT HIM WHEN WE'S DONE. STOOPIT DAG.
PREDICAMENT, AIN'T IT, DAVEY?
AH'M SICK A' THET ANIMAL ANYWAYS!
ADIÓS, DAG!

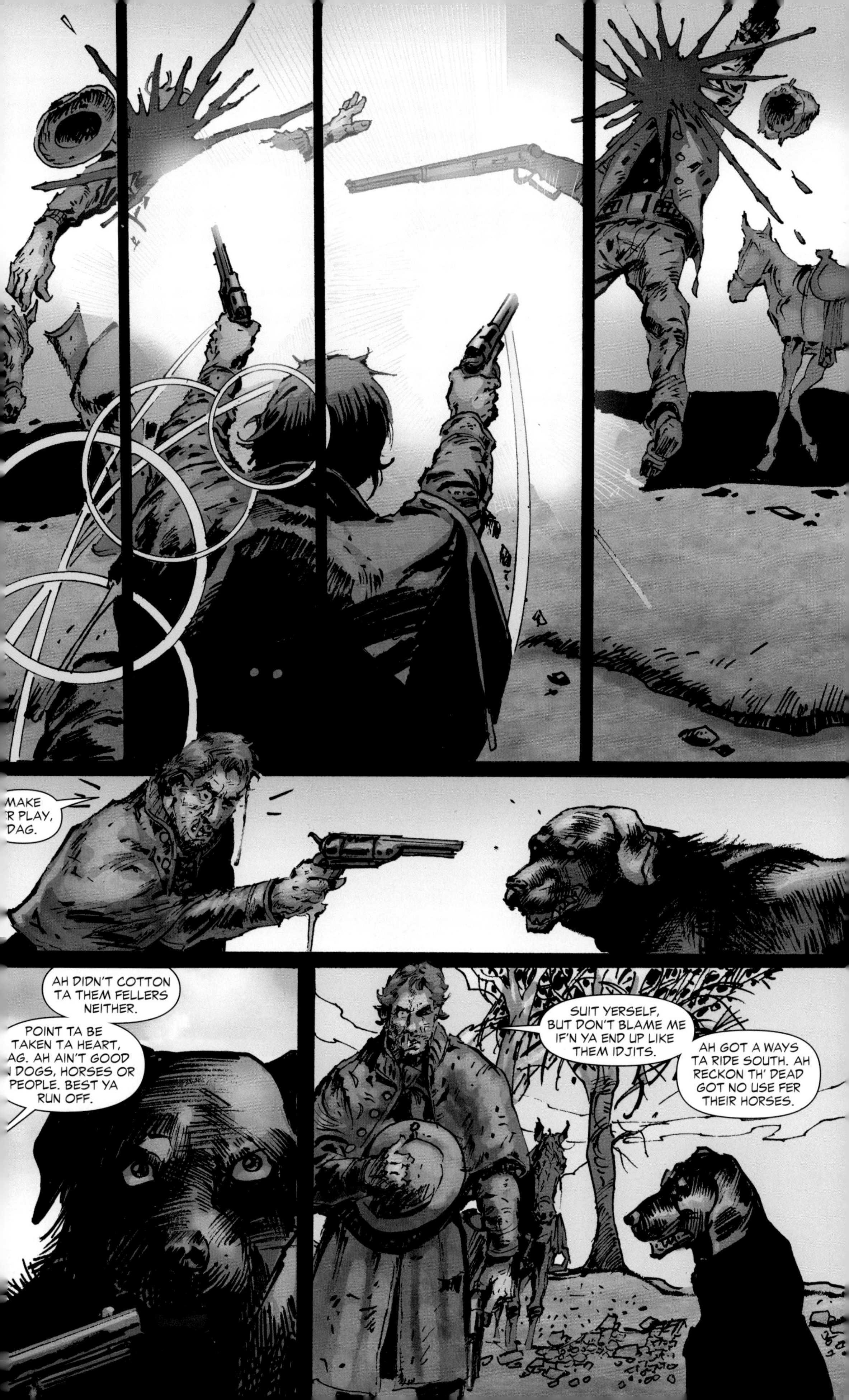
MAKE
R PLAY,
DAG.
AH DIDN'T COTTON TA THEM FELLERS NEITHER.
POINT TA BE TAKEN TA HEART, AG. AH AIN'T GOOD N DOGS, HORSES OR PEOPLE. BEST YA RUN OFF.
SUIT YERSELF, BUT DON'T BLAME ME IF'N YA END UP LIKE THEM IDJITS.
AH GOT A WAYS TA RIDE SOUTH. AH RECKON TH' DEAD GOT NO USE FER THEIR HORSES.

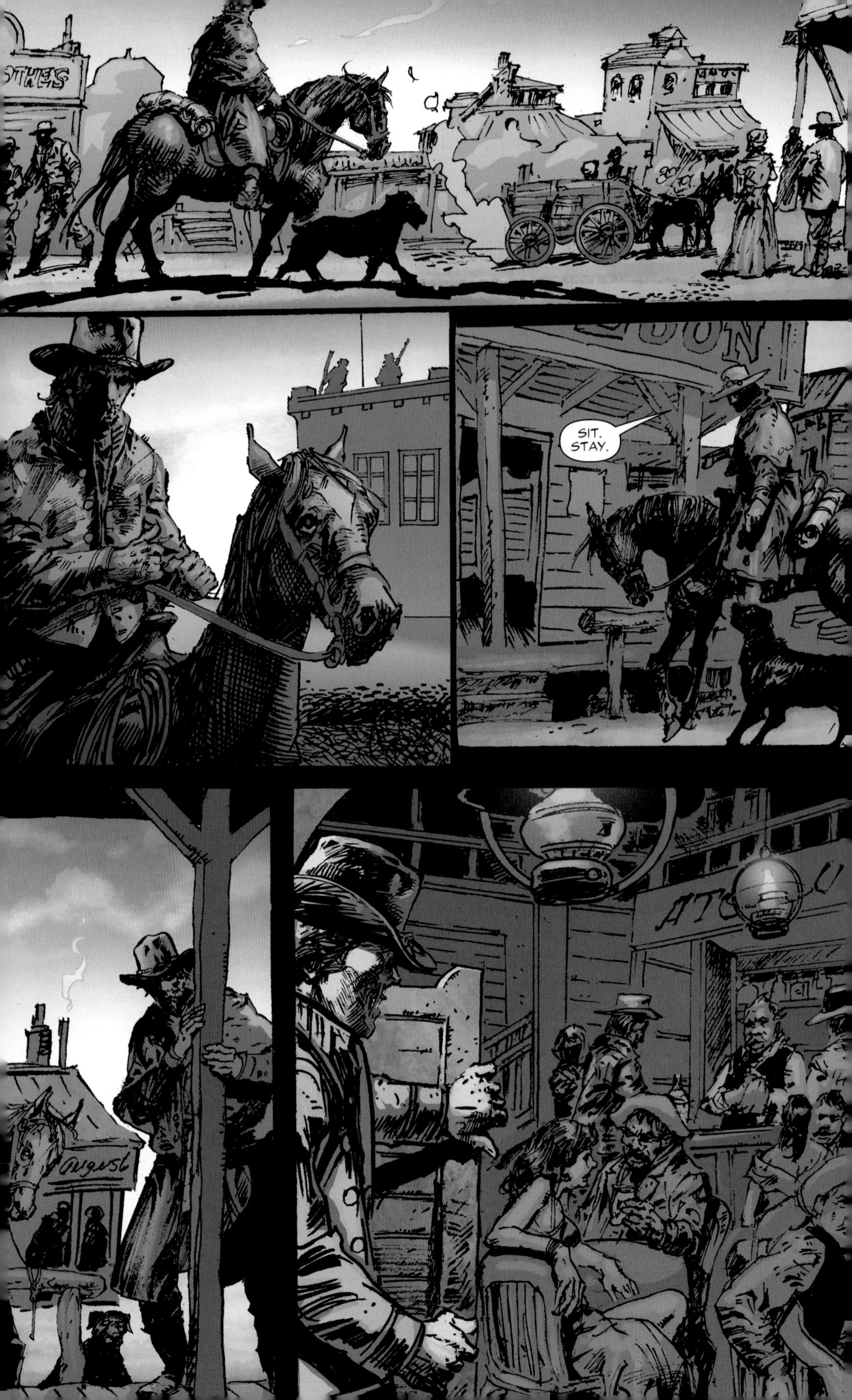
SIT. STAY.

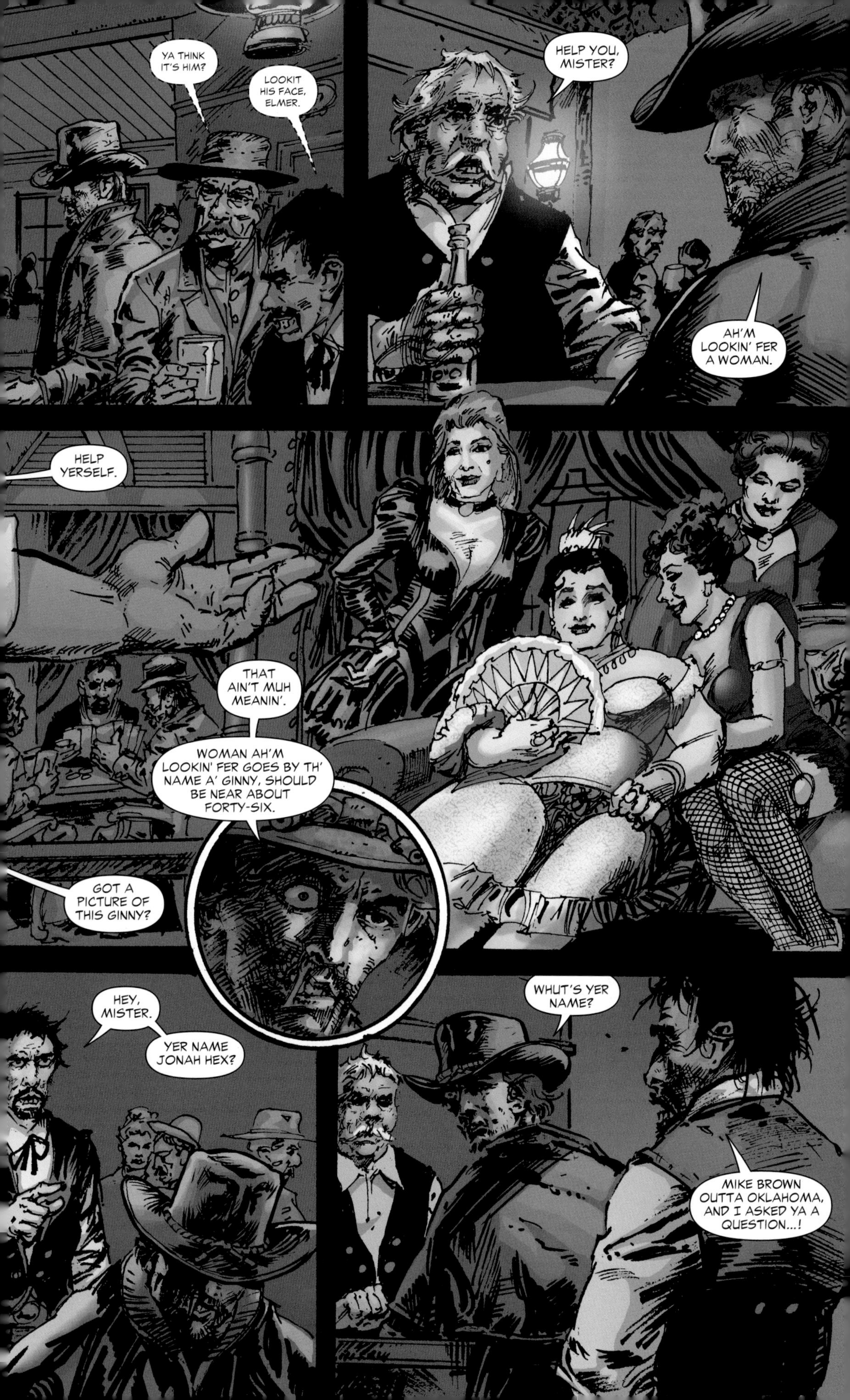
YA THINK IT'S HIM?
LOOKIT HIS FACE, ELMER.
HELP YOU, MISTER?
AH'M LOOKIN' FER A WOMAN.
HELP YERSELF.
THAT AIN'T MUH MEANIN'.
WOMAN AH'M LOOKIN' FER GOES BY TH' NAME A' GINNY, SHOULD BE NEAR ABOUT FORTY-SIX.
GOT A PICTURE OF THIS GINNY?
HEY, MISTER.
YER NAME JONAH HEX?
WHUT'S YER NAME?
MIKE BROWN OUTTA OKLAHOMA, AND I ASKED YA A QUESTION...!

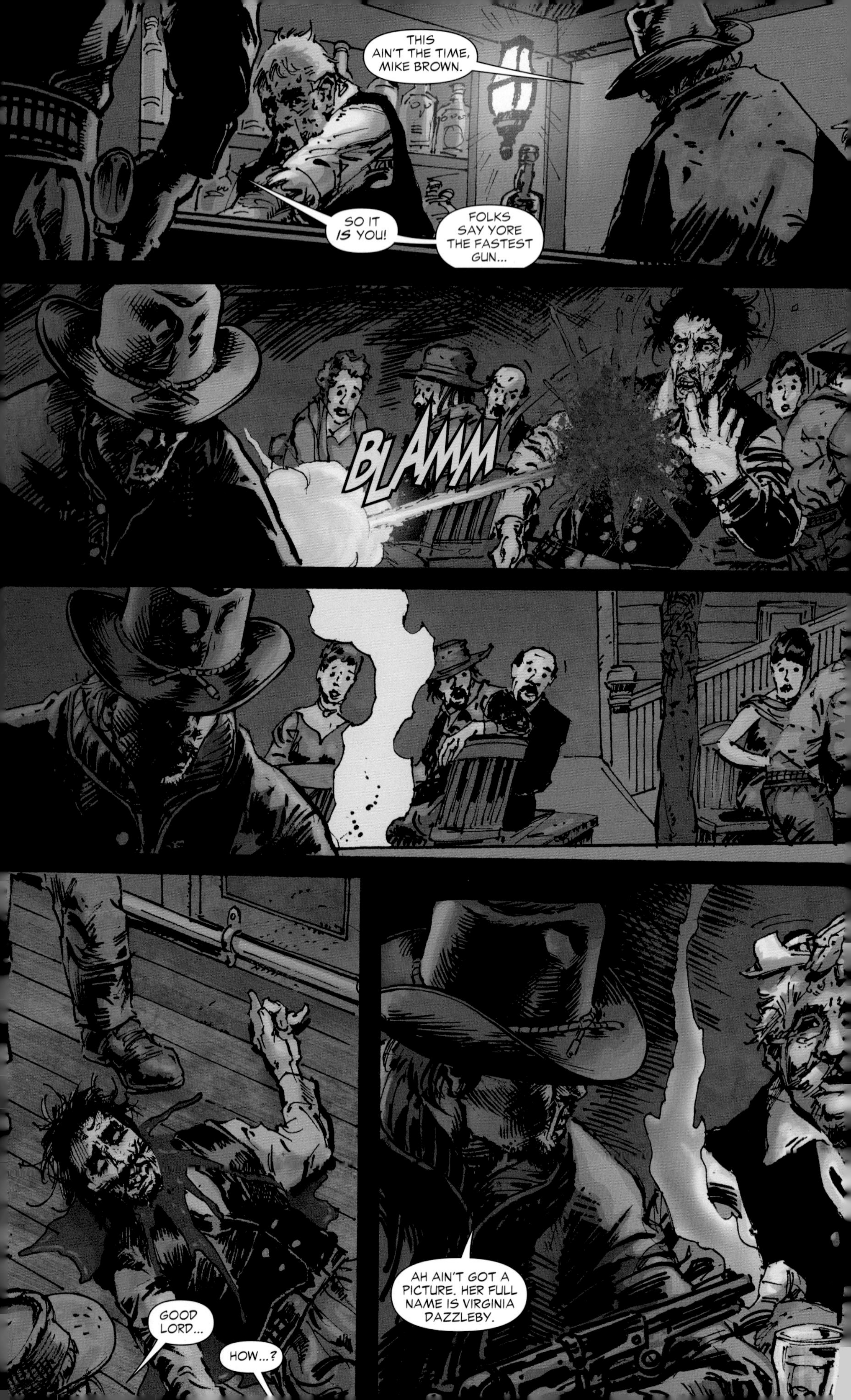
THIS AIN'T THE TIME, MIKE BROWN.
SO IT *IS* YOU!
FOLKS SAY YORE THE FASTEST GUN...
BLAMM
GOOD LORD...
HOW...?
AH AIN'T GOT A PICTURE. HER FULL NAME IS VIRGINIA DAZZLEBY.

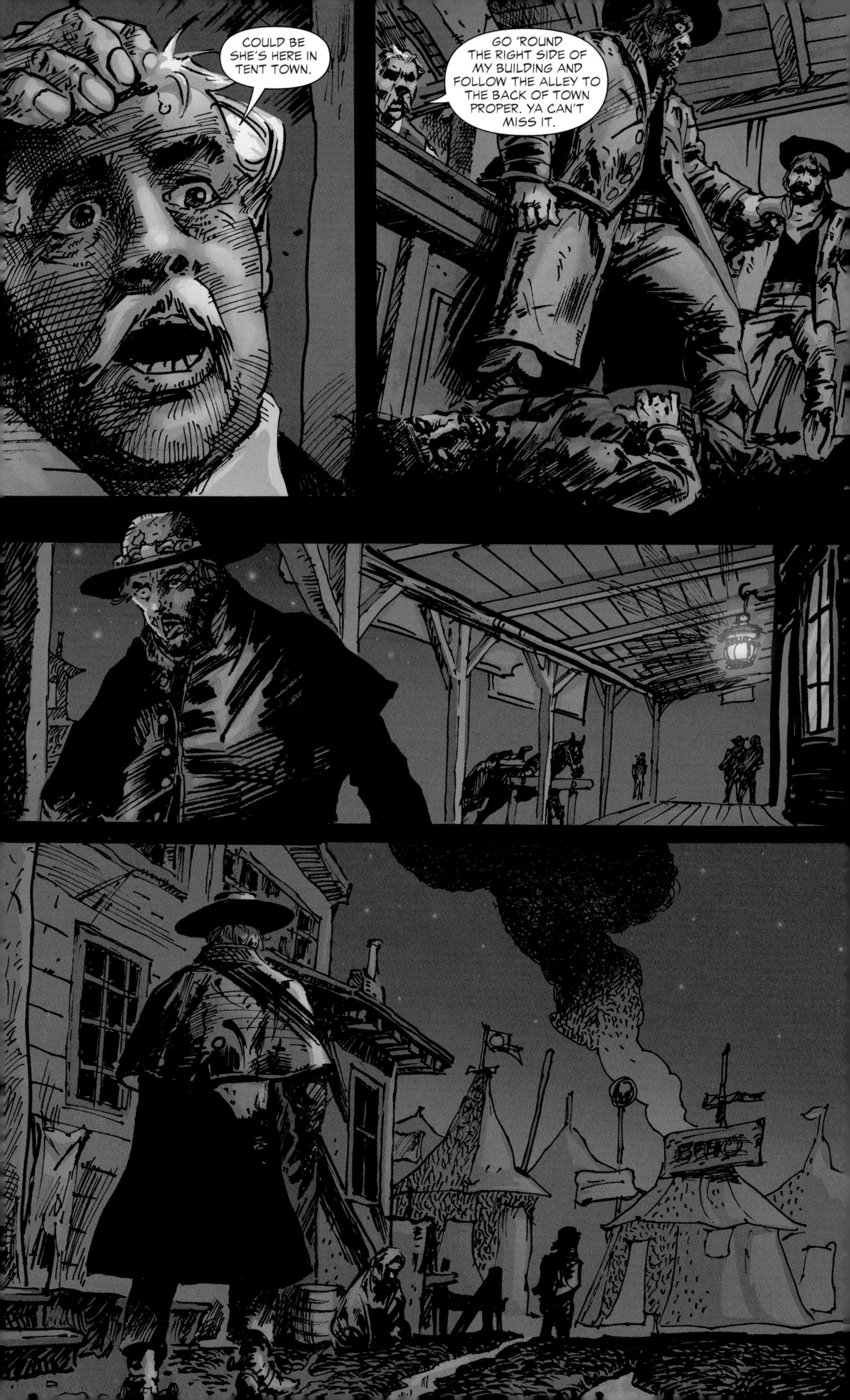
COULD BE SHE'S HERE IN TENT TOWN.
GO 'ROUND THE RIGHT SIDE OF MY BUILDING AND FOLLOW THE ALLEY TO THE BACK OF TOWN PROPER. YA CAN'T MISS IT.

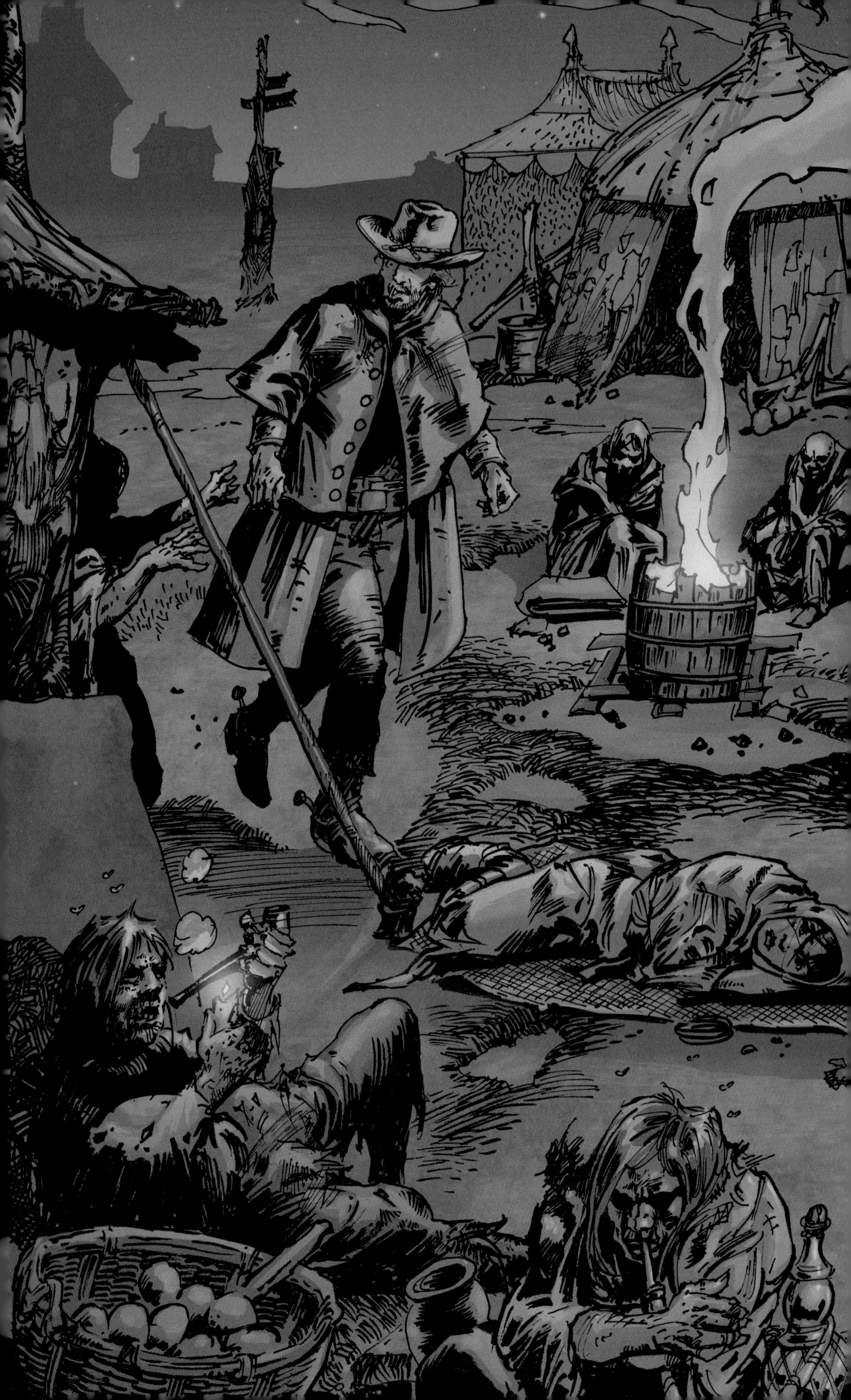

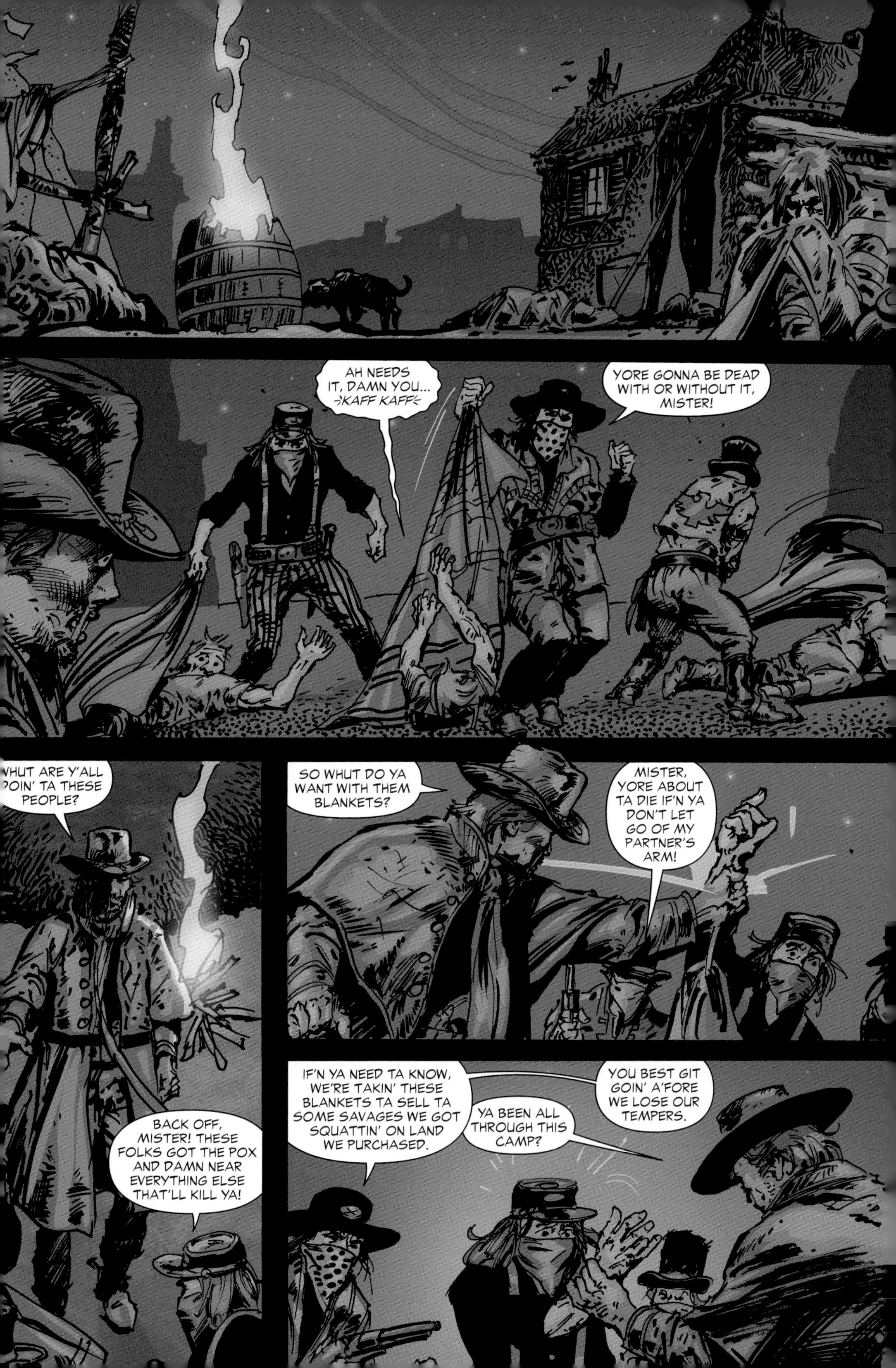
AH NEEDS IT, DAMN YOU... *KAFF KAFF*
YORE GONNA BE DEAD WITH OR WITHOUT IT, MISTER!
WHUT ARE Y'ALL DOIN' TA THESE PEOPLE?
BACK OFF, MISTER! THESE FOLKS GOT THE POX AND DAMN NEAR EVERYTHING ELSE THAT'LL KILL YA!
SO WHUT DO YA WANT WITH THEM BLANKETS?
MISTER, YORE ABOUT TA DIE IF'N YA DON'T LET GO OF MY PARTNER'S ARM!
IF'N YA NEED TA KNOW, WE'RE TAKIN' THESE BLANKETS TA SELL TA SOME SAVAGES WE GOT SQUATTIN' ON LAND WE PURCHASED.
YOU BEST GIT GOIN' A'FORE WE LOSE OUR TEMPERS.
YA BEEN ALL THROUGH THIS CAMP?

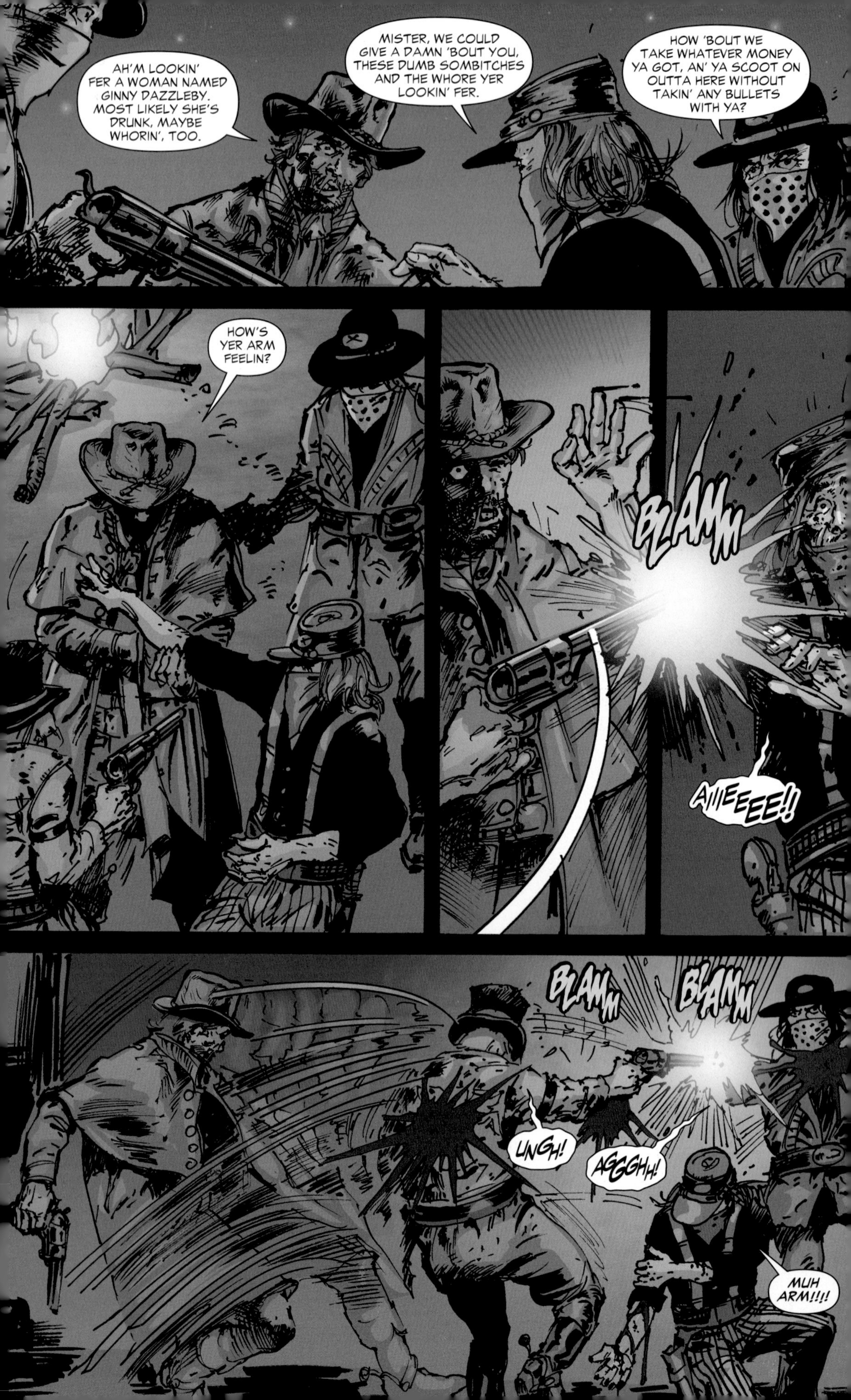
AH'M LOOKIN' FER A WOMAN NAMED GINNY DAZZLEBY. MOST LIKELY SHE'S DRUNK, MAYBE WHORIN', TOO.
MISTER, WE COULD GIVE A DAMN 'BOUT YOU, THESE DUMB SOMBITCHES AND THE WHORE YER LOOKIN' FER.
HOW 'BOUT WE TAKE WHATEVER MONEY YA GOT, AN' YA SCOOT ON OUTTA HERE WITHOUT TAKIN' ANY BULLETS WITH YA?
HOW'S YER ARM FEELIN?
BLAMM
AIIEEEEE!!
BLAMM
BLAMM
UNGH!
AGGGHH!
MUH ARM!!!!

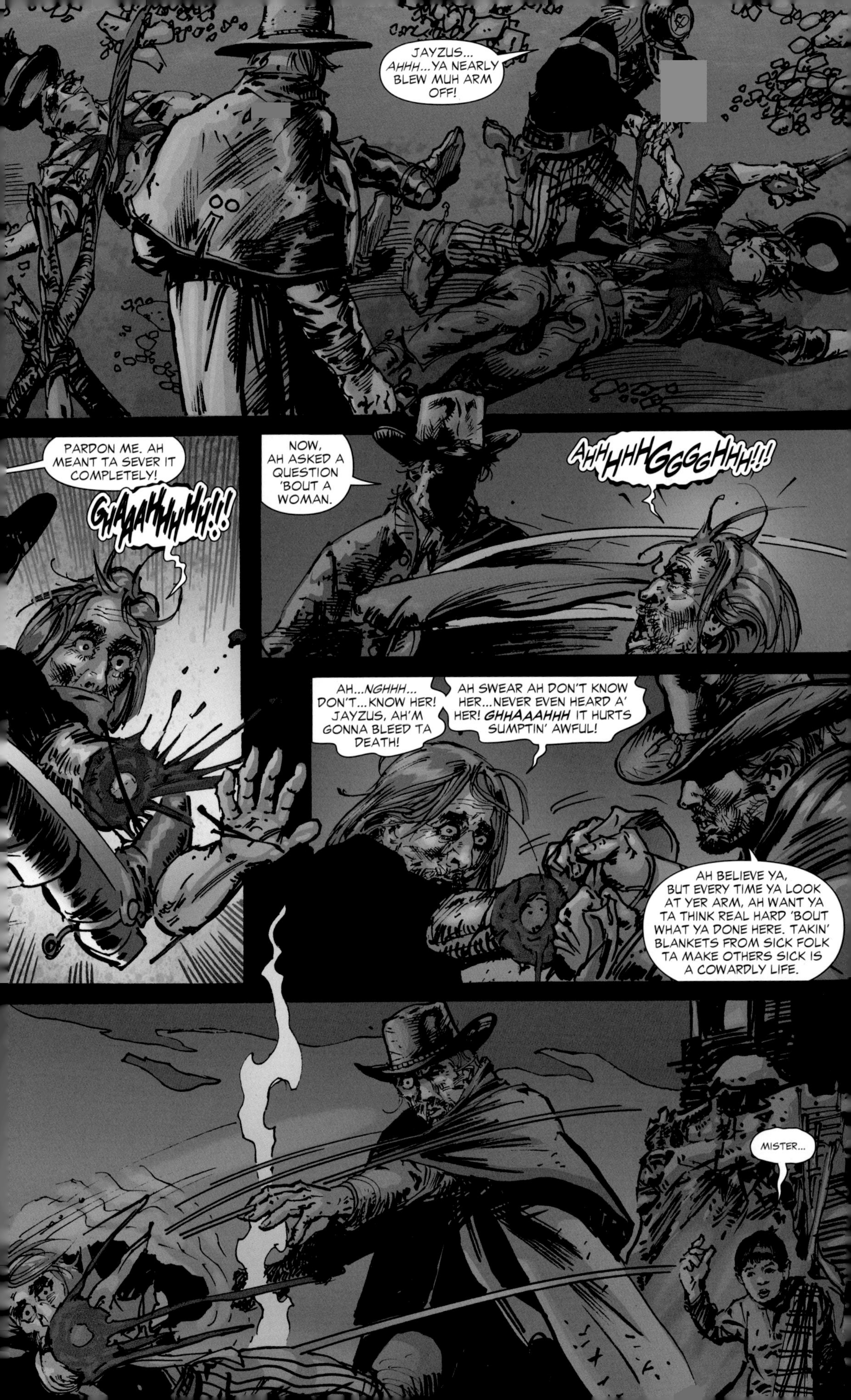

JAYZUS... AHHH...YA NEARLY BLEW MUH ARM OFF!
PARDON ME. AH MEANT TA SEVER IT COMPLETELY!
GHAAAAKHHHHH!!!
NOW, AH ASKED A QUESTION 'BOUT A WOMAN.
AHHHHHGGGGHHH!!!
AH...NGHHH... DON'T...KNOW HER! JAYZUS, AH'M GONNA BLEED TA DEATH!
AH SWEAR AH DON'T KNOW HER...NEVER EVEN HEARD A' HER! GHHAAAHHH IT HURTS SUMPTIN' AWFUL!
AH BELIEVE YA, BUT EVERY TIME YA LOOK AT YER ARM, AH WANT YA TA THINK REAL HARD 'BOUT WHAT YA DONE HERE. TAKIN' BLANKETS FROM SICK FOLK TA MAKE OTHERS SICK IS A COWARDLY LIFE.
MISTER...

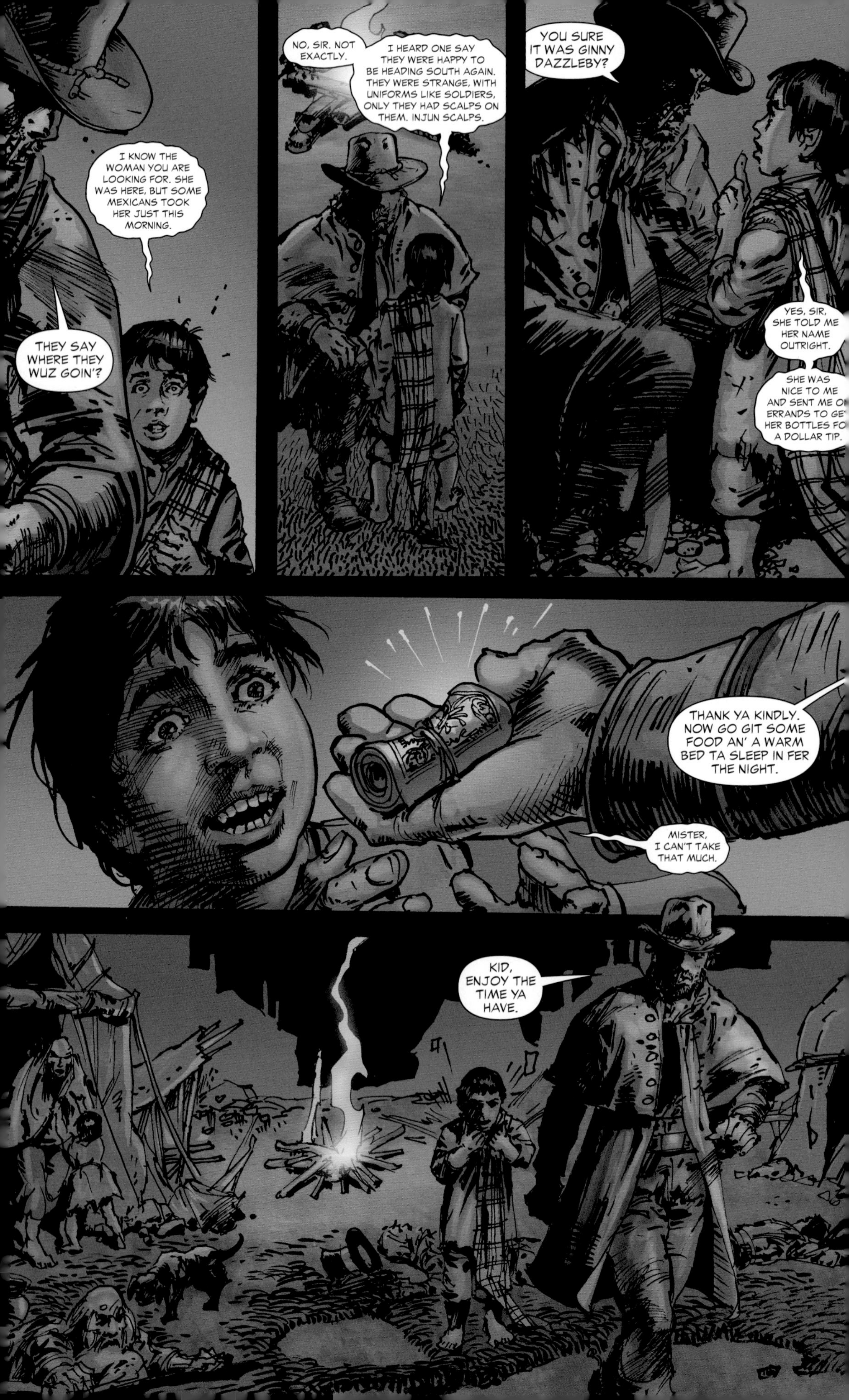
I KNOW THE WOMAN YOU ARE LOOKING FOR. SHE WAS HERE, BUT SOME MEXICANS TOOK HER JUST THIS MORNING.
THEY SAY WHERE THEY WUZ GOIN'?
NO, SIR. NOT EXACTLY.
I HEARD ONE SAY THEY WERE HAPPY TO BE HEADING SOUTH AGAIN. THEY WERE STRANGE, WITH UNIFORMS LIKE SOLDIERS, ONLY THEY HAD SCALPS ON THEM. INJUN SCALPS.
YOU SURE IT WAS GINNY DAZZLEBY?
YES, SIR, SHE TOLD ME HER NAME OUTRIGHT.
THANK YA KINDLY. NOW GO GIT SOME FOOD AN' A WARM BED TA SLEEP IN FER THE NIGHT.
MISTER, I CAN'T TAKE THAT MUCH.
KID, ENJOY THE TIME YA HAVE.

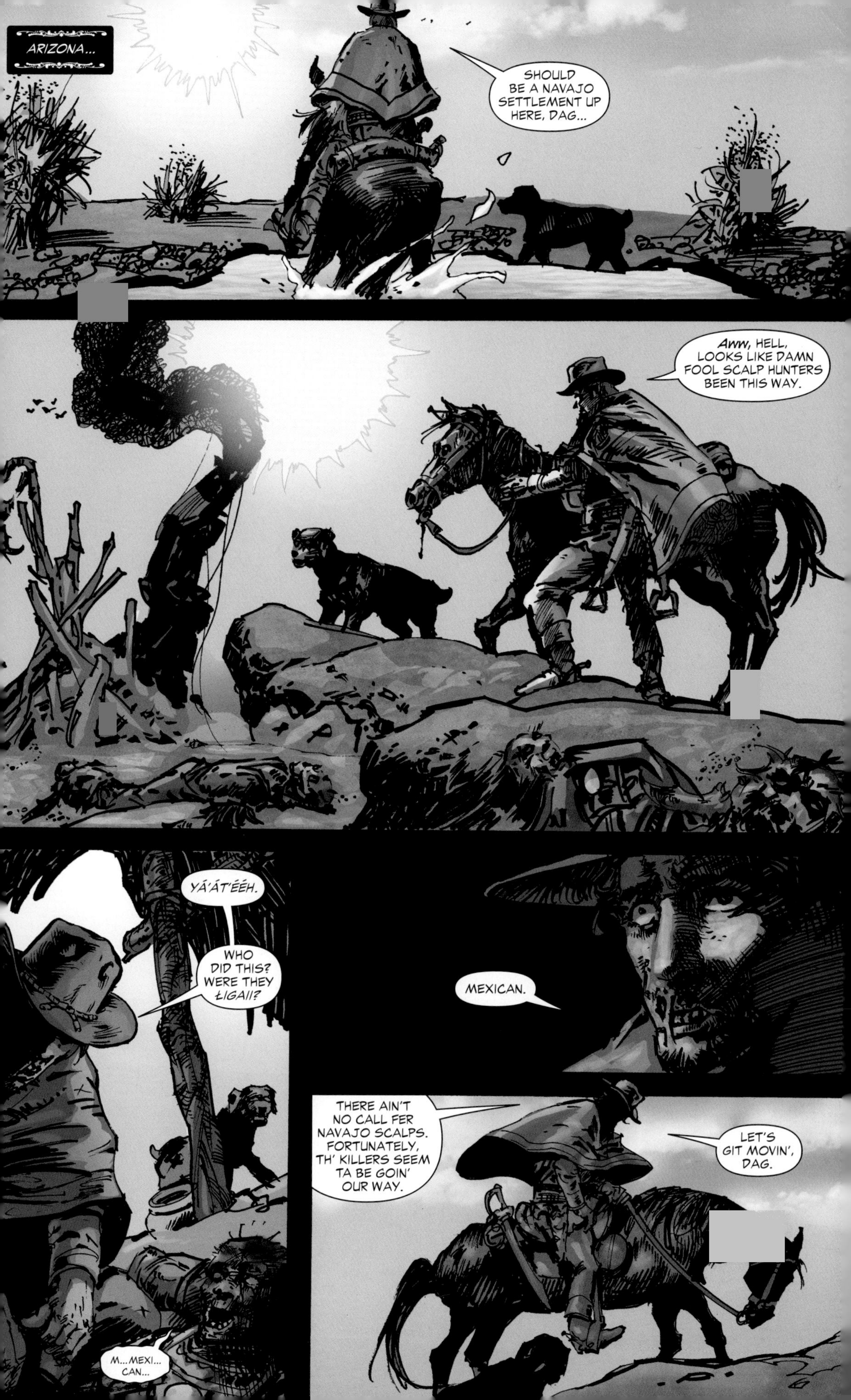
ARIZONA...
SHOULD BE A NAVAJO SETTLEMENT UP HERE, DAG...
AWW, HELL, LOOKS LIKE DAMN FOOL SCALP HUNTERS BEEN THIS WAY.
YÁ'ÁT'ÉÉH.
WHO DID THIS? WERE THEY ŁIGAII?
M...MEXI... CAN...
MEXICAN.
THERE AIN'T NO CALL FER NAVAJO SCALPS. FORTUNATELY, TH' KILLERS SEEM TA BE GOIN' OUR WAY.
LET'S GIT MOVIN', DAG.

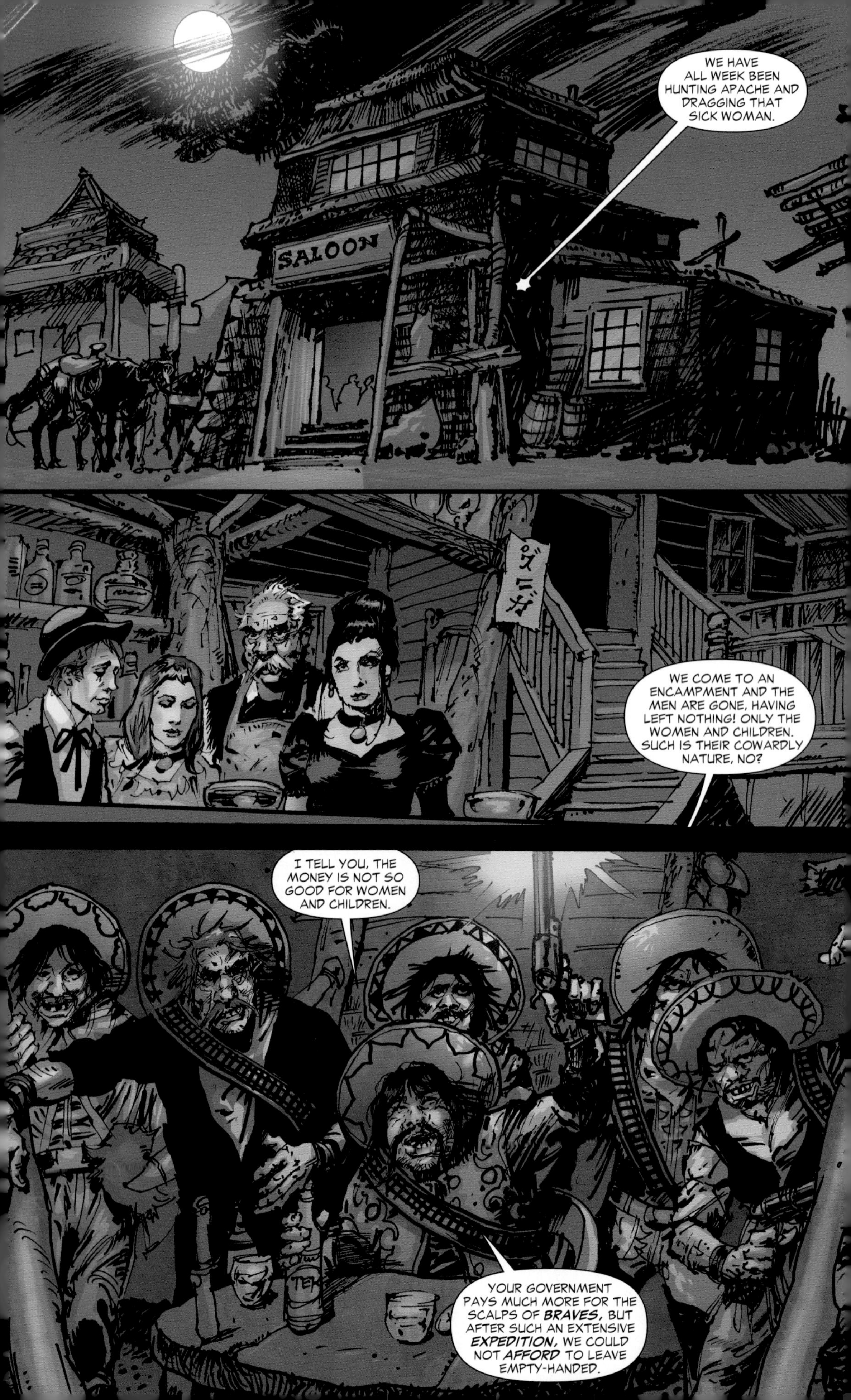
SALOON
WE HAVE ALL WEEK BEEN HUNTING APACHE AND DRAGGING THAT SICK WOMAN.
WE COME TO AN ENCAMPMENT AND THE MEN ARE GONE, HAVING LEFT NOTHING! ONLY THE WOMEN AND CHILDREN. SUCH IS THEIR COWARDLY NATURE, NO?
I TELL YOU, THE MONEY IS NOT SO GOOD FOR WOMEN AND CHILDREN.
YOUR GOVERNMENT PAYS MUCH MORE FOR THE SCALPS OF BRAVES, BUT AFTER SUCH AN EXTENSIVE EXPEDITION, WE COULD NOT AFFORD TO LEAVE EMPTY-HANDED.

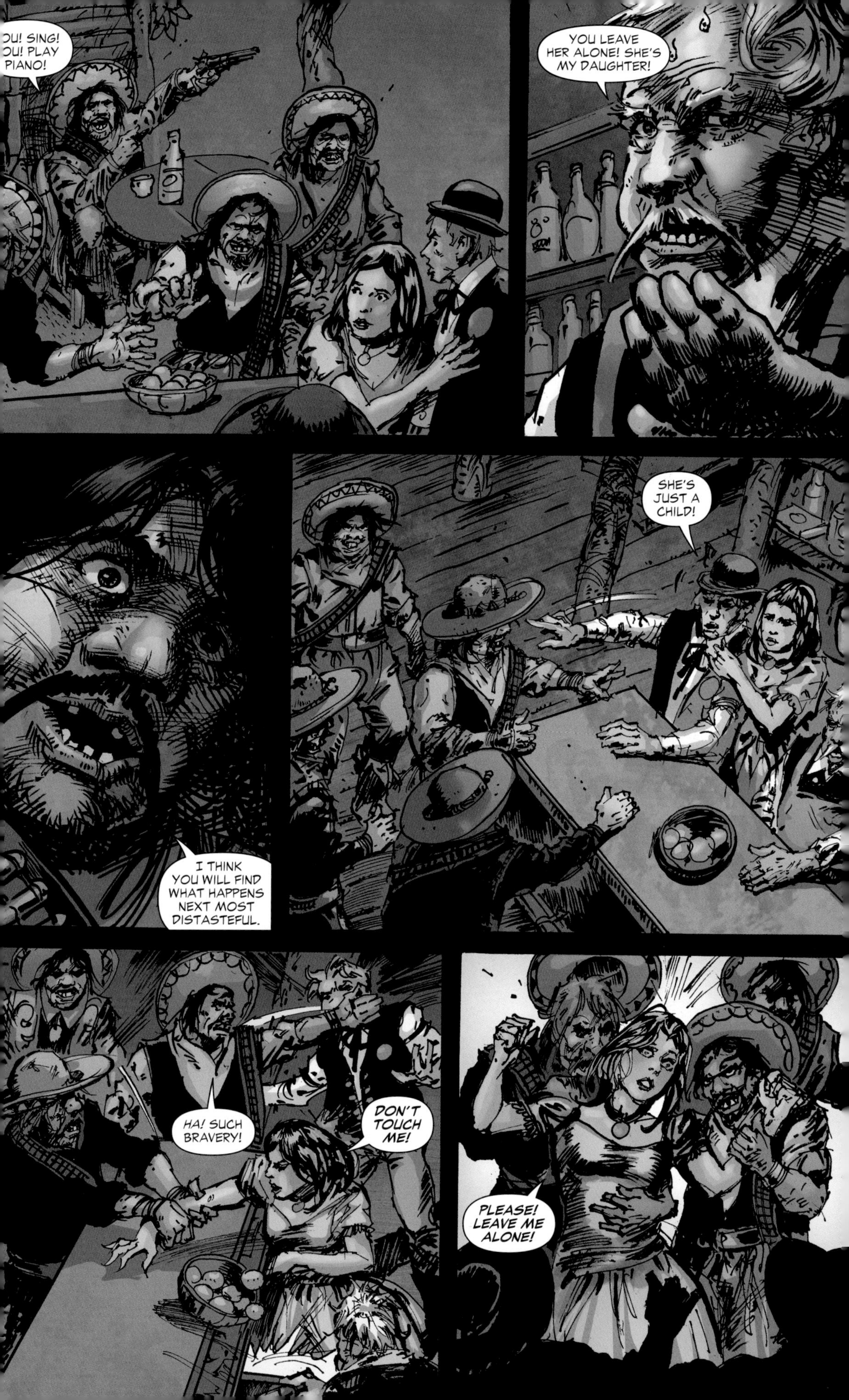
OU! SING! OU! PLAY PIANO!
YOU LEAVE HER ALONE! SHE'S MY DAUGHTER!
SHE'S JUST A CHILD!
I THINK YOU WILL FIND WHAT HAPPENS NEXT MOST DISTASTEFUL.
HA! SUCH BRAVERY!
DON'T TOUCH ME!
PLEASE! LEAVE ME ALONE!

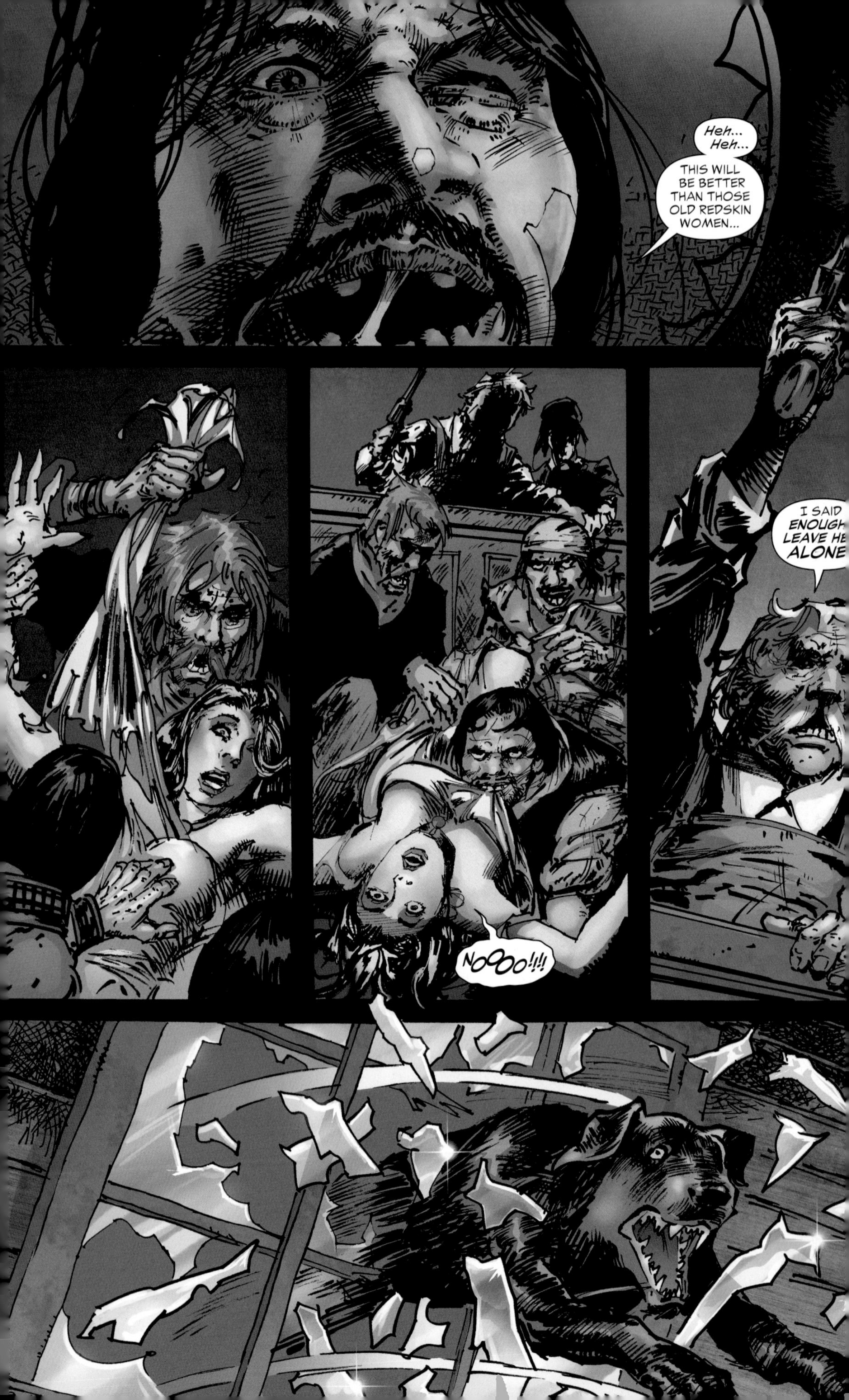
Heh... Heh...
THIS WILL BE BETTER THAN THOSE OLD REDSKIN WOMEN...
NOOOO!!!!
I SAID ENOUGH LEAVE HE ALONE

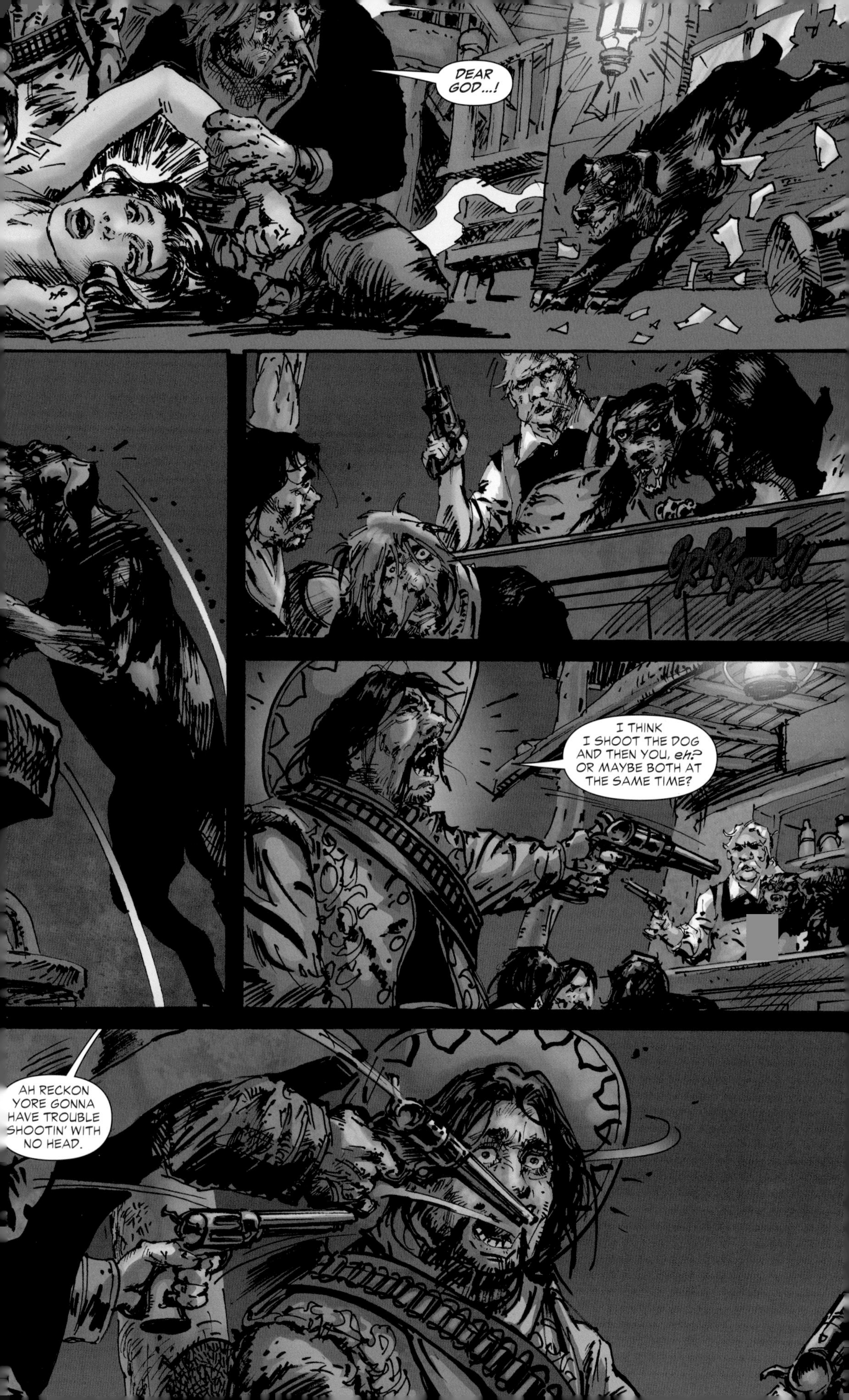
DEAR GOD...!
I THINK I SHOOT THE DOG AND THEN YOU, *eh?* OR MAYBE BOTH AT THE SAME TIME?
AH RECKON YORE GONNA HAVE TROUBLE SHOOTIN' WITH NO HEAD.

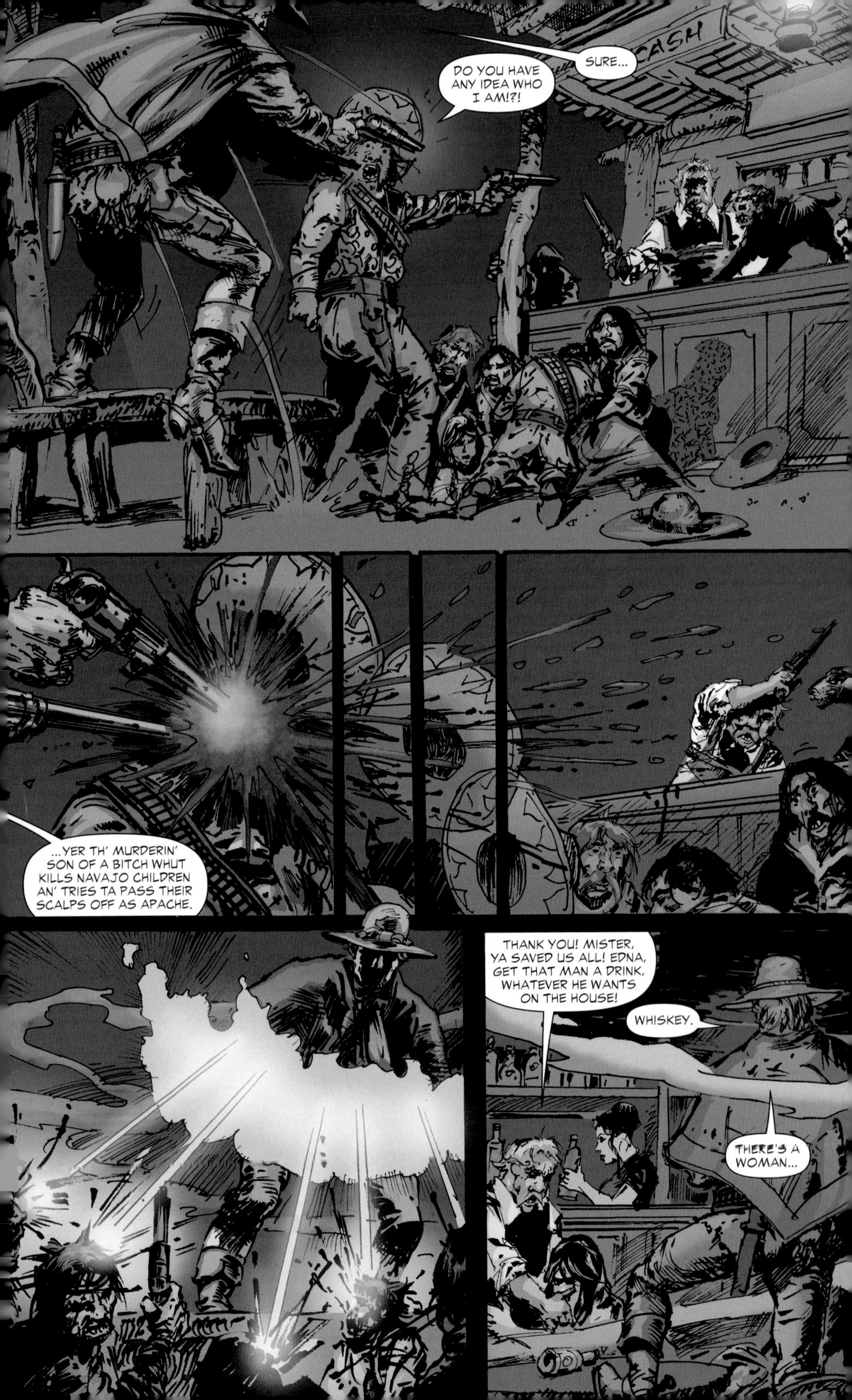
DO YOU HAVE ANY IDEA WHO I AM!?!
SURE...
...YER TH' MURDERIN' SON OF A BITCH WHUT KILLS NAVAJO CHILDREN AN' TRIES TA PASS THEIR SCALPS OFF AS APACHE.
THANK YOU! MISTER, YA SAVED US ALL! EDNA, GET THAT MAN A DRINK, WHATEVER HE WANTS ON THE HOUSE!
WHISKEY.
THERE'S A WOMAN...

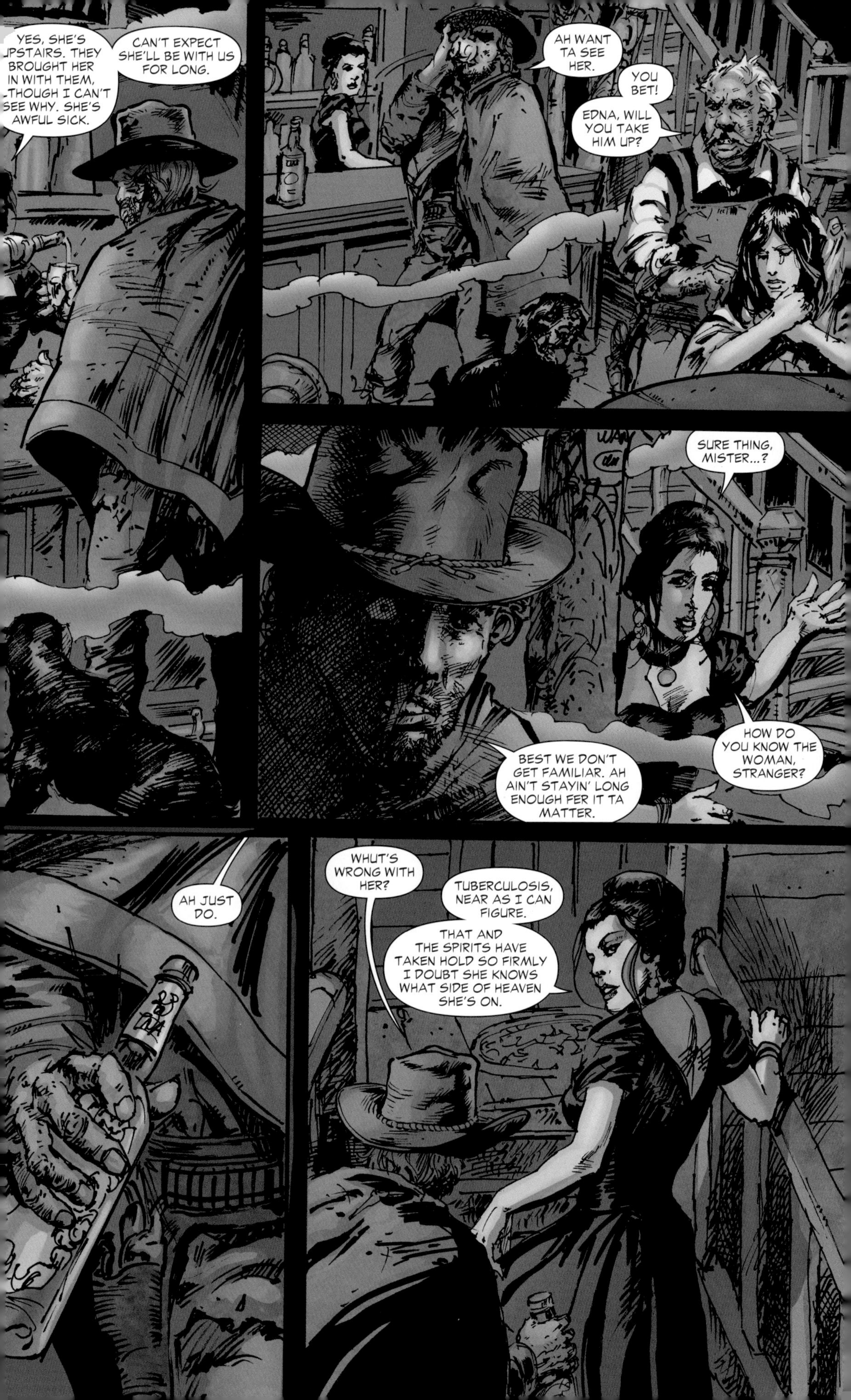
YES, SHE'S UPSTAIRS. THEY BROUGHT HER IN WITH THEM, THOUGH I CAN'T SEE WHY. SHE'S AWFUL SICK.
CAN'T EXPECT SHE'LL BE WITH US FOR LONG.
AH WANT TA SEE HER.
YOU BET!
EDNA, WILL YOU TAKE HIM UP?
SURE THING, MISTER...?
BEST WE DON'T GET FAMILIAR. AH AIN'T STAYIN' LONG ENOUGH FER IT TA MATTER.
HOW DO YOU KNOW THE WOMAN, STRANGER?
AH JUST DO.
WHUT'S WRONG WITH HER?
TUBERCULOSIS, NEAR AS I CAN FIGURE.
THAT AND THE SPIRITS HAVE TAKEN HOLD SO FIRMLY I DOUBT SHE KNOWS WHAT SIDE OF HEAVEN SHE'S ON.

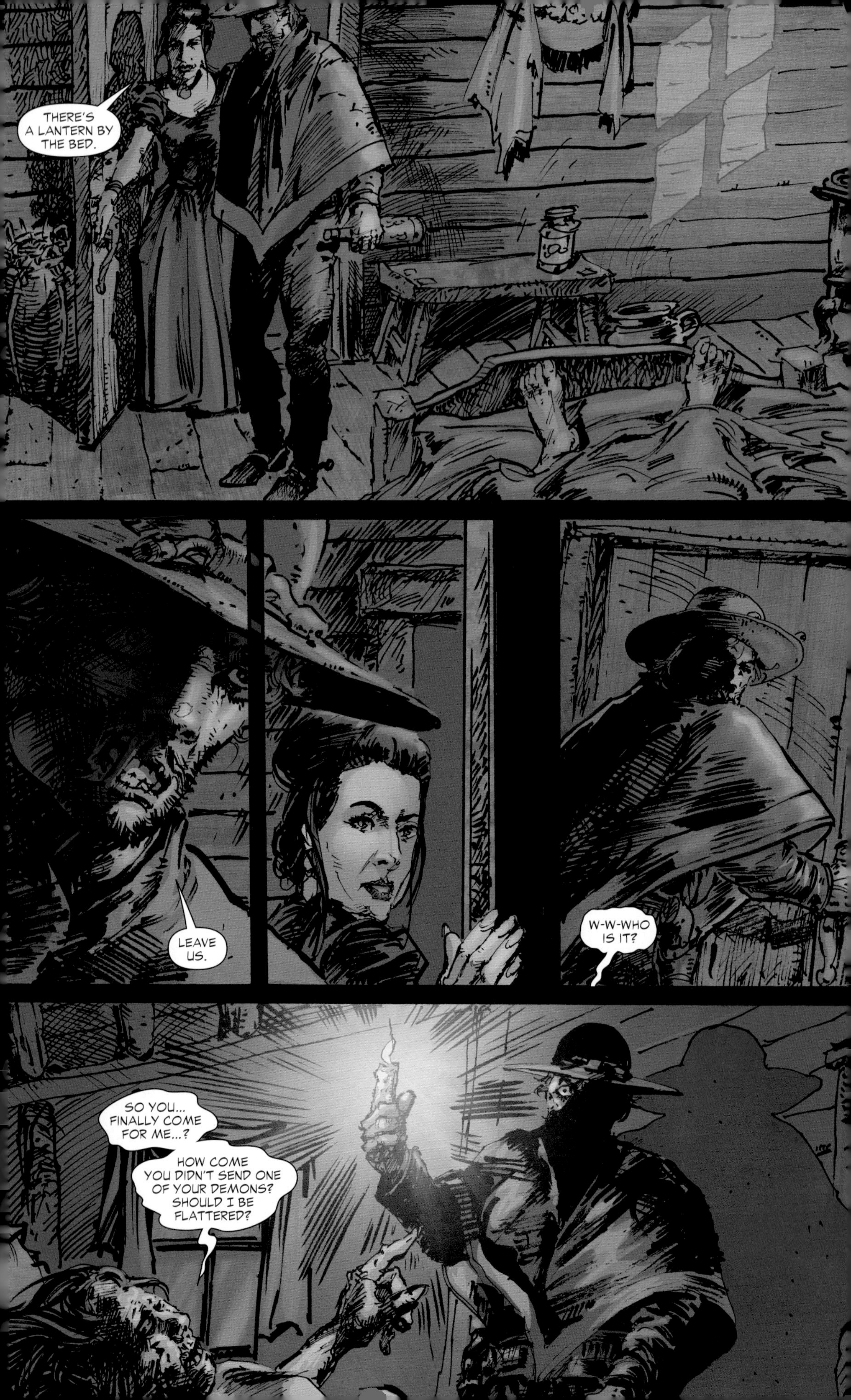
THERE'S A LANTERN BY THE BED.
LEAVE US.
W-W-WHO IS IT?
SO YOU... FINALLY COME FOR ME...?
HOW COME YOU DIDN'T SEND ONE OF YOUR DEMONS? SHOULD I BE FLATTERED?

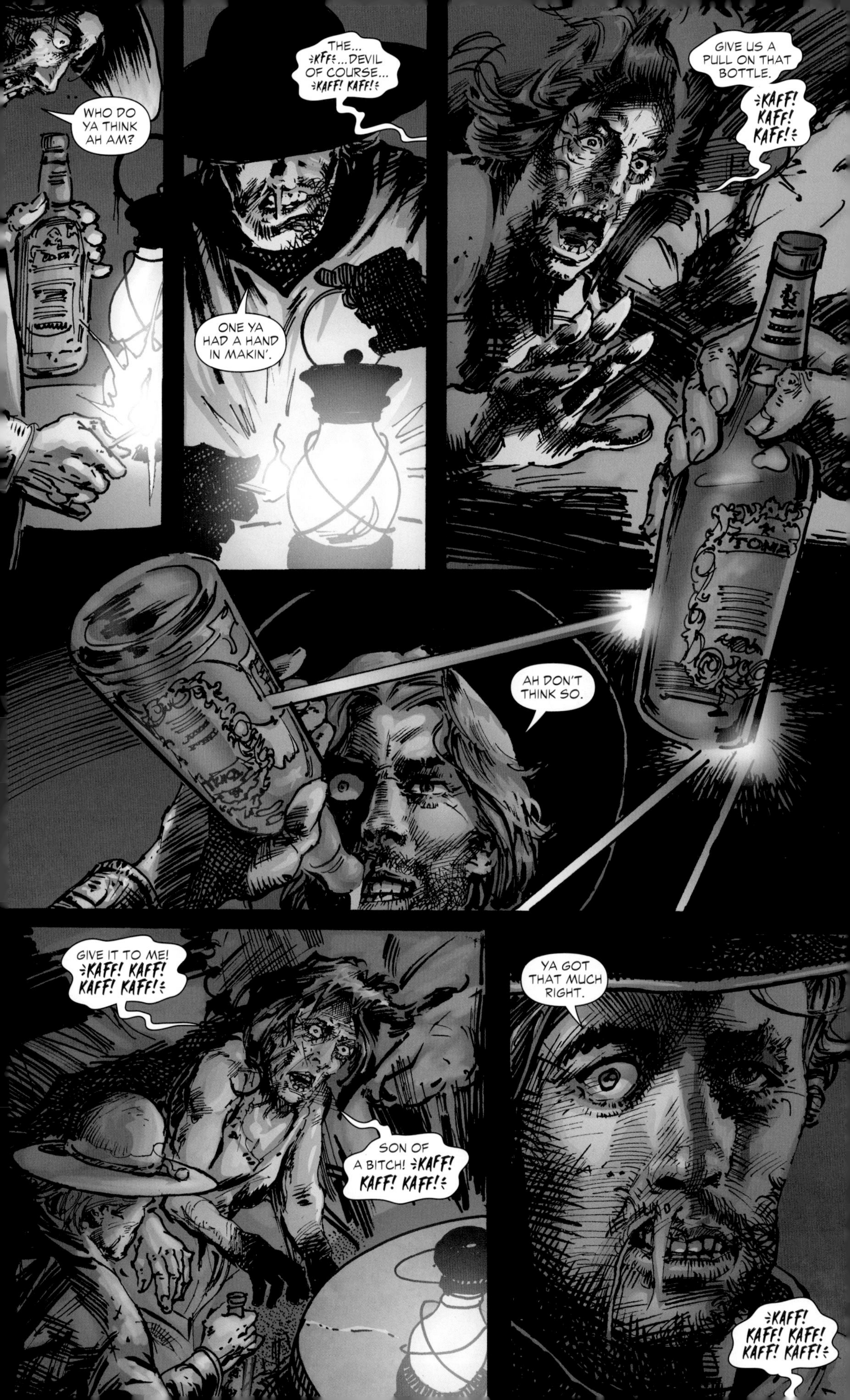
WHO DO YA THINK AH AM?
THE... KFF ...DEVIL OF COURSE... KAFF! KAFF!
ONE YA HAD A HAND IN MAKIN'.
GIVE US A PULL ON THAT BOTTLE.
KAFF! KAFF! KAFF!
AH DON'T THINK SO.
GIVE IT TO ME! KAFF! KAFF! KAFF! KAFF!
SON OF A BITCH! KAFF! KAFF! KAFF!
YA GOT THAT MUCH RIGHT.
KAFF! KAFF! KAFF! KAFF! KAFF!

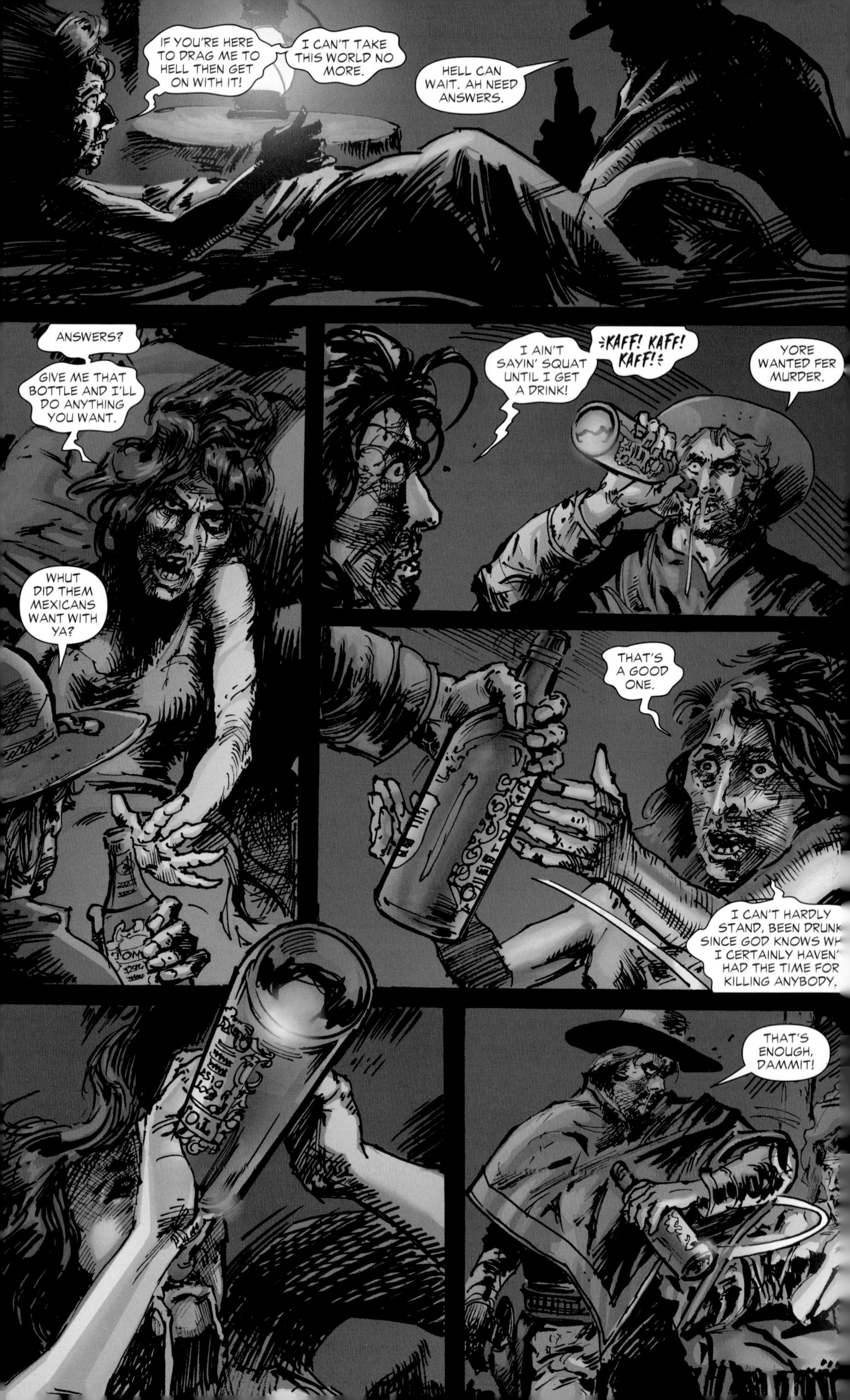

IF YOU'RE HERE TO DRAG ME TO HELL THEN GET ON WITH IT!
I CAN'T TAKE THIS WORLD NO MORE.
HELL CAN WAIT. AH NEED ANSWERS.
ANSWERS?
GIVE ME THAT BOTTLE AND I'LL DO ANYTHING YOU WANT.
WHUT DID THEM MEXICANS WANT WITH YA?
I AIN'T SAYIN' SQUAT UNTIL I GET A DRINK!
KAFF! KAFF! KAFF!
YORE WANTED FER MURDER.
THAT'S A GOOD ONE.
I CAN'T HARDLY STAND, BEEN DRUNK SINCE GOD KNOWS WH I CERTAINLY HAVEN' HAD THE TIME FOR KILLING ANYBODY.
THAT'S ENOUGH, DAMMIT!

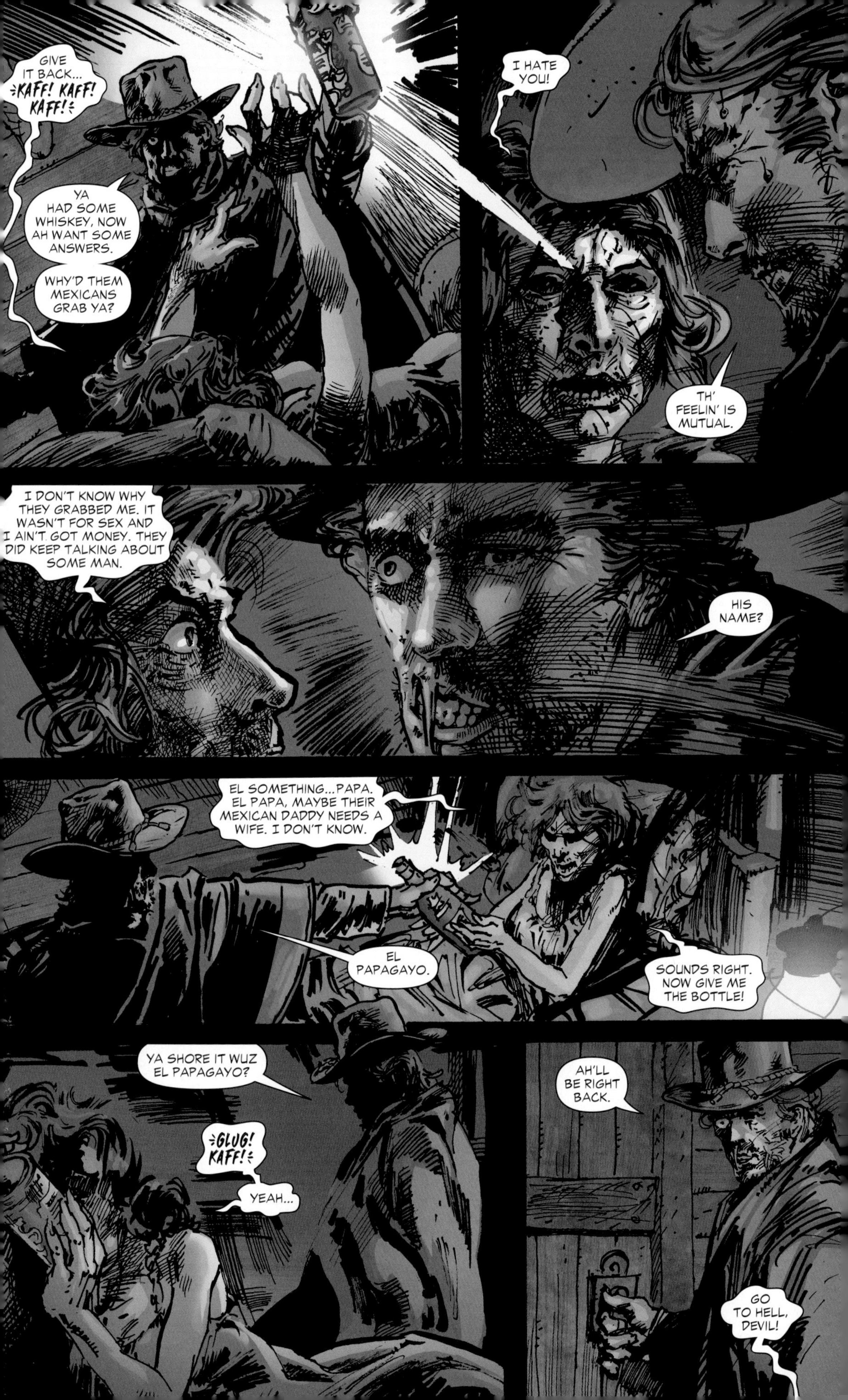
GIVE IT BACK... KAFF! KAFF! KAFF!
YA HAD SOME WHISKEY, NOW AH WANT SOME ANSWERS.
WHY'D THEM MEXICANS GRAB YA?
I HATE YOU!
TH' FEELIN' IS MUTUAL.
I DON'T KNOW WHY THEY GRABBED ME. IT WASN'T FOR SEX AND I AIN'T GOT MONEY. THEY DID KEEP TALKING ABOUT SOME MAN.
HIS NAME?
EL SOMETHING...PAPA. EL PAPA, MAYBE THEIR MEXICAN DADDY NEEDS A WIFE. I DON'T KNOW.
EL PAPAGAYO.
SOUNDS RIGHT. NOW GIVE ME THE BOTTLE!
YA SHORE IT WUZ EL PAPAGAYO?
GLUG! KAFF!
YEAH...
AH'LL BE RIGHT BACK.
GO TO HELL, DEVIL!

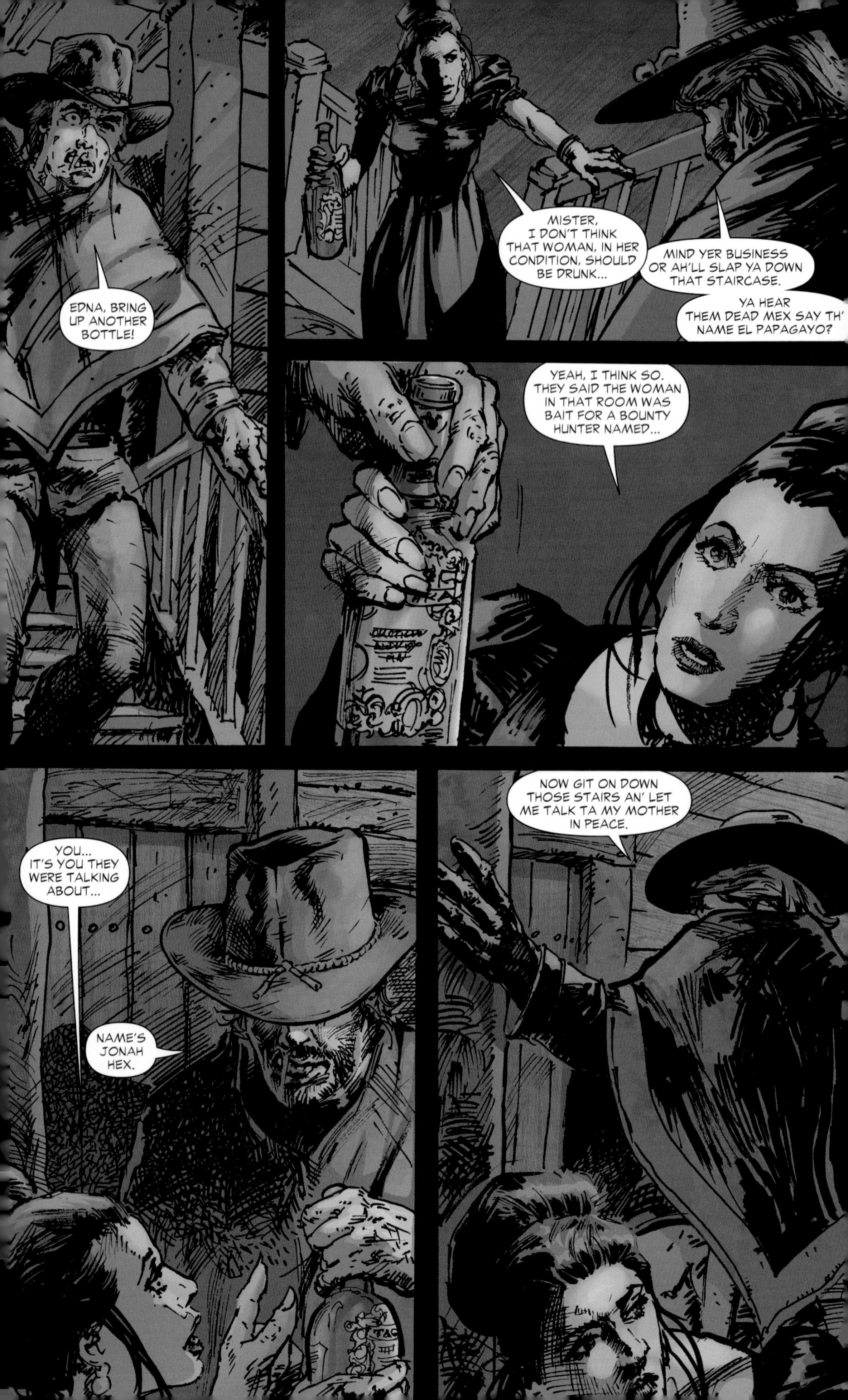
EDNA, BRING UP ANOTHER BOTTLE!
MISTER, I DON'T THINK THAT WOMAN, IN HER CONDITION, SHOULD BE DRUNK...
MIND YER BUSINESS OR AH'LL SLAP YA DOWN THAT STAIRCASE.
YA HEAR THEM DEAD MEX SAY TH' NAME EL PAPAGAYO?
YEAH, I THINK SO. THEY SAID THE WOMAN IN THAT ROOM WAS BAIT FOR A BOUNTY HUNTER NAMED...
YOU... IT'S YOU THEY WERE TALKING ABOUT...
NAME'S JONAH HEX.
NOW GIT ON DOWN THOSE STAIRS AN' LET ME TALK TA MY MOTHER IN PEACE.

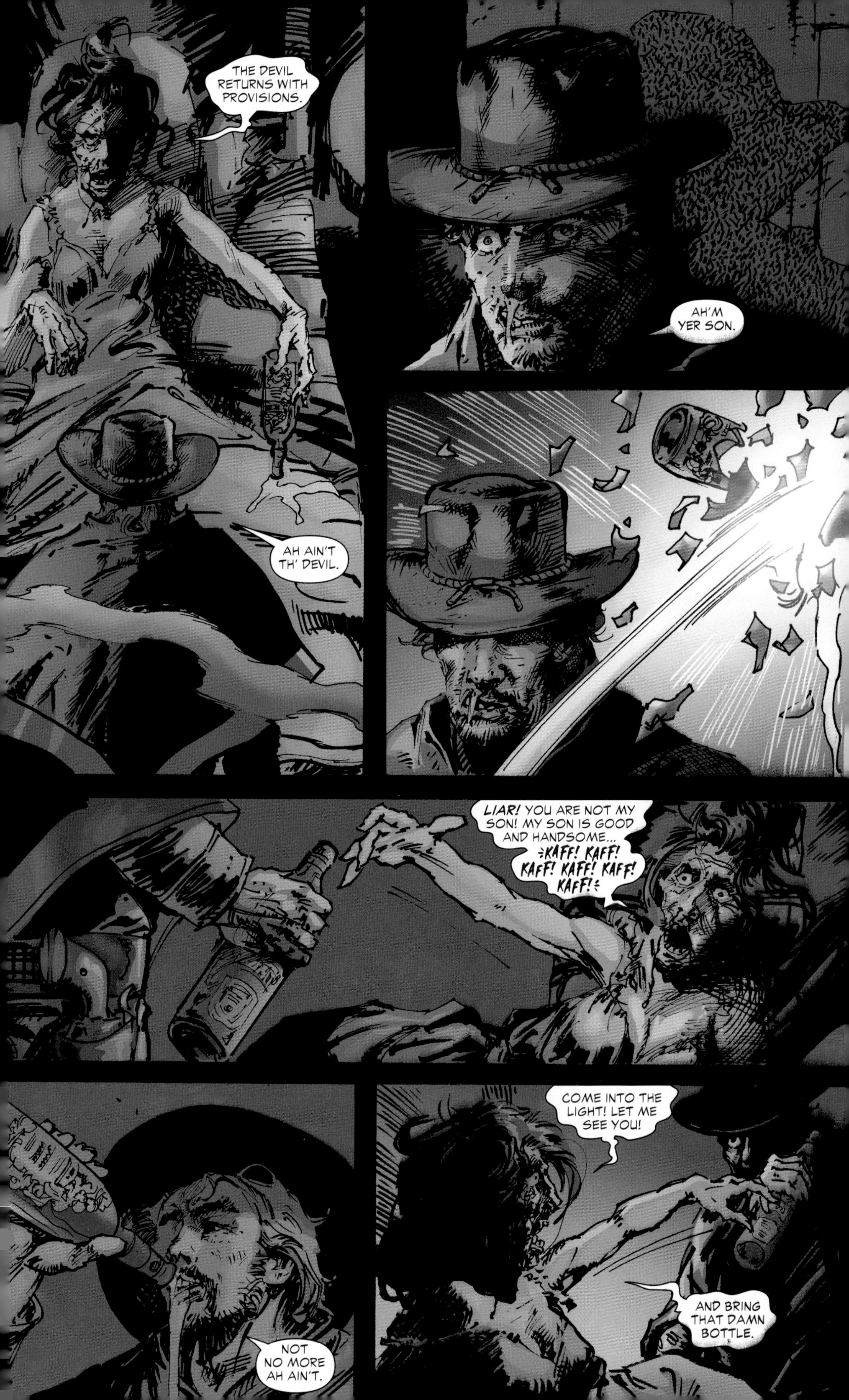
THE DEVIL RETURNS WITH PROVISIONS.
AH AIN'T TH' DEVIL.
AH'M YER SON.
LIAR! YOU ARE NOT MY SON! MY SON IS GOOD AND HANDSOME...
KAFF! KAFF! KAFF! KAFF! KAFF! KAFF!
NOT NO MORE AH AIN'T.
COME INTO THE LIGHT! LET ME SEE YOU!
AND BRING THAT DAMN BOTTLE.

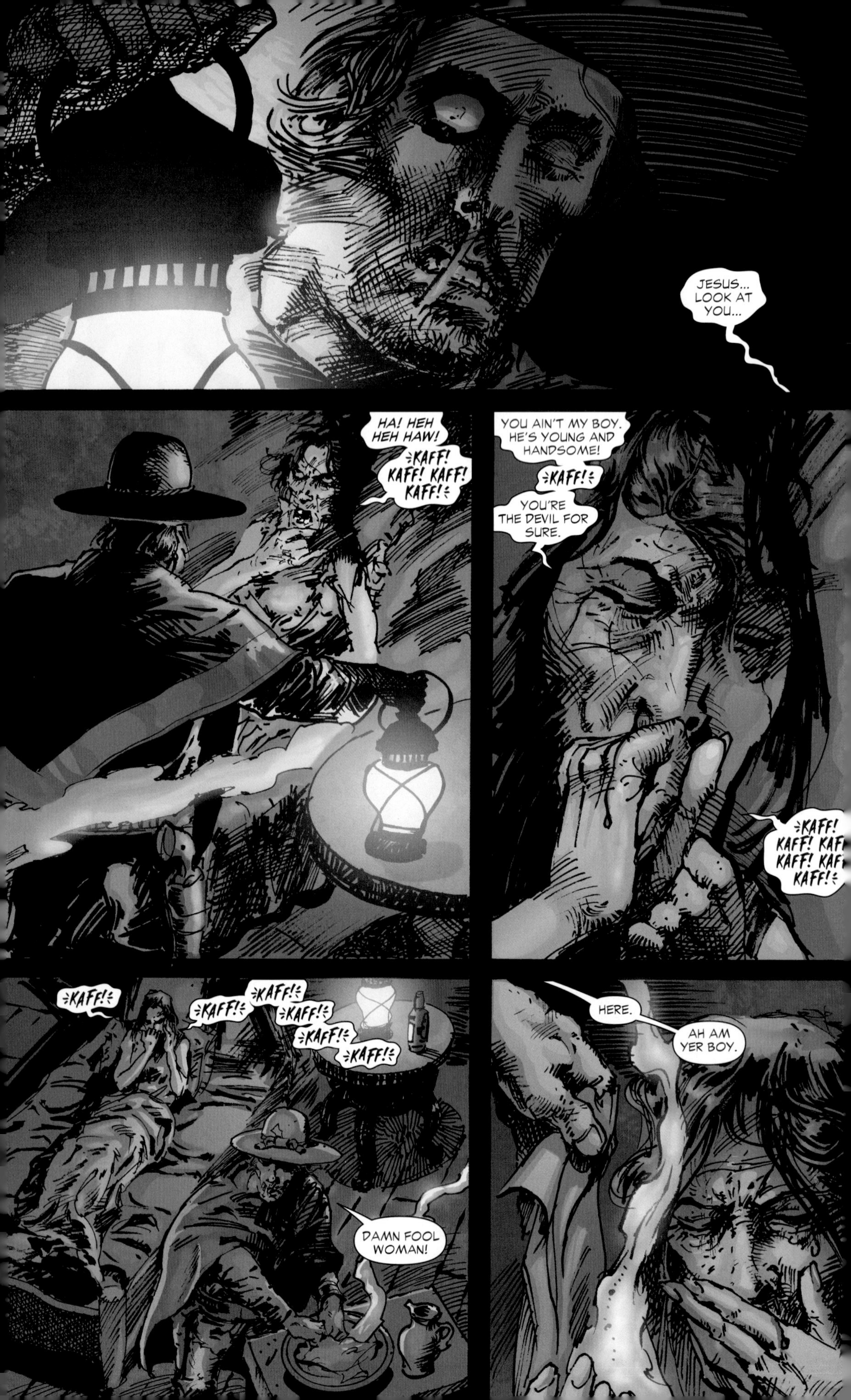
JESUS... LOOK AT YOU...
HA! HEH HEH HAW!
KAFF! KAFF! KAFF! KAFF!
YOU AIN'T MY BOY. HE'S YOUNG AND HANDSOME!
KAFF!
YOU'RE THE DEVIL FOR SURE.
KAFF! KAFF! KAFF! KAFF! KAFF! KAFF!
KAFF!
KAFF!
KAFF!
KAFF!
KAFF!
KAFF!
DAMN FOOL WOMAN!
HERE.
AH AM YER BOY.

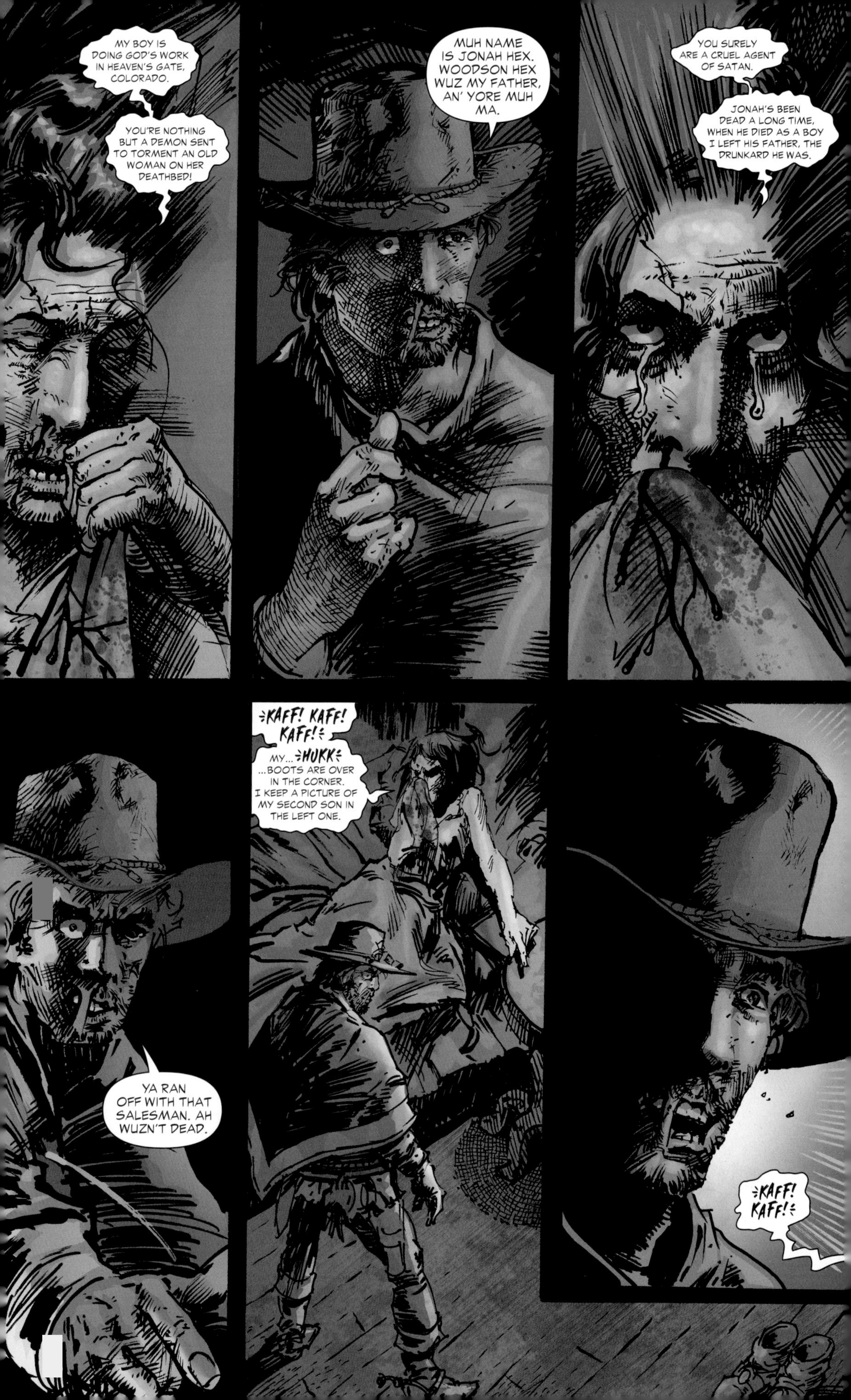
MY BOY IS DOING GOD'S WORK IN HEAVEN'S GATE, COLORADO.
YOU'RE NOTHING BUT A DEMON SENT TO TORMENT AN OLD WOMAN ON HER DEATHBED!
MUH NAME IS JONAH HEX. WOODSON HEX WUZ MY FATHER, AN' YORE MUH MA.
YOU SURELY ARE A CRUEL AGENT OF SATAN.
JONAH'S BEEN DEAD A LONG TIME, WHEN HE DIED AS A BOY I LEFT HIS FATHER, THE DRUNKARD HE WAS.
YA RAN OFF WITH THAT SALESMAN. AH WUZN'T DEAD.
KAFF! KAFF! KAFF!
MY... HUKK ...BOOTS ARE OVER IN THE CORNER. I KEEP A PICTURE OF MY SECOND SON IN THE LEFT ONE.
KAFF! KAFF!

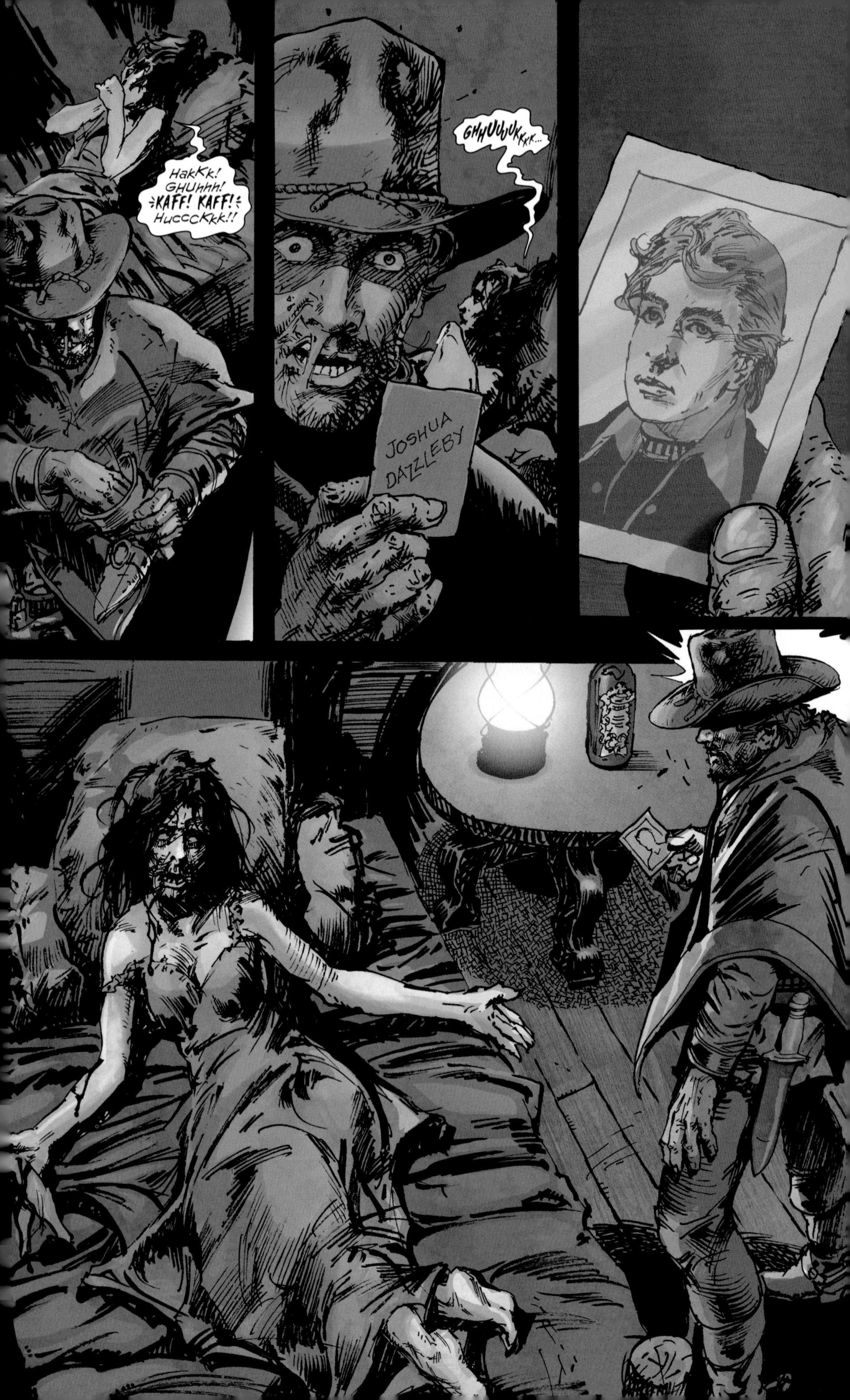
HakKk! GHUhhh! KAFF! KAFF! HuccckKk!!
GHHUUUUKKKK...
JOSHUA DAZZLEBY

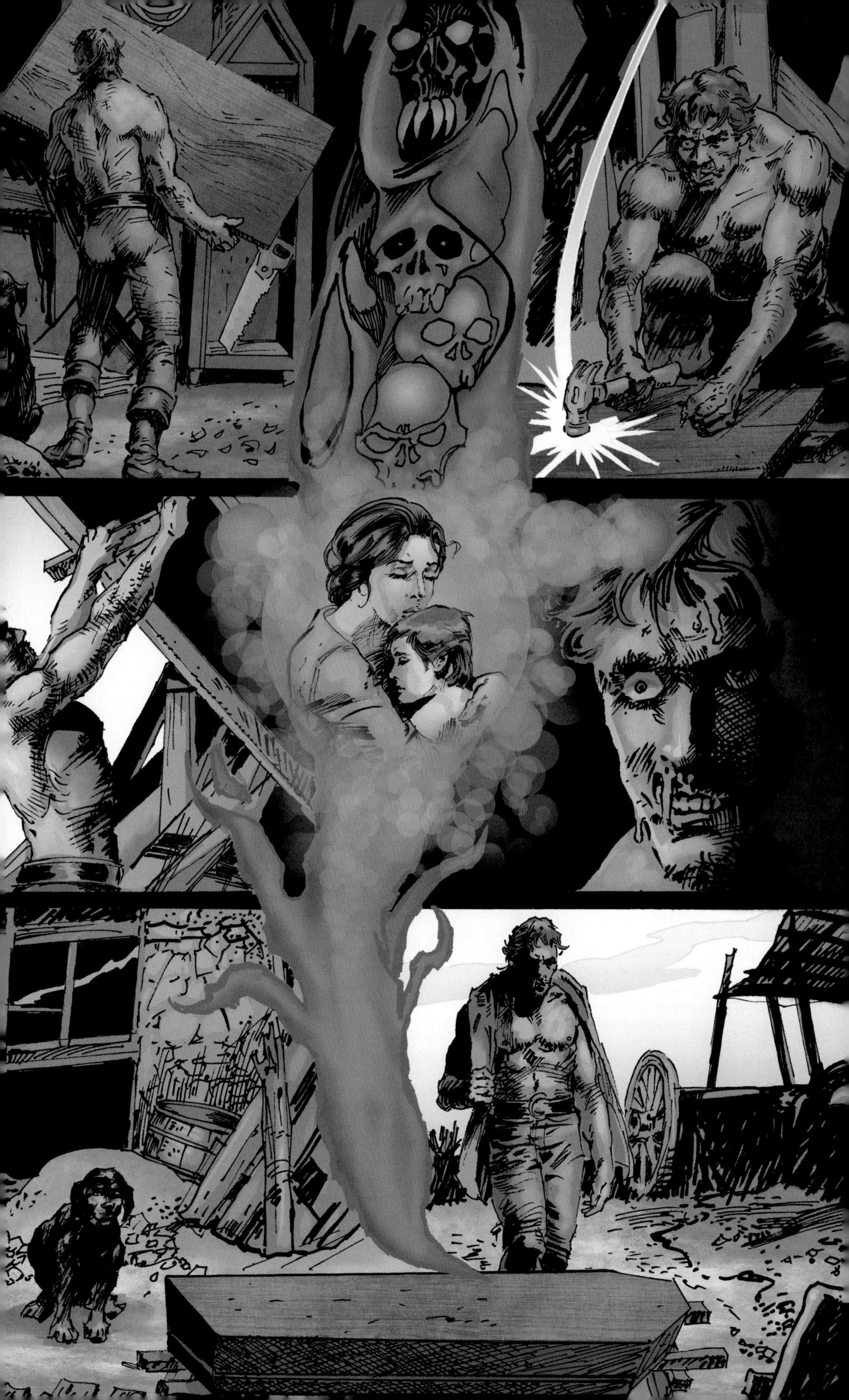

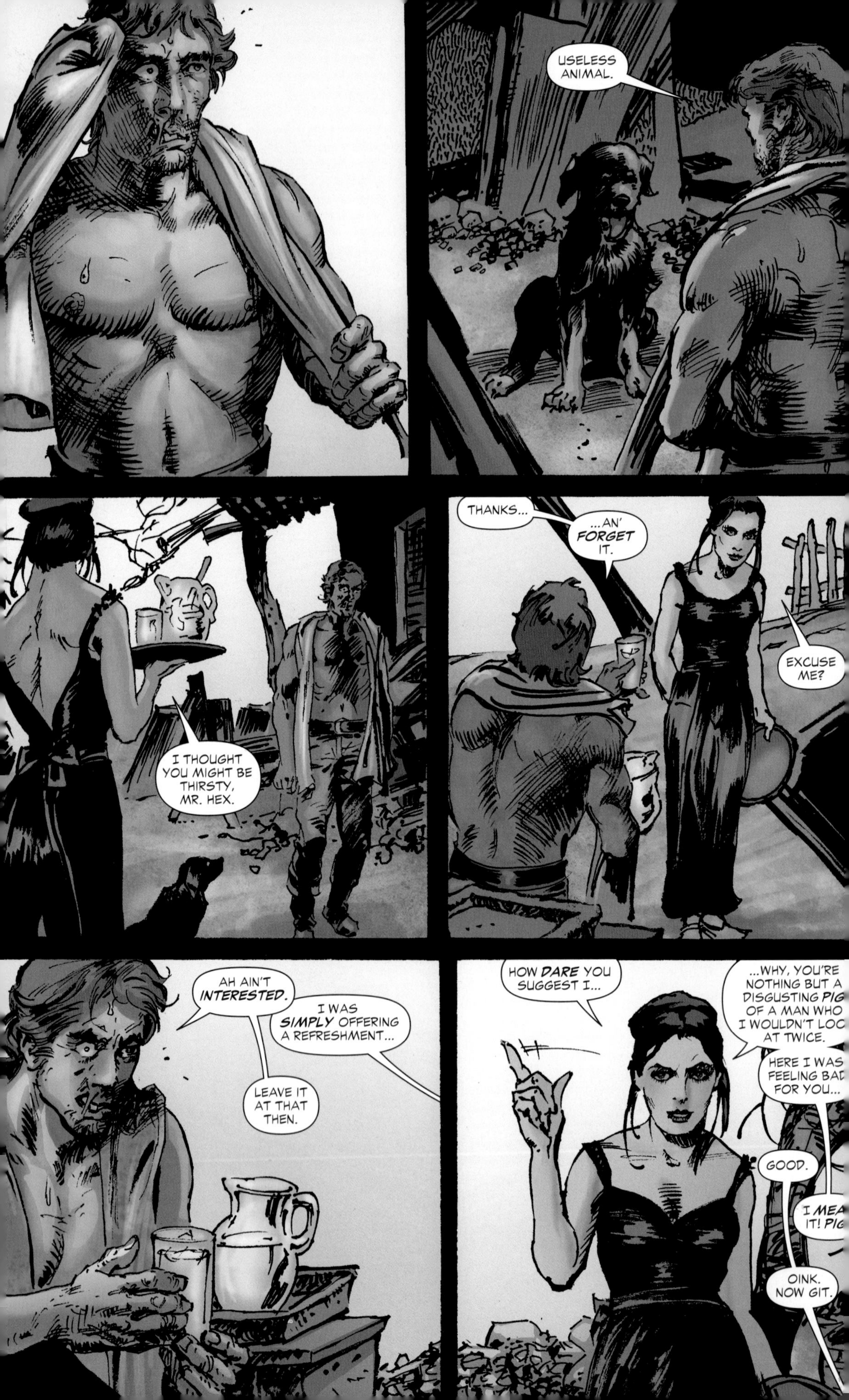
USELESS ANIMAL.
I THOUGHT YOU MIGHT BE THIRSTY, MR. HEX.
THANKS...
...AN' FORGET IT.
EXCUSE ME?
I WAS SIMPLY OFFERING A REFRESHMENT...
AH AIN'T INTERESTED.
LEAVE IT AT THAT THEN.
HOW DARE YOU SUGGEST I...
...WHY, YOU'RE NOTHING BUT A DISGUSTING PIG OF A MAN WHO I WOULDN'T LOO AT TWICE.
HERE I WAS FEELING BAD FOR YOU...
GOOD.
I MEA IT! PIG
OINK. NOW GIT.

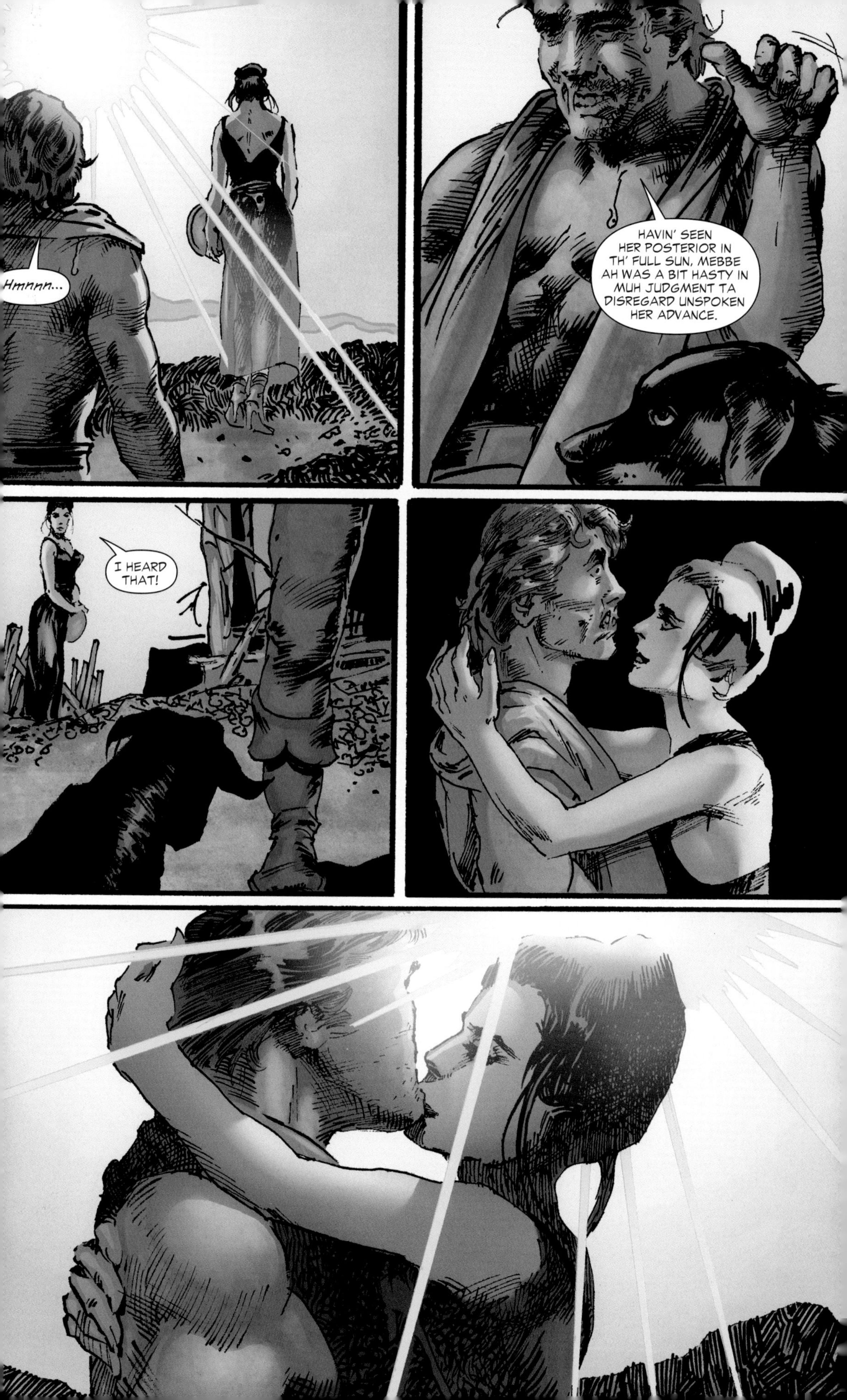
Hmnnn...
HAVIN' SEEN HER POSTERIOR IN TH' FULL SUN, MEBBE AH WAS A BIT HASTY IN MUH JUDGMENT TA DISREGARD UNSPOKEN HER ADVANCE.
I HEARD THAT!

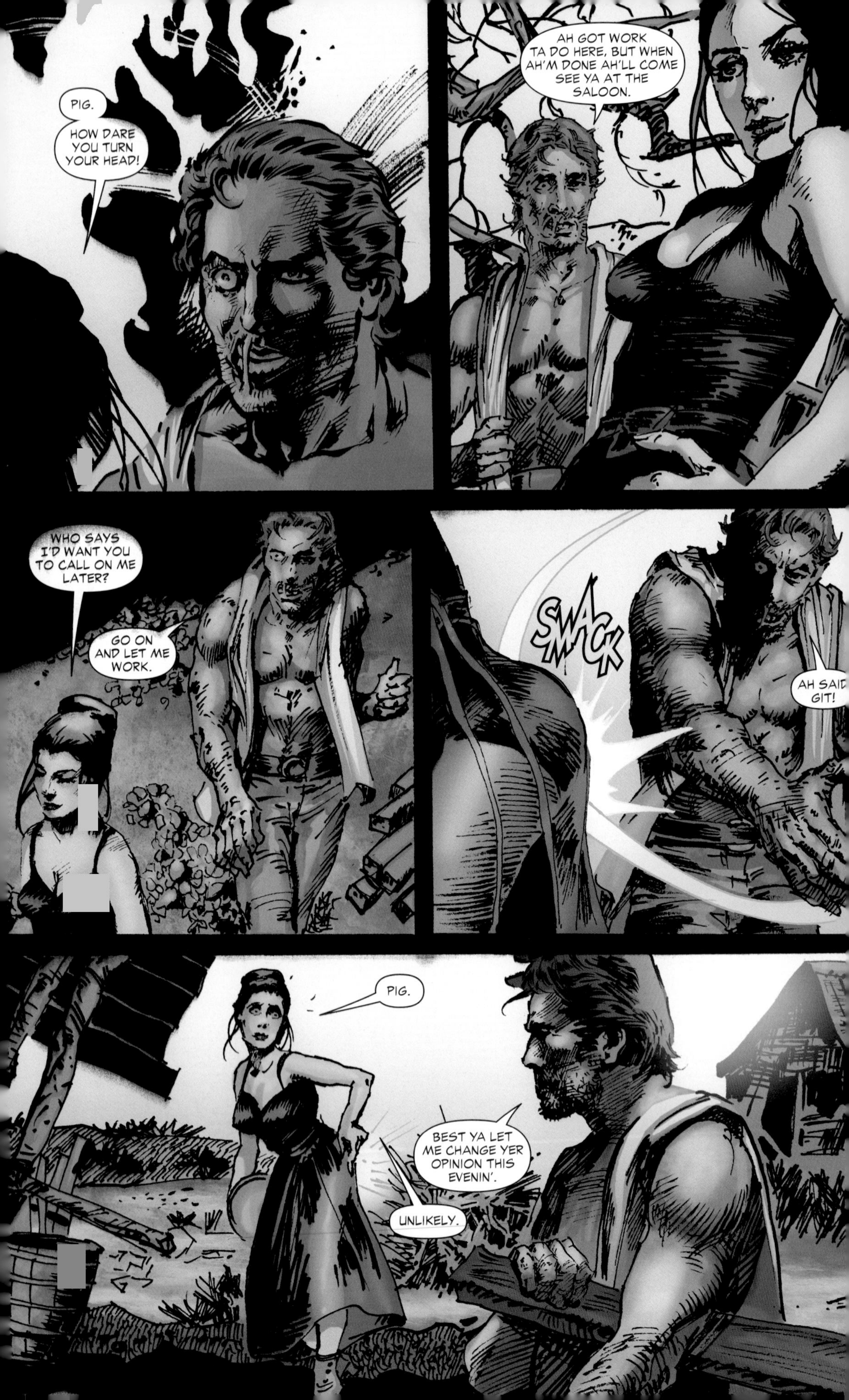
PIG.
HOW DARE YOU TURN YOUR HEAD!
AH GOT WORK TA DO HERE, BUT WHEN AH'M DONE AH'LL COME SEE YA AT THE SALOON.
WHO SAYS I'D WANT YOU TO CALL ON ME LATER?
GO ON AND LET ME WORK.
SMACK
AH SAID GIT!
PIG.
BEST YA LET ME CHANGE YER OPINION THIS EVENIN'.
UNLIKELY.

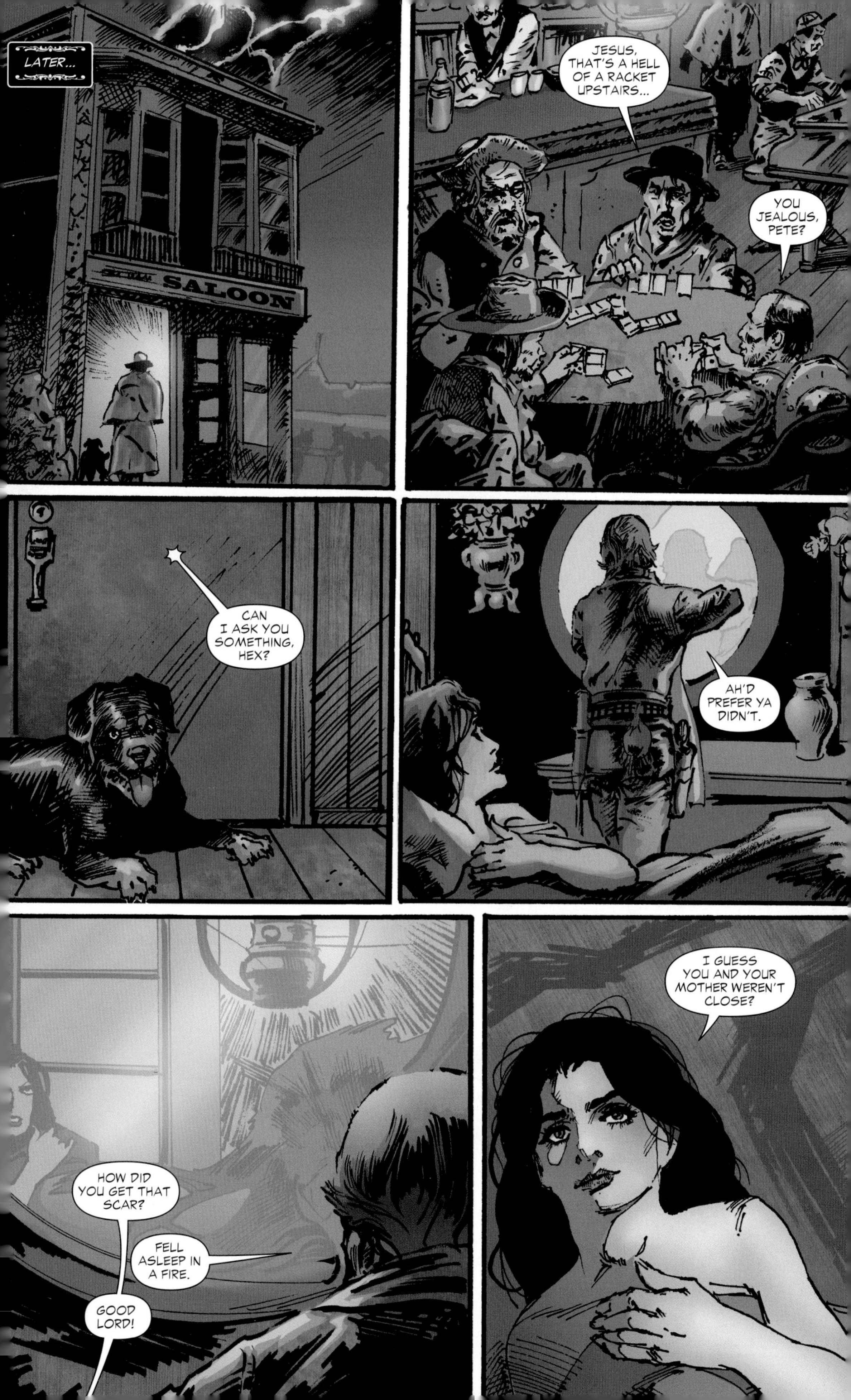
LATER...
SALOON
JESUS, THAT'S A HELL OF A RACKET UPSTAIRS...
YOU JEALOUS, PETE?
CAN I ASK YOU SOMETHING, HEX?
AH'D PREFER YA DIDN'T.
HOW DID YOU GET THAT SCAR?
FELL ASLEEP IN A FIRE.
GOOD LORD!
I GUESS YOU AND YOUR MOTHER WEREN'T CLOSE?

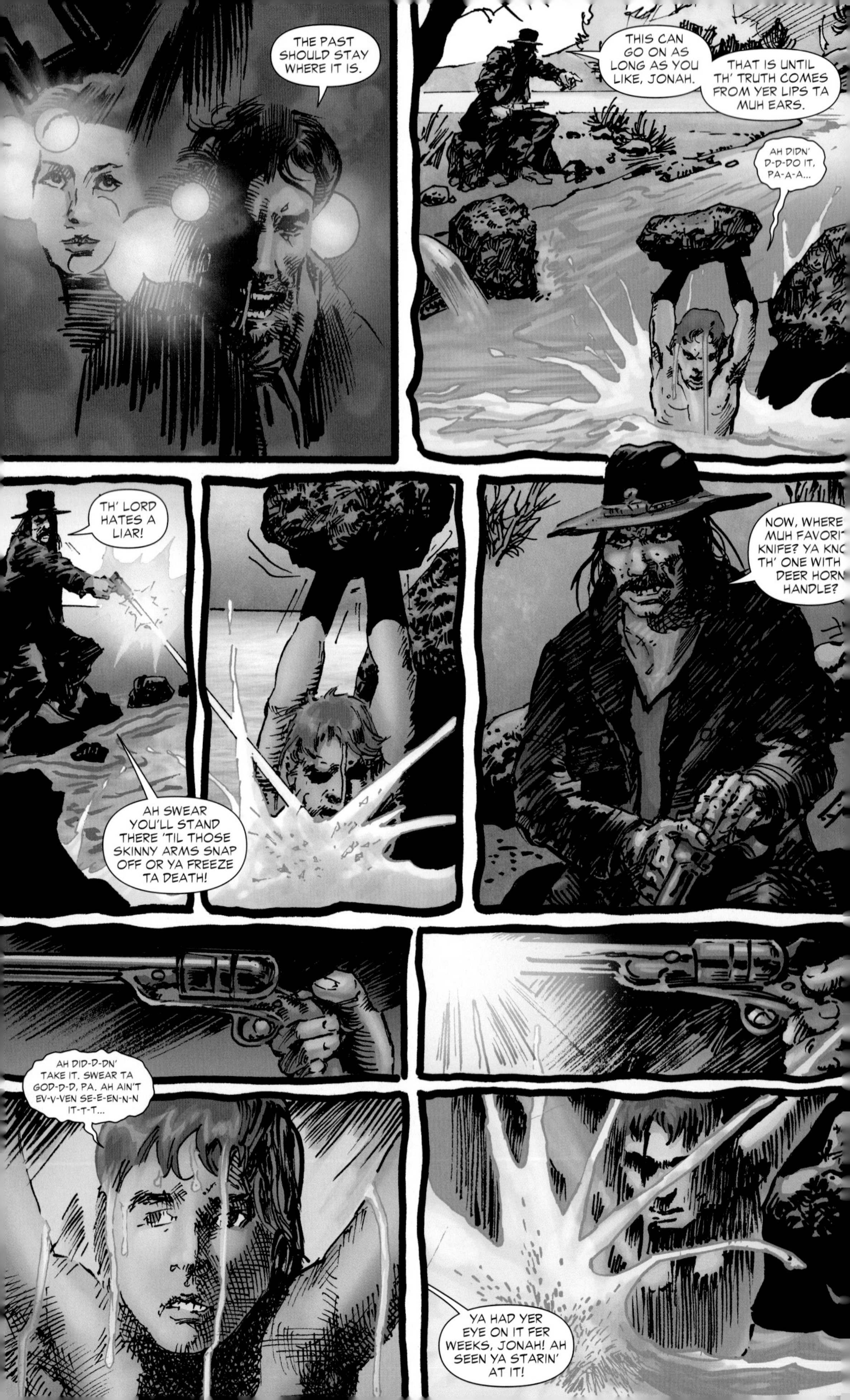
THE PAST SHOULD STAY WHERE IT IS.
THIS CAN GO ON AS LONG AS YOU LIKE, JONAH.
THAT IS UNTIL TH' TRUTH COMES FROM YER LIPS TA MUH EARS.
AH DIDN' D-D-DO IT, PA-A-A...
TH' LORD HATES A LIAR!
AH SWEAR YOU'LL STAND THERE 'TIL THOSE SKINNY ARMS SNAP OFF OR YA FREEZE TA DEATH!
NOW, WHERE MUH FAVORIT KNIFE? YA KNO TH' ONE WITH DEER HORN HANDLE?
AH DID-D-DN' TAKE IT. SWEAR TA GOD-D-D, PA. AH AIN'T EV-V-VEN SE-E-EN-N-N IT-T-T...
YA HAD YER EYE ON IT FER WEEKS, JONAH! AH SEEN YA STARIN' AT IT!

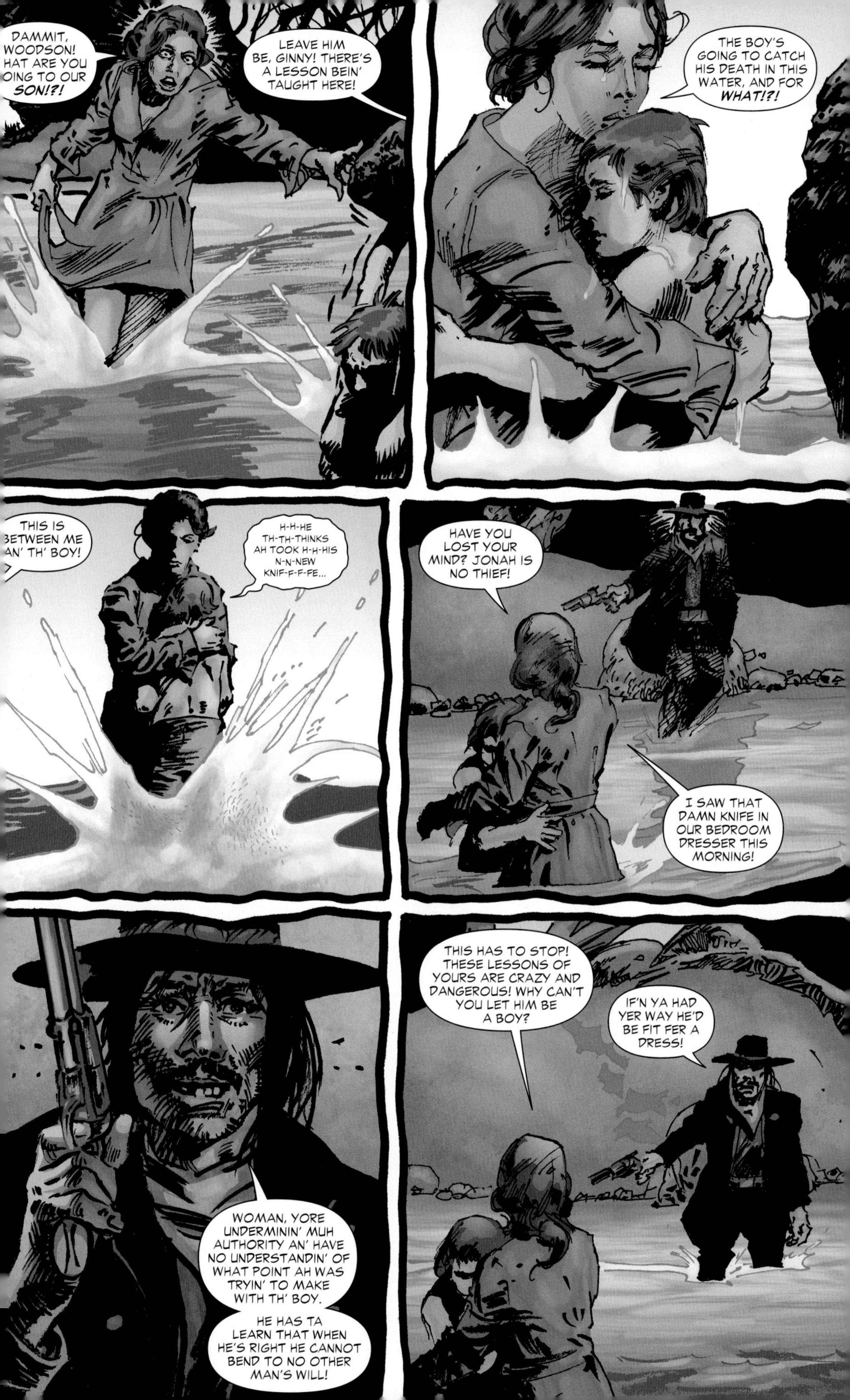

DAMMIT, WOODSON! HAT ARE YOU OING TO OUR SON!?!
LEAVE HIM BE, GINNY! THERE'S A LESSON BEIN' TAUGHT HERE!
THE BOY'S GOING TO CATCH HIS DEATH IN THIS WATER, AND FOR WHAT!?!
THIS IS BETWEEN ME AN' TH' BOY!
H-H-HE TH-TH-THINKS AH TOOK H-H-HIS N-N-NEW KNIF-F-F-FE...
HAVE YOU LOST YOUR MIND? JONAH IS NO THIEF!
I SAW THAT DAMN KNIFE IN OUR BEDROOM DRESSER THIS MORNING!
WOMAN, YORE UNDERMININ' MUH AUTHORITY AN' HAVE NO UNDERSTANDIN' OF WHAT POINT AH WAS TRYIN' TO MAKE WITH TH' BOY.
HE HAS TA LEARN THAT WHEN HE'S RIGHT HE CANNOT BEND TO NO OTHER MAN'S WILL!
THIS HAS TO STOP! THESE LESSONS OF YOURS ARE CRAZY AND DANGEROUS! WHY CAN'T YOU LET HIM BE A BOY?
IF'N YA HAD YER WAY HE'D BE FIT FER A DRESS!

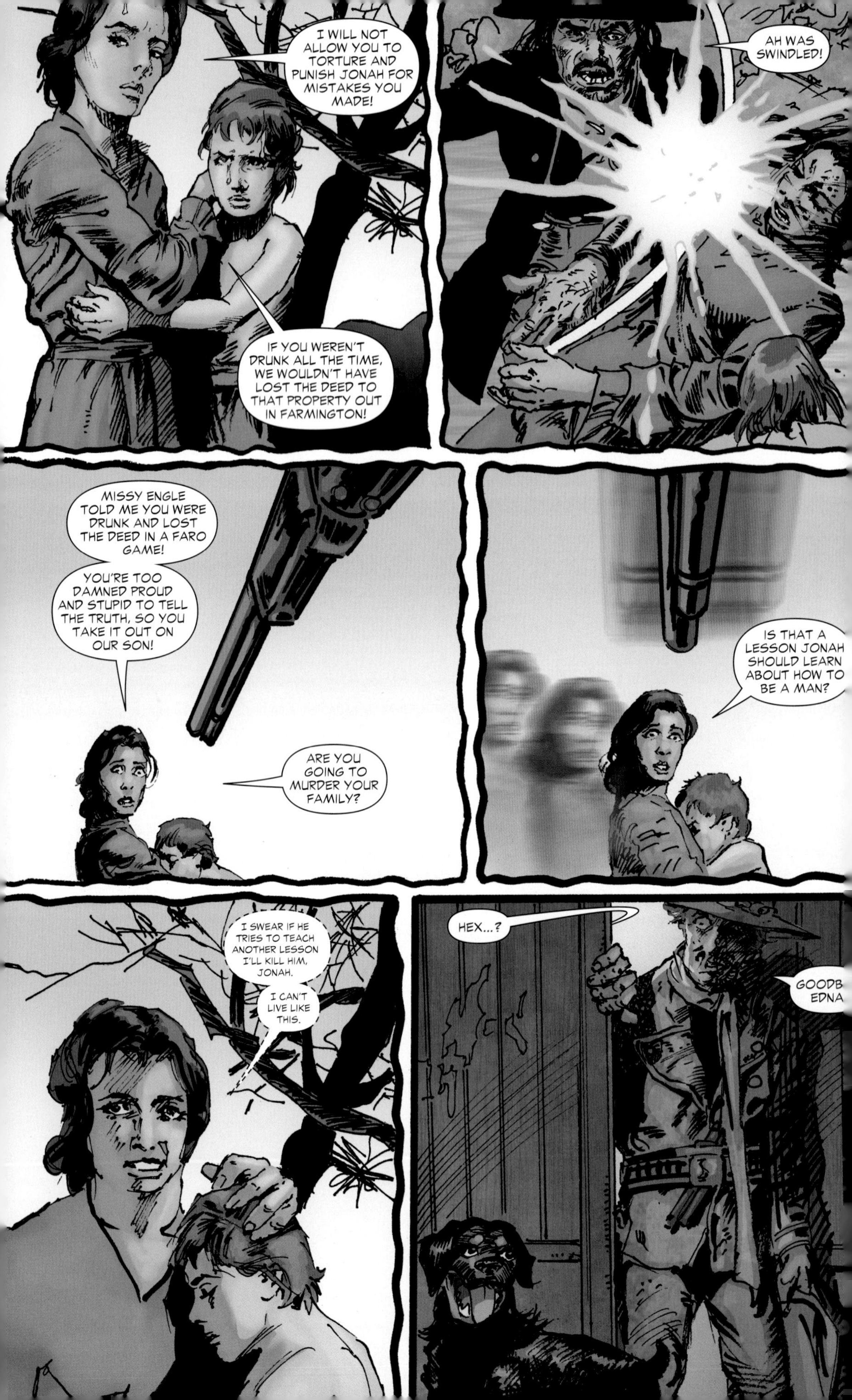
I WILL NOT ALLOW YOU TO TORTURE AND PUNISH JONAH FOR MISTAKES YOU MADE!
IF YOU WEREN'T DRUNK ALL THE TIME, WE WOULDN'T HAVE LOST THE DEED TO THAT PROPERTY OUT IN FARMINGTON!
AH WAS SWINDLED!
MISSY ENGLE TOLD ME YOU WERE DRUNK AND LOST THE DEED IN A FARO GAME!
YOU'RE TOO DAMNED PROUD AND STUPID TO TELL THE TRUTH, SO YOU TAKE IT OUT ON OUR SON!
ARE YOU GOING TO MURDER YOUR FAMILY?
IS THAT A LESSON JONAH SHOULD LEARN ABOUT HOW TO BE A MAN?
I SWEAR IF HE TRIES TO TEACH ANOTHER LESSON I'LL KILL HIM, JONAH.
I CAN'T LIVE LIKE THIS.
HEX...?
GOODB
EDNA

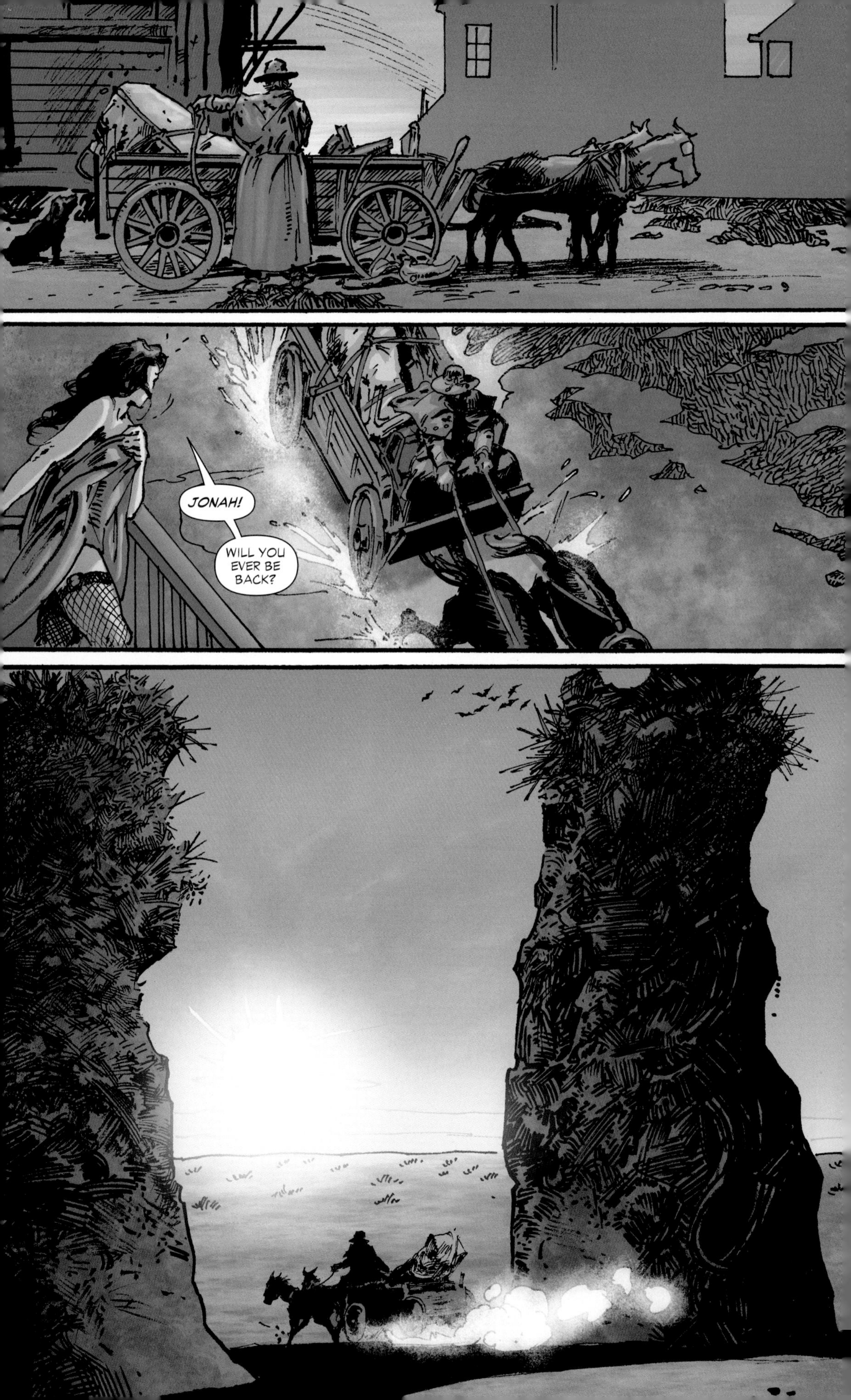
JONAH!
WILL YOU EVER BE BACK?

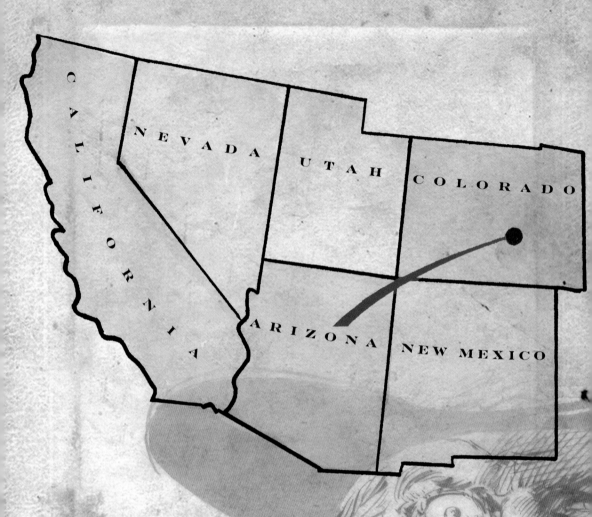

CALIFORNIA

NEVADA

UTAH

COLORADO

ARIZONA

NEW MEXICO

Summit

North Park

South River

Weld

Sand Hills

Larimer

Freemont-Butte

COLORADO

Arapahoe

Lake Park

Rocky Mountains

Freemont

Cheyenne

El Paso

Costilla

Conejos

Heaven's Gate

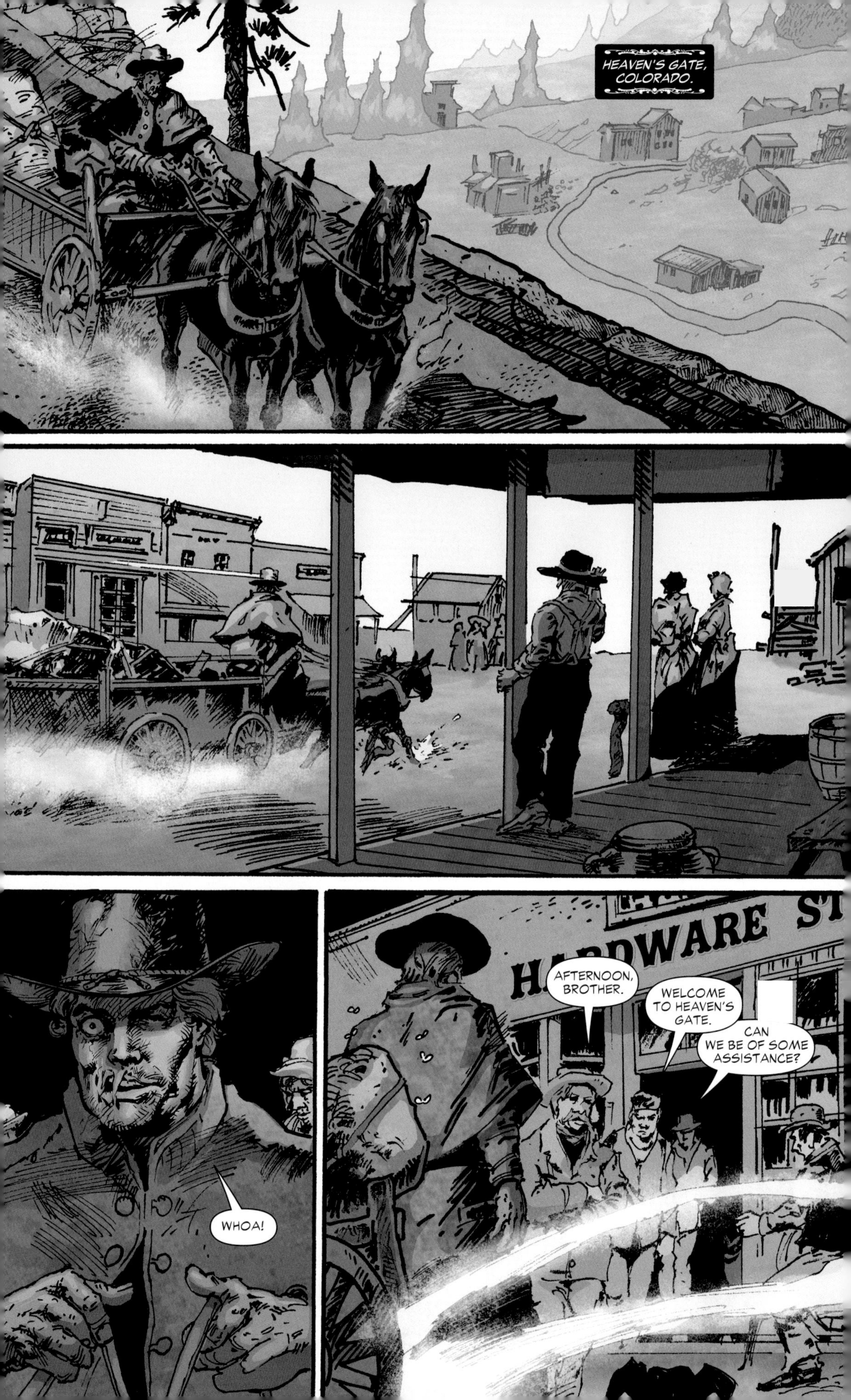
HEAVEN'S GATE, COLORADO.
WHOA!
AFTERNOON, BROTHER.
WELCOME TO HEAVEN'S GATE.
CAN WE BE OF SOME ASSISTANCE?

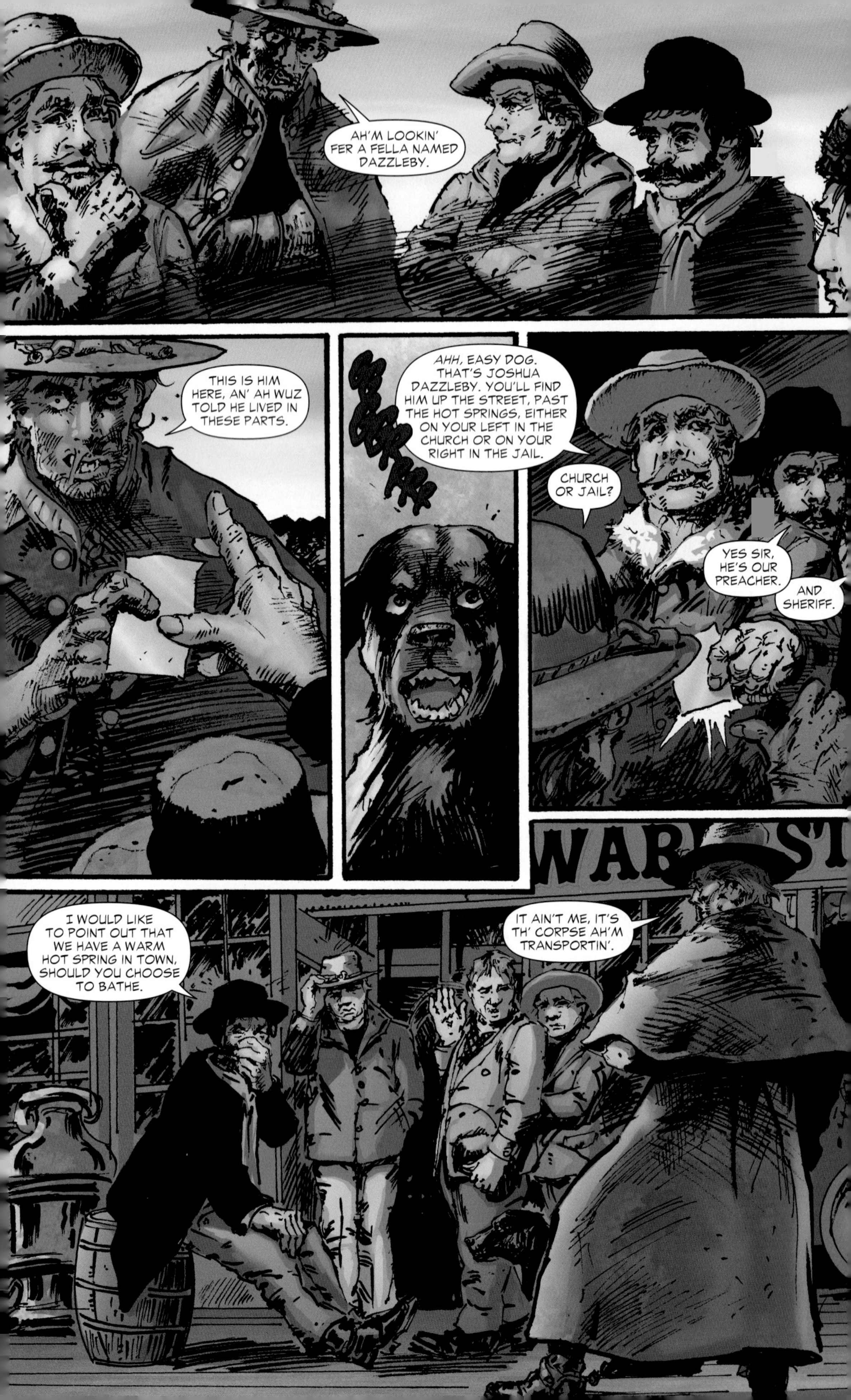
AH'M LOOKIN' FER A FELLA NAMED DAZZLEBY.
THIS IS HIM HERE, AN' AH WUZ TOLD HE LIVED IN THESE PARTS.
GRRRRR
AHH, EASY DOG. THAT'S JOSHUA DAZZLEBY. YOU'LL FIND HIM UP THE STREET, PAST THE HOT SPRINGS, EITHER ON YOUR LEFT IN THE CHURCH OR ON YOUR RIGHT IN THE JAIL.
CHURCH OR JAIL?
YES SIR, HE'S OUR PREACHER.
AND SHERIFF.
I WOULD LIKE TO POINT OUT THAT WE HAVE A WARM HOT SPRING IN TOWN, SHOULD YOU CHOOSE TO BATHE.
IT AIN'T ME, IT'S TH' CORPSE AH'M TRANSPORTIN'.

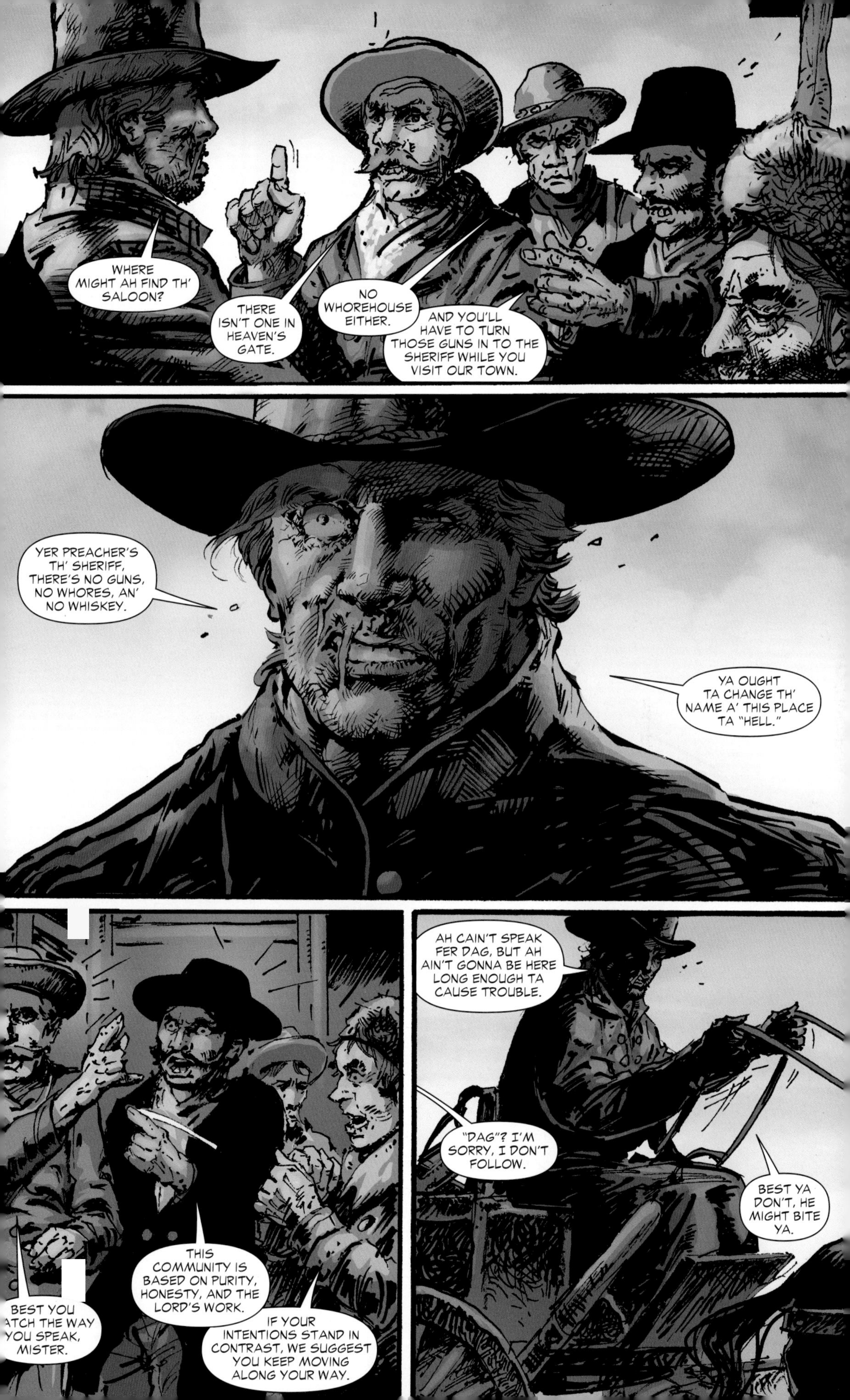
WHERE MIGHT AH FIND TH' SALOON?
THERE ISN'T ONE IN HEAVEN'S GATE.
NO WHOREHOUSE EITHER.
AND YOU'LL HAVE TO TURN THOSE GUNS IN TO THE SHERIFF WHILE YOU VISIT OUR TOWN.
YER PREACHER'S TH' SHERIFF, THERE'S NO GUNS, NO WHORES, AN' NO WHISKEY.
YA OUGHT TA CHANGE TH' NAME A' THIS PLACE TA "HELL."
BEST YOU ATCH THE WAY YOU SPEAK, MISTER.
THIS COMMUNITY IS BASED ON PURITY, HONESTY, AND THE LORD'S WORK.
IF YOUR INTENTIONS STAND IN CONTRAST, WE SUGGEST YOU KEEP MOVING ALONG YOUR WAY.
AH CAIN'T SPEAK FER DAG, BUT AH AIN'T GONNA BE HERE LONG ENOUGH TA CAUSE TROUBLE.
"DAG"? I'M SORRY, I DON'T FOLLOW.
BEST YA DON'T, HE MIGHT BITE YA.

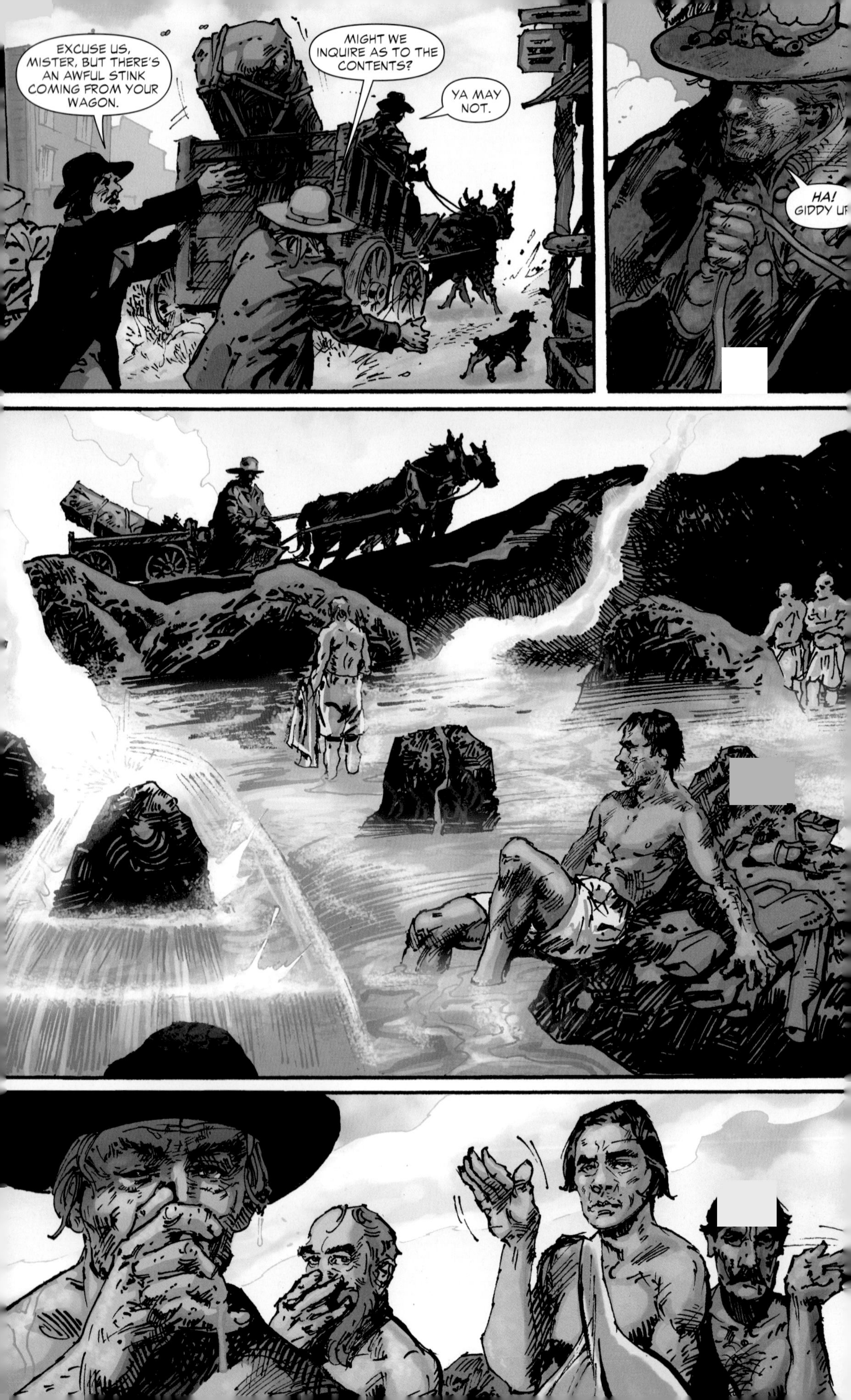
EXCUSE US, MISTER, BUT THERE'S AN AWFUL STINK COMING FROM YOUR WAGON.
MIGHT WE INQUIRE AS TO THE CONTENTS?
YA MAY NOT.
HA! GIDDY UP

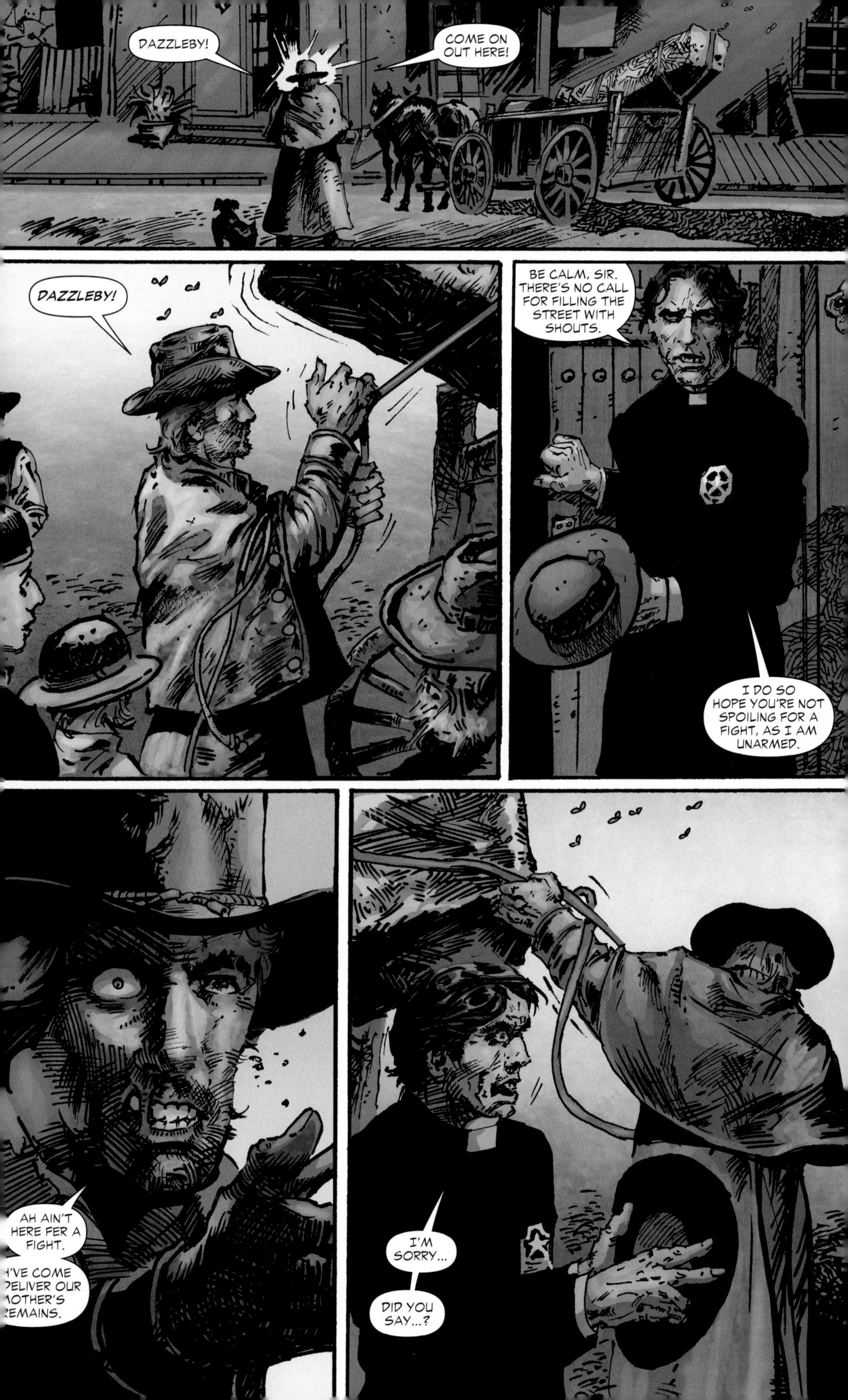
DAZZLEBY!
COME ON OUT HERE!
DAZZLEBY!
BE CALM, SIR. THERE'S NO CALL FOR FILLING THE STREET WITH SHOUTS.
I DO SO HOPE YOU'RE NOT SPOILING FOR A FIGHT, AS I AM UNARMED.
AH AIN'T HERE FER A FIGHT.
I'VE COME DELIVER OUR MOTHER'S REMAINS.
I'M SORRY...
DID YOU SAY...?

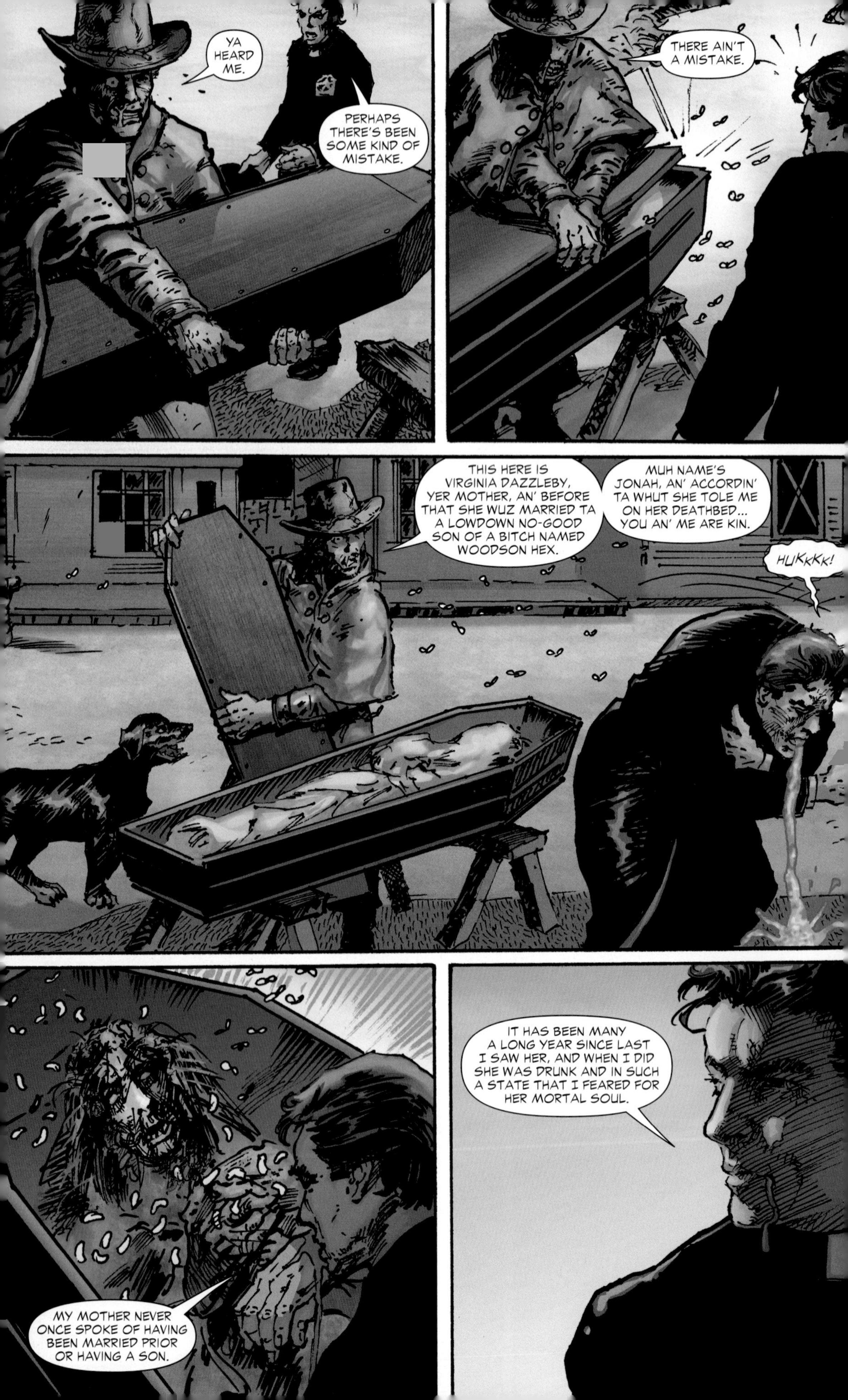
YA HEARD ME.
PERHAPS THERE'S BEEN SOME KIND OF MISTAKE.
THERE AIN'T A MISTAKE.
THIS HERE IS VIRGINIA DAZZLEBY, YER MOTHER, AN' BEFORE THAT SHE WUZ MARRIED TA A LOWDOWN NO-GOOD SON OF A BITCH NAMED WOODSON HEX.
MUH NAME'S JONAH, AN' ACCORDIN' TA WHUT SHE TOLE ME ON HER DEATHBED... YOU AN' ME ARE KIN.
HUKKKK!
MY MOTHER NEVER ONCE SPOKE OF HAVING BEEN MARRIED PRIOR OR HAVING A SON.
IT HAS BEEN MANY A LONG YEAR SINCE LAST I SAW HER, AND WHEN I DID SHE WAS DRUNK AND IN SUCH A STATE THAT I FEARED FOR HER MORTAL SOUL.

AN' NOW SHE'S DEAD AN' ALL YERS TA BURY AS YA SEE FIT.

WHERE ARE YOU GOING?

MOVIN' ON TA A PROPER TOWN WITH WHISKEY AN' WHORES.

YOU DON'T WANT ANYTHING?

HELL, REVEREND SHERIFF, BY TH' LOOK OF IT YA AIN'T GOT ANYTHIN' GOOD IN THIS TOWN.

WELL, IF YOU TRULY ARE MY HALF BROTHER, WOULDN'T YOU WANT TO STAY FOR OUR MOTHER'S FUNERAL?

SURELY THERE ARE QUESTIONS THAT PLAGUE YOU ABOUT MYSELF AND...?

AN' WHUT?

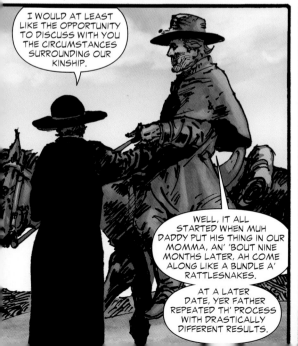

I WOULD AT LEAST LIKE THE OPPORTUNITY TO DISCUSS WITH YOU THE CIRCUMSTANCES SURROUNDING OUR KINSHIP.

WELL, IT ALL STARTED WHEN MUH DADDY PUT HIS THING IN OUR MOMMA, AN' 'BOUT NINE MONTHS LATER, AH COME ALONG LIKE A BUNDLE A' RATTLESNAKES.

AT A LATER DATE, YER FATHER REPEATED TH' PROCESS WITH DRASTICALLY DIFFERENT RESULTS.

THAT 'BOUT ANSWER YER QUESTIONS?

I FEEL AS IF I CAN UNDERSTAND YOUR ANGER, AND IN OBSERVING YOUR PERSONAGE, WITH THE INCLUSION OF THAT SCAR AND THOSE CONFEDERATE GRAYS...

CLEARLY THE LORD HAS SET A ROUGH TRAIL BEFORE YOU, JONAH.

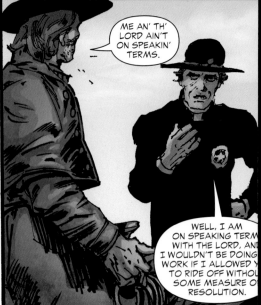

ME AN' TH' LORD AIN'T ON SPEAKIN' TERMS.

WELL, I AM ON SPEAKING TERMS WITH THE LORD, AND I WOULDN'T BE DOING WORK IF I ALLOWED YO TO RIDE OFF WITHOUT SOME MEASURE OF RESOLUTION.

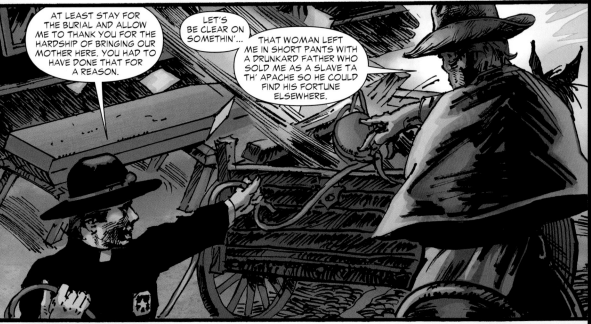

AT LEAST STAY FOR THE BURIAL AND ALLOW ME TO THANK YOU FOR THE HARDSHIP OF BRINGING OUR MOTHER HERE. YOU HAD TO HAVE DONE THAT FOR A REASON.

LET'S BE CLEAR ON SOMETHIN'... THAT WOMAN LEFT ME IN SHORT PANTS WITH A DRUNKARD FATHER WHO SOLD ME AS A SLAVE TA TH' APACHE SO HE COULD FIND HIS FORTUNE ELSEWHERE.

ALL THE MORE REASON TO STAY SO WE CAN GET TO KNOW EACH OTHER BETTER. I HAVE NO FAMILY LEFT TO ME, AND I SUSPECT WITH OUR MOTHER'S PASSING THE SAME CAN BE SAID OF YOU.

AM I CORRECT?

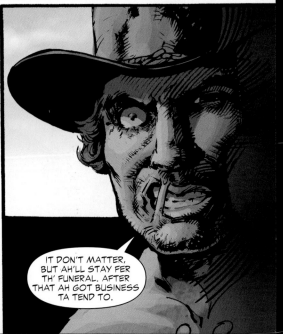

IT DON'T MATTER, BUT AH'LL STAY FER TH' FUNERAL. AFTER THAT AH GOT BUSINESS TA TEND TO.

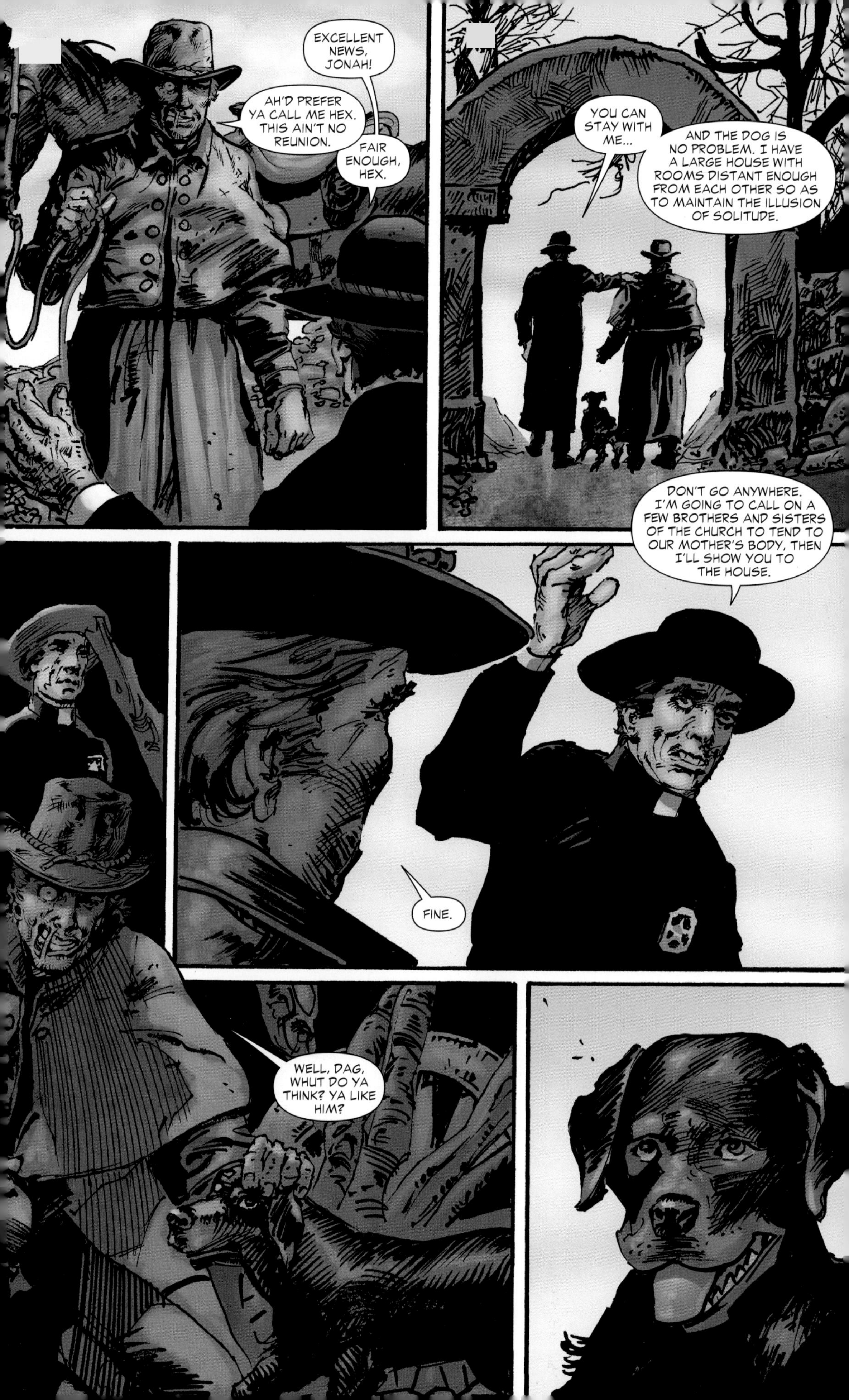
EXCELLENT NEWS, JONAH!
AH'D PREFER YA CALL ME HEX. THIS AIN'T NO REUNION.
FAIR ENOUGH, HEX.
YOU CAN STAY WITH ME...
AND THE DOG IS NO PROBLEM. I HAVE A LARGE HOUSE WITH ROOMS DISTANT ENOUGH FROM EACH OTHER SO AS TO MAINTAIN THE ILLUSION OF SOLITUDE.
DON'T GO ANYWHERE. I'M GOING TO CALL ON A FEW BROTHERS AND SISTERS OF THE CHURCH TO TEND TO OUR MOTHER'S BODY, THEN I'LL SHOW YOU TO THE HOUSE.
FINE.
WELL, DAG, WHUT DO YA THINK? YA LIKE HIM?

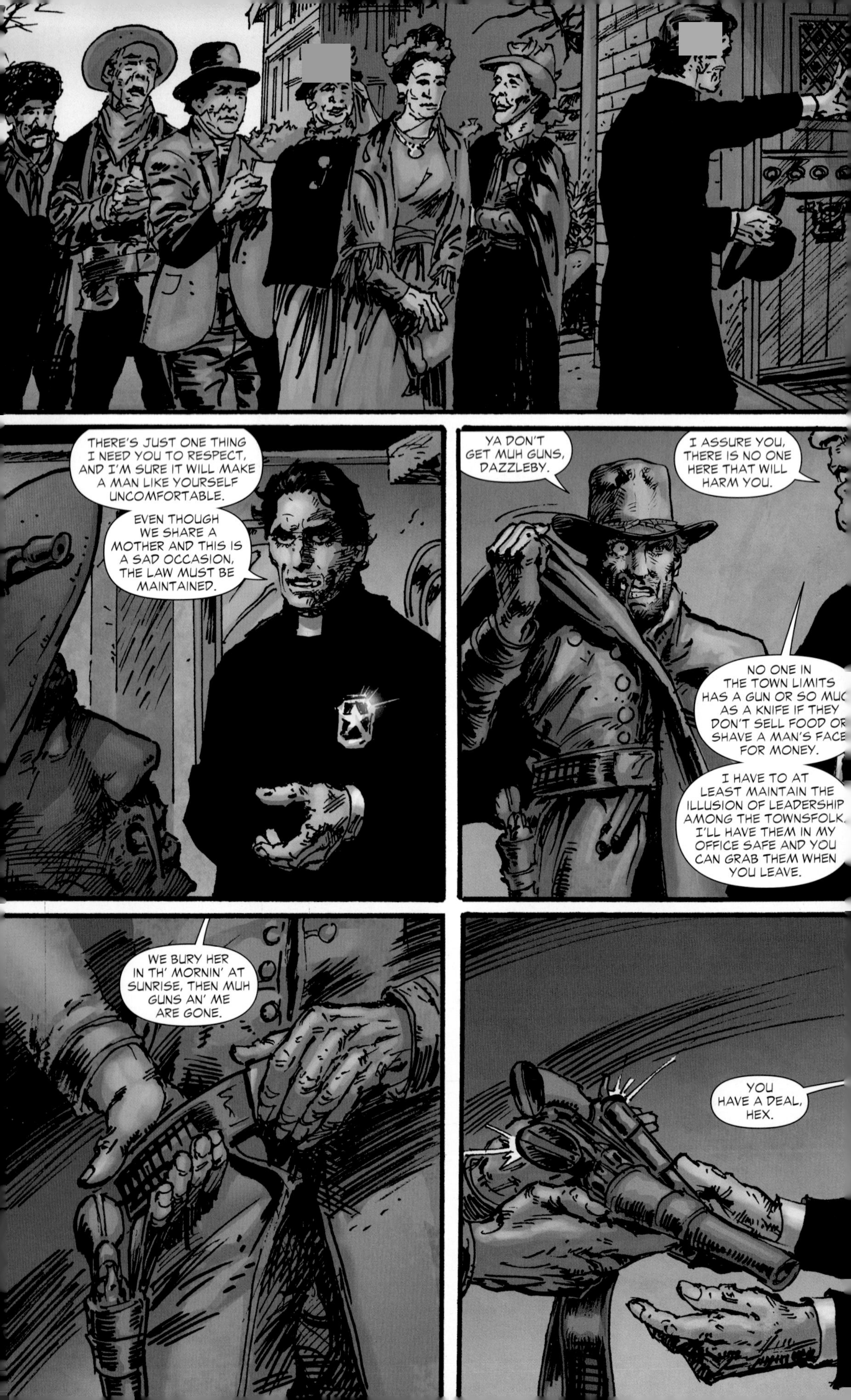
THERE'S JUST ONE THING I NEED YOU TO RESPECT, AND I'M SURE IT WILL MAKE A MAN LIKE YOURSELF UNCOMFORTABLE.
EVEN THOUGH WE SHARE A MOTHER AND THIS IS A SAD OCCASION, THE LAW MUST BE MAINTAINED.
YA DON'T GET MUH GUNS, DAZZLEBY.
I ASSURE YOU, THERE IS NO ONE HERE THAT WILL HARM YOU.
NO ONE IN THE TOWN LIMITS HAS A GUN OR SO MUC AS A KNIFE IF THEY DON'T SELL FOOD OR SHAVE A MAN'S FACE FOR MONEY.
I HAVE TO AT LEAST MAINTAIN THE ILLUSION OF LEADERSHIP AMONG THE TOWNSFOLK. I'LL HAVE THEM IN MY OFFICE SAFE AND YOU CAN GRAB THEM WHEN YOU LEAVE.
WE BURY HER IN TH' MORNIN' AT SUNRISE, THEN MUH GUNS AN' ME ARE GONE.
YOU HAVE A DEAL, HEX.

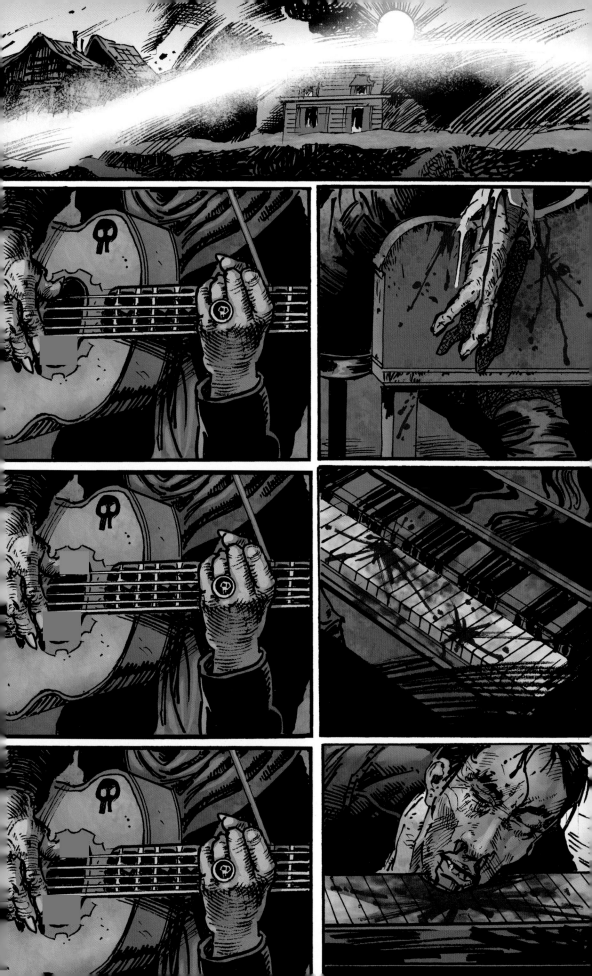

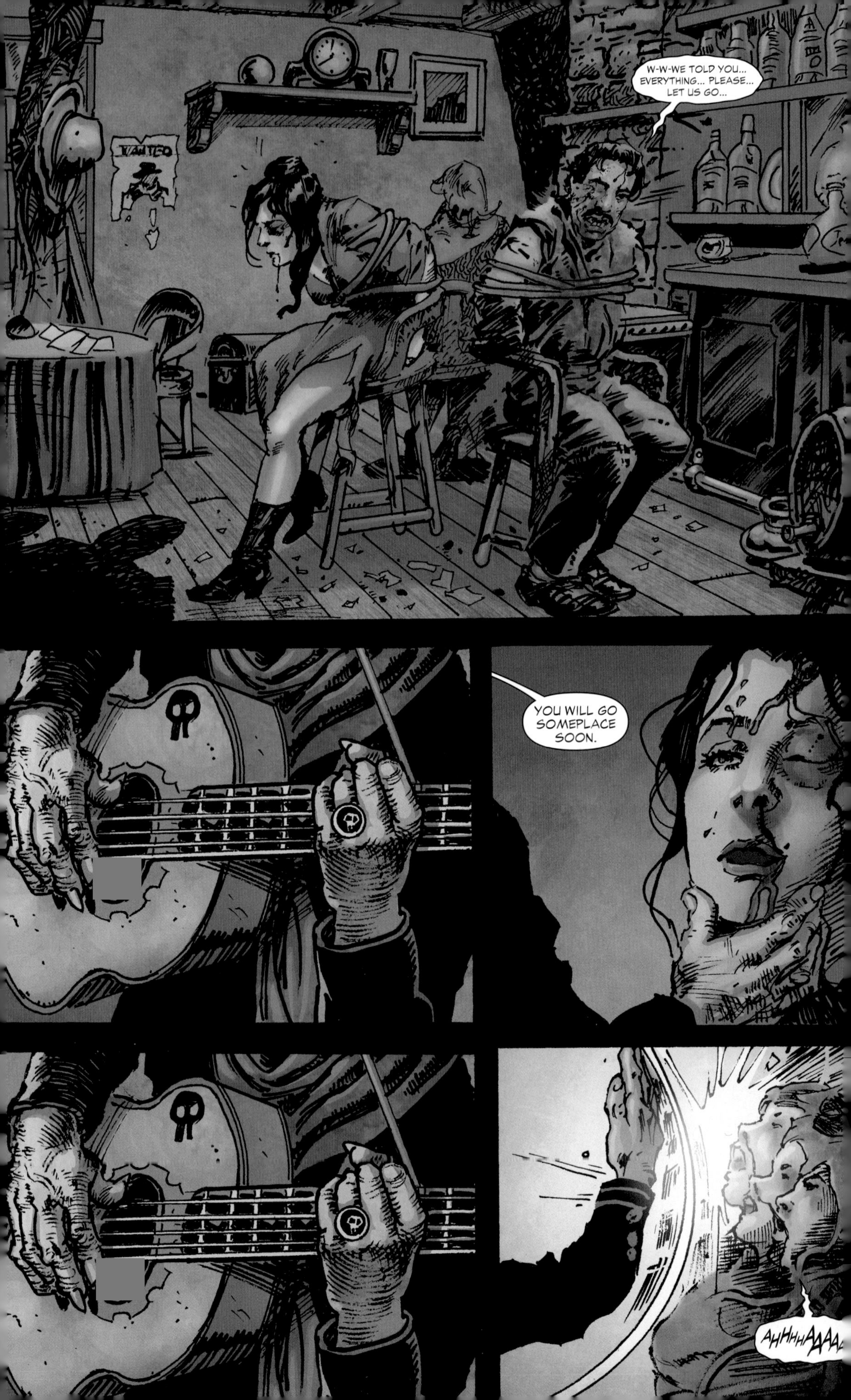
W-W-WE TOLD YOU... EVERYTHING... PLEASE... LET US GO...
YOU WILL GO SOMEPLACE SOON.
AHHHHAAAA

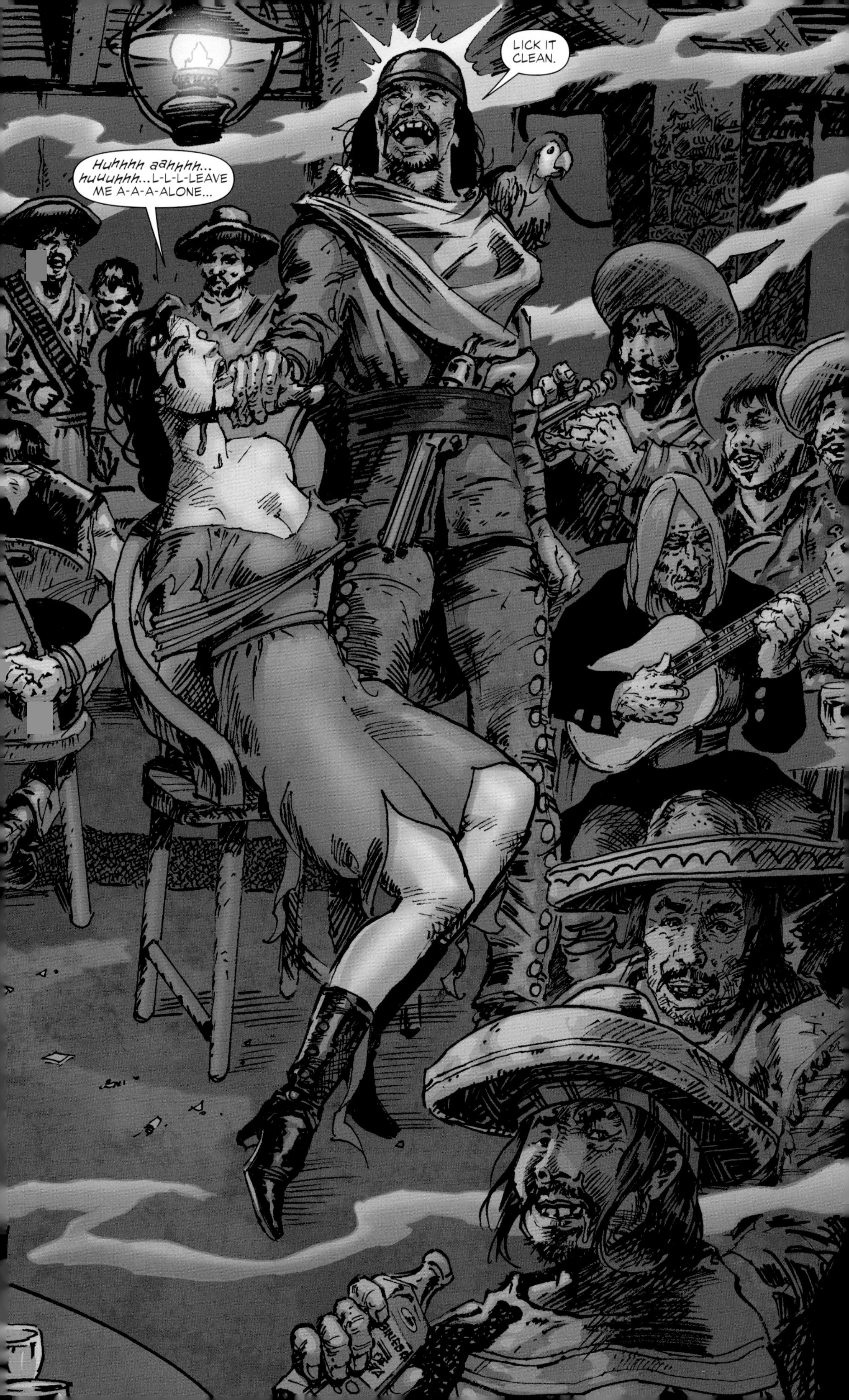
LICK IT CLEAN.
Huhhhh aahhhh... huuuhhh...L-L-L-LEAVE ME A-A-A-ALONE...

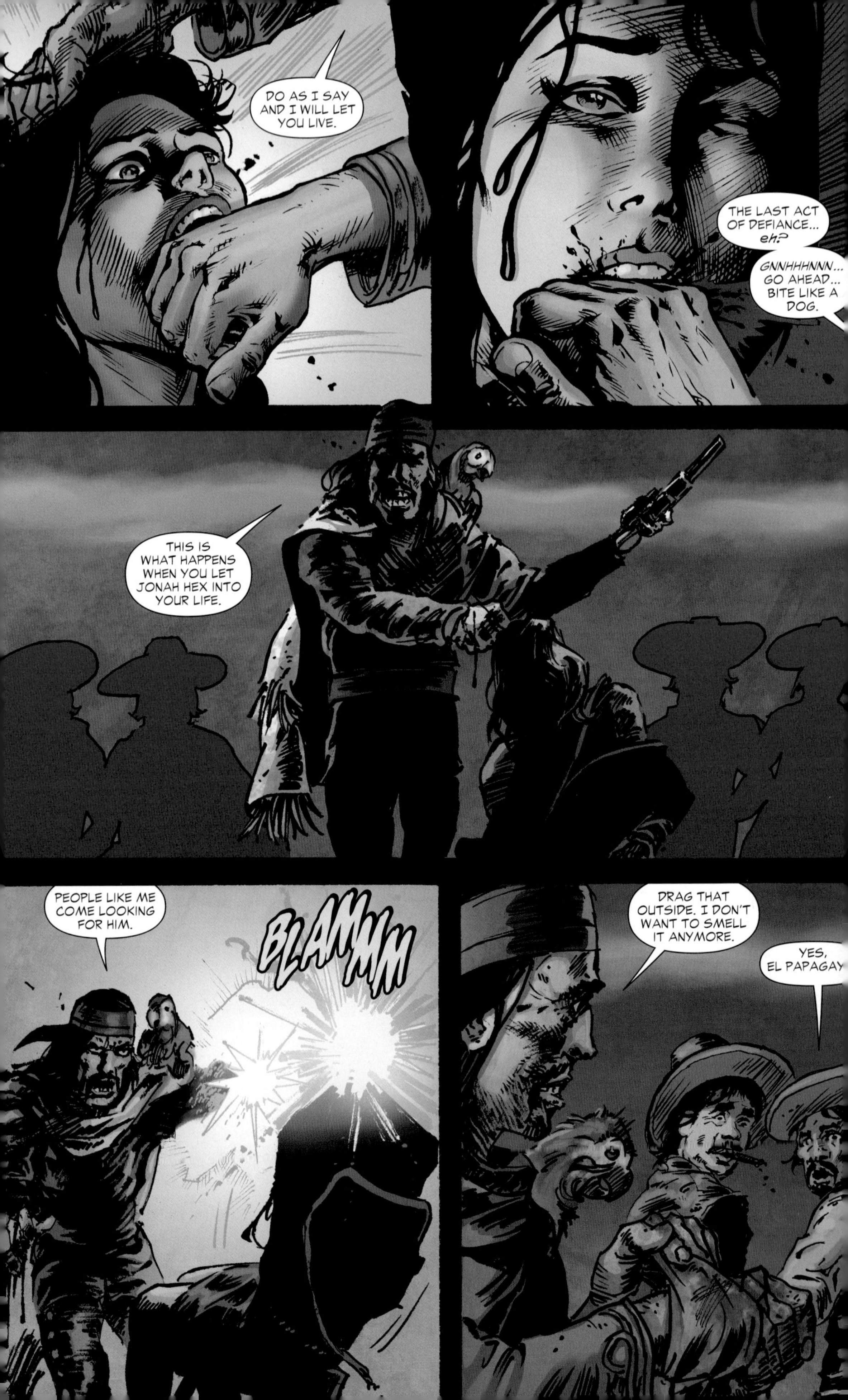
DO AS I SAY AND I WILL LET YOU LIVE.
THE LAST ACT OF DEFIANCE... eh?
GNNHHHHNNN... GO AHEAD... BITE LIKE A DOG.
THIS IS WHAT HAPPENS WHEN YOU LET JONAH HEX INTO YOUR LIFE.
PEOPLE LIKE ME COME LOOKING FOR HIM.
BLAMMM
DRAG THAT OUTSIDE. I DON'T WANT TO SMELL IT ANYMORE.
YES, EL PAPAGAY

WHY ARE YOU DOING THIS? WE DIDN'T KILL YOUR MEN...

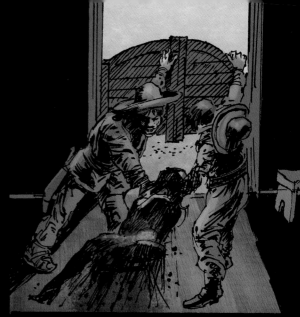

SMACK

PLEASE STOP!

PLEASE DON'T HURT HIM ANYMORE!

I'LL DO ANYTHING.

I KNOW YOU WILL.

EVEN THINGS YOU'D NEVER IMAGINED YOU WOULD, BUT THAT IS FOR LATER.

GET THE GIRL SOMETHING TO DRINK.

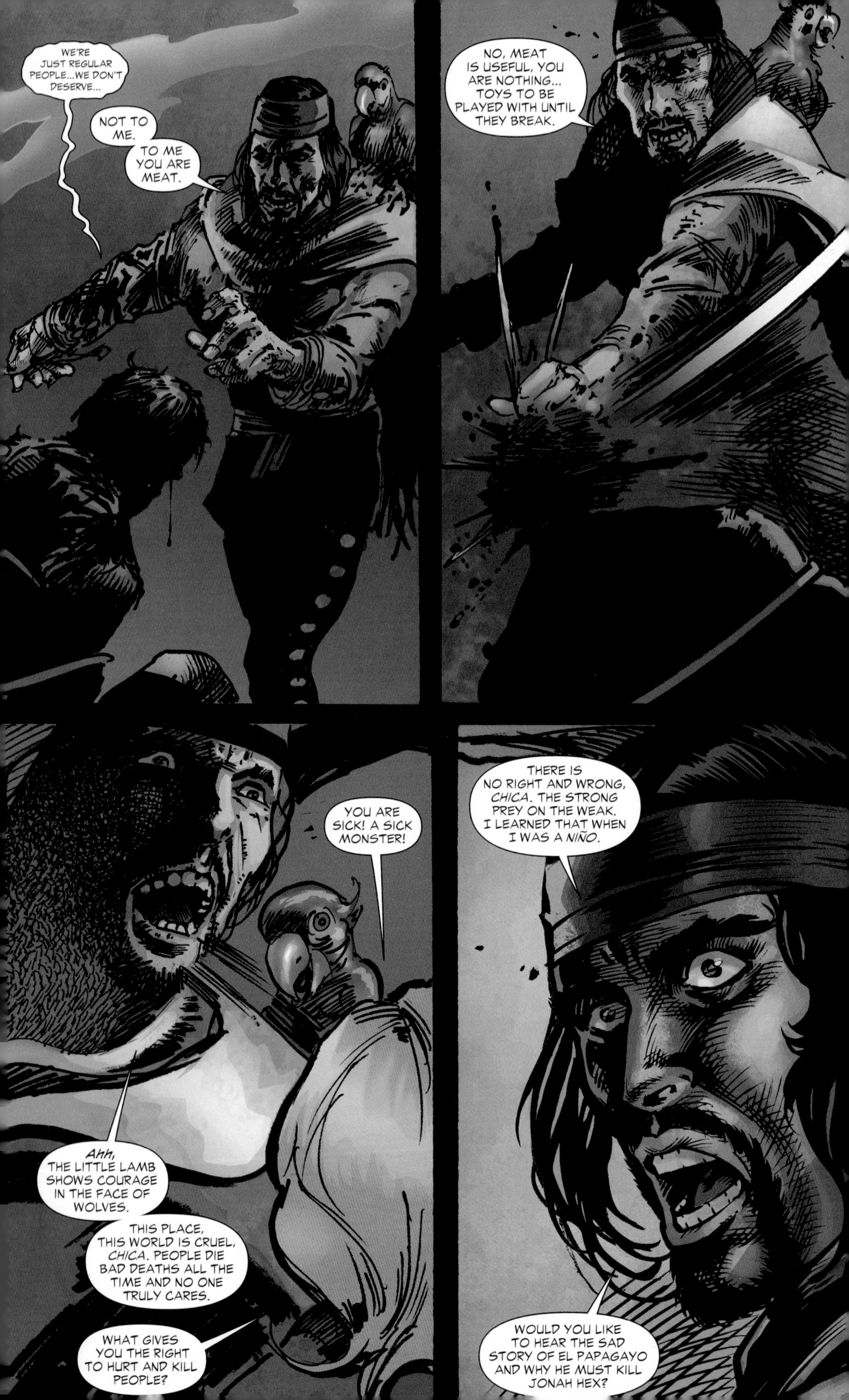
WE'RE JUST REGULAR PEOPLE...WE DON'T DESERVE...
NOT TO ME.
TO ME YOU ARE MEAT.
NO, MEAT IS USEFUL, YOU ARE NOTHING... TOYS TO BE PLAYED WITH UNTIL THEY BREAK.
YOU ARE SICK! A SICK MONSTER!
Ahh, THE LITTLE LAMB SHOWS COURAGE IN THE FACE OF WOLVES.
THIS PLACE, THIS WORLD IS CRUEL, *CHICA*. PEOPLE DIE BAD DEATHS ALL THE TIME AND NO ONE TRULY CARES.
WHAT GIVES YOU THE RIGHT TO HURT AND KILL PEOPLE?
THERE IS NO RIGHT AND WRONG, *CHICA*. THE STRONG PREY ON THE WEAK. I LEARNED THAT WHEN I WAS A *NIÑO*.
WOULD YOU LIKE TO HEAR THE SAD STORY OF EL PAPAGAYO AND WHY HE MUST KILL JONAH HEX?

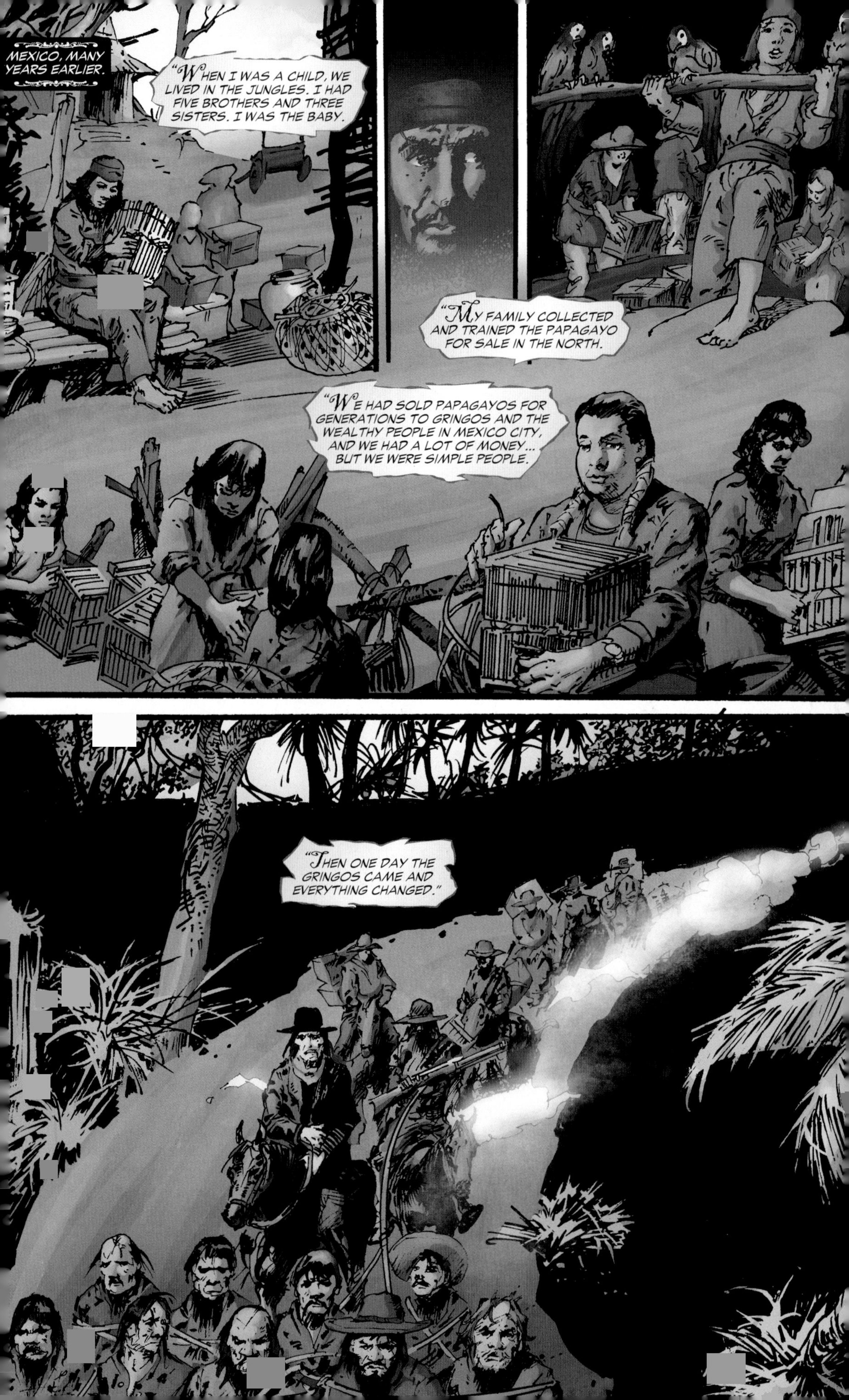
MEXICO, MANY YEARS EARLIER.
"WHEN I WAS A CHILD, WE LIVED IN THE JUNGLES. I HAD FIVE BROTHERS AND THREE SISTERS. I WAS THE BABY.
"MY FAMILY COLLECTED AND TRAINED THE PAPAGAYO FOR SALE IN THE NORTH.
"WE HAD SOLD PAPAGAYOS FOR GENERATIONS TO GRINGOS AND THE WEALTHY PEOPLE IN MEXICO CITY, AND WE HAD A LOT OF MONEY... BUT WE WERE SIMPLE PEOPLE.
"THEN ONE DAY THE GRINGOS CAME AND EVERYTHING CHANGED."

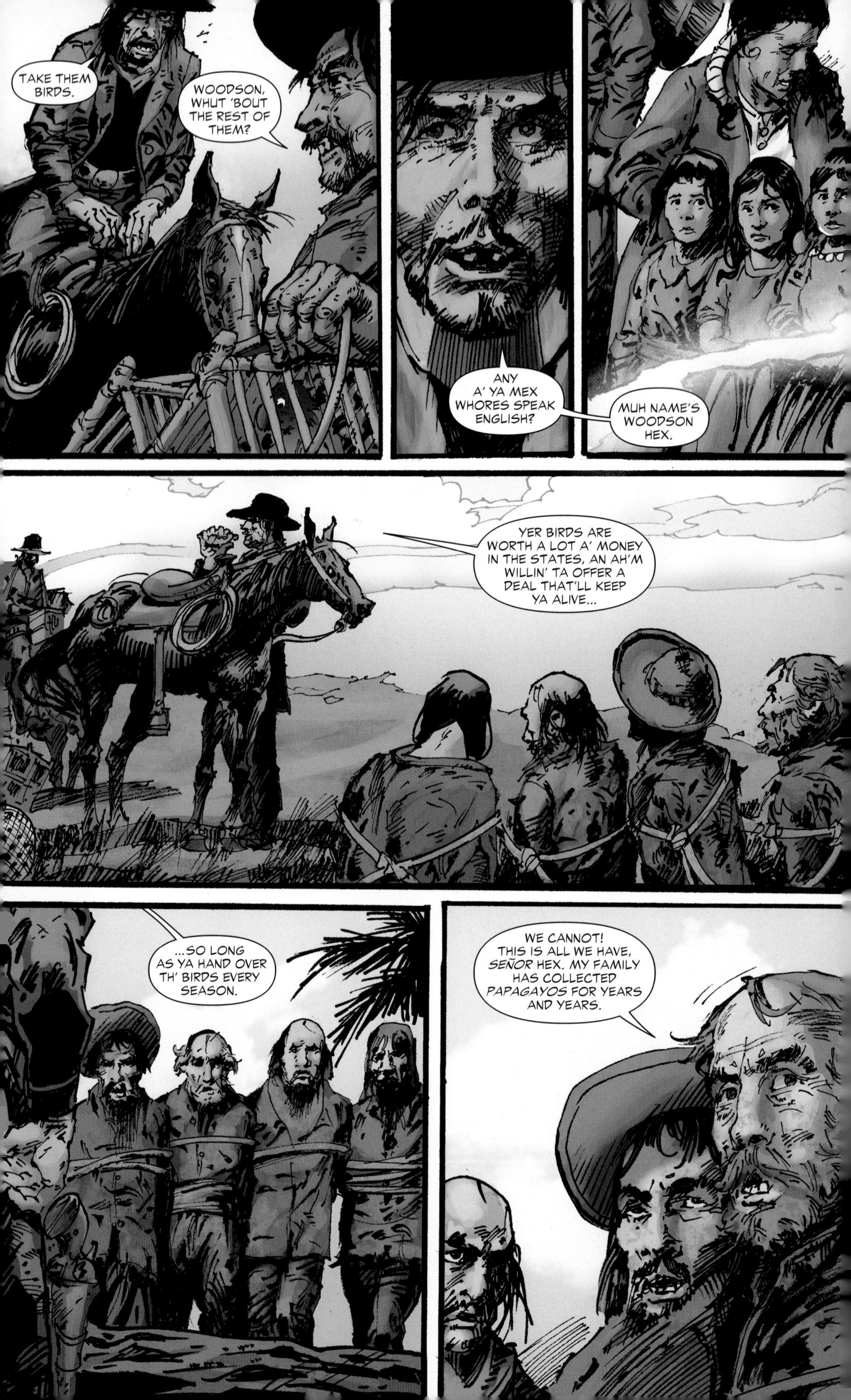
TAKE THEM BIRDS.
WOODSON, WHUT 'BOUT THE REST OF THEM?
ANY A' YA MEX WHORES SPEAK ENGLISH?
MUH NAME'S WOODSON HEX.
YER BIRDS ARE WORTH A LOT A' MONEY IN THE STATES, AN AH'M WILLIN' TA OFFER A DEAL THAT'LL KEEP YA ALIVE...
...SO LONG AS YA HAND OVER TH' BIRDS EVERY SEASON.
WE CANNOT! THIS IS ALL WE HAVE, *SEÑOR* HEX. MY FAMILY HAS COLLECTED *PAPAGAYOS* FOR YEARS AND YEARS.

BLAMMM

AH AIN'T NEGOTIATIN'.

WAY AH FIGGER, AH DON'T NEED NONE A' YA MEN NOR BOYS. SEEMS THE WOMEN ARE PLENTY CAPABLE A' SHOWIN' US THE PLACES YA FIND THEM BIRDS.

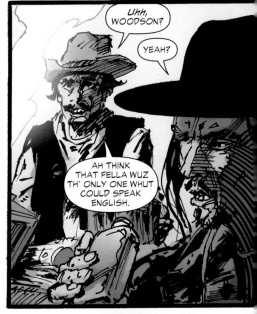

Uhh, WOODSON?

YEAH?

AH THINK THAT FELLA WUZ TH' ONLY ONE WHUT COULD SPEAK ENGLISH.

Aww, HELL. JUST KILL EVERYONE 'CEPTIN' TH' THREE WOMEN, AN' BURN DOWN EVERYTHIN'!

WE'LL KEEP THEM MEX WHORES TA SHOW US TH' SPOTS FER BIRDS.

KILL EVEN THE YOUNG'UNS?

'SPECIALLY TH' YOUNG ONES. AH HATE CHILDREN.

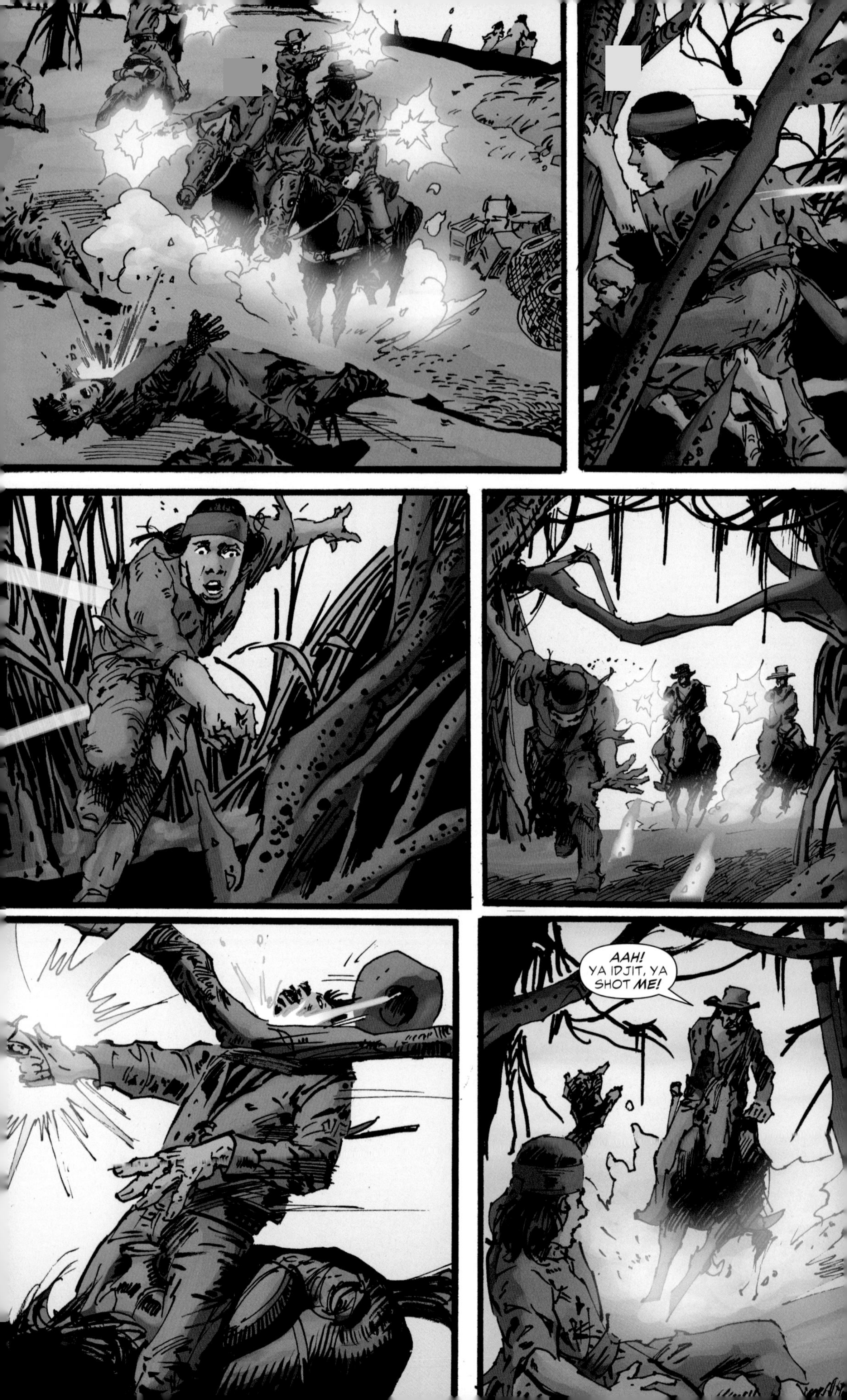
AAH! YA IDJIT, YA SHOT ME!

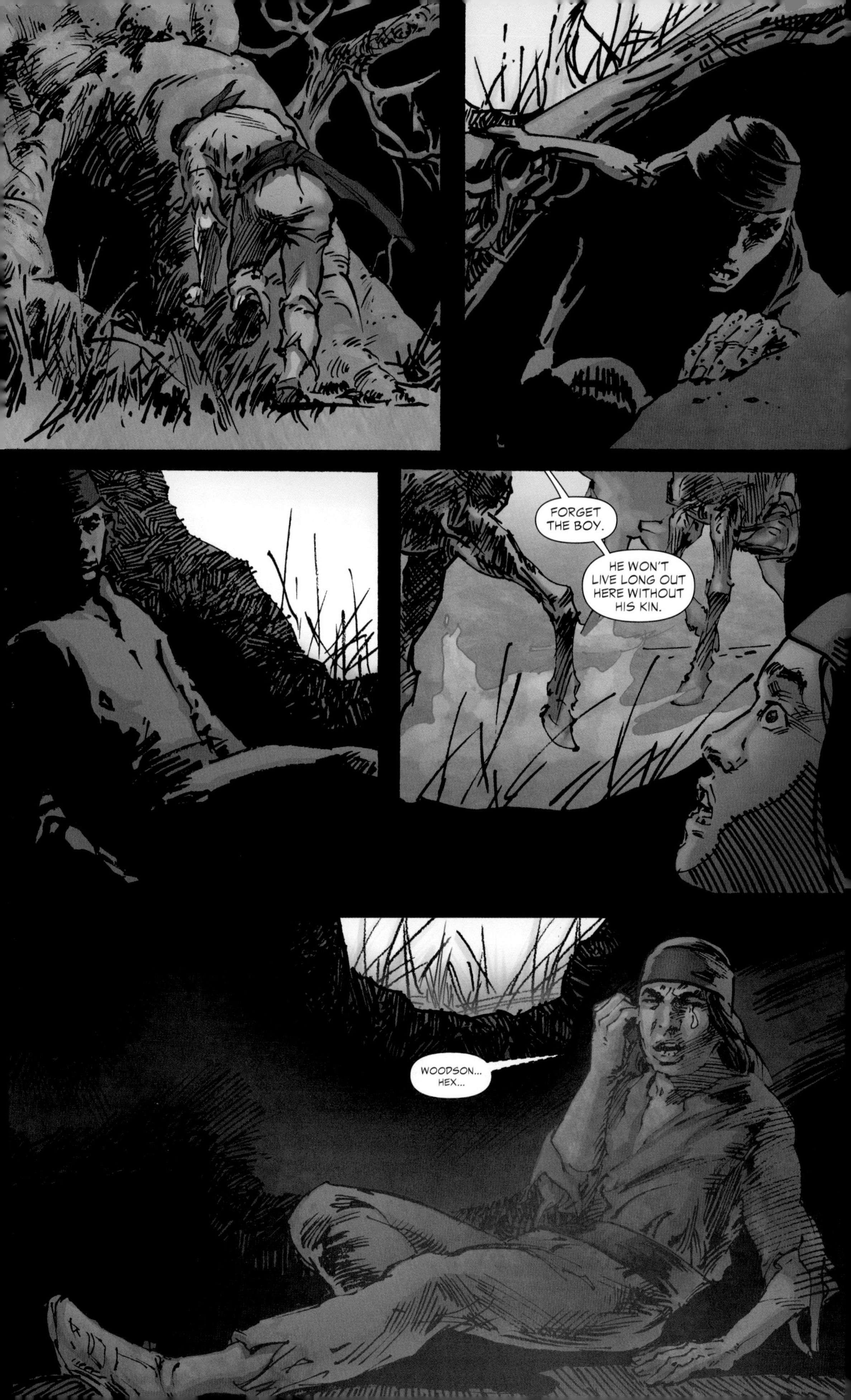

FORGET THE BOY.
HE WON'T LIVE LONG OUT HERE WITHOUT HIS KIN.
WOODSON... HEX...

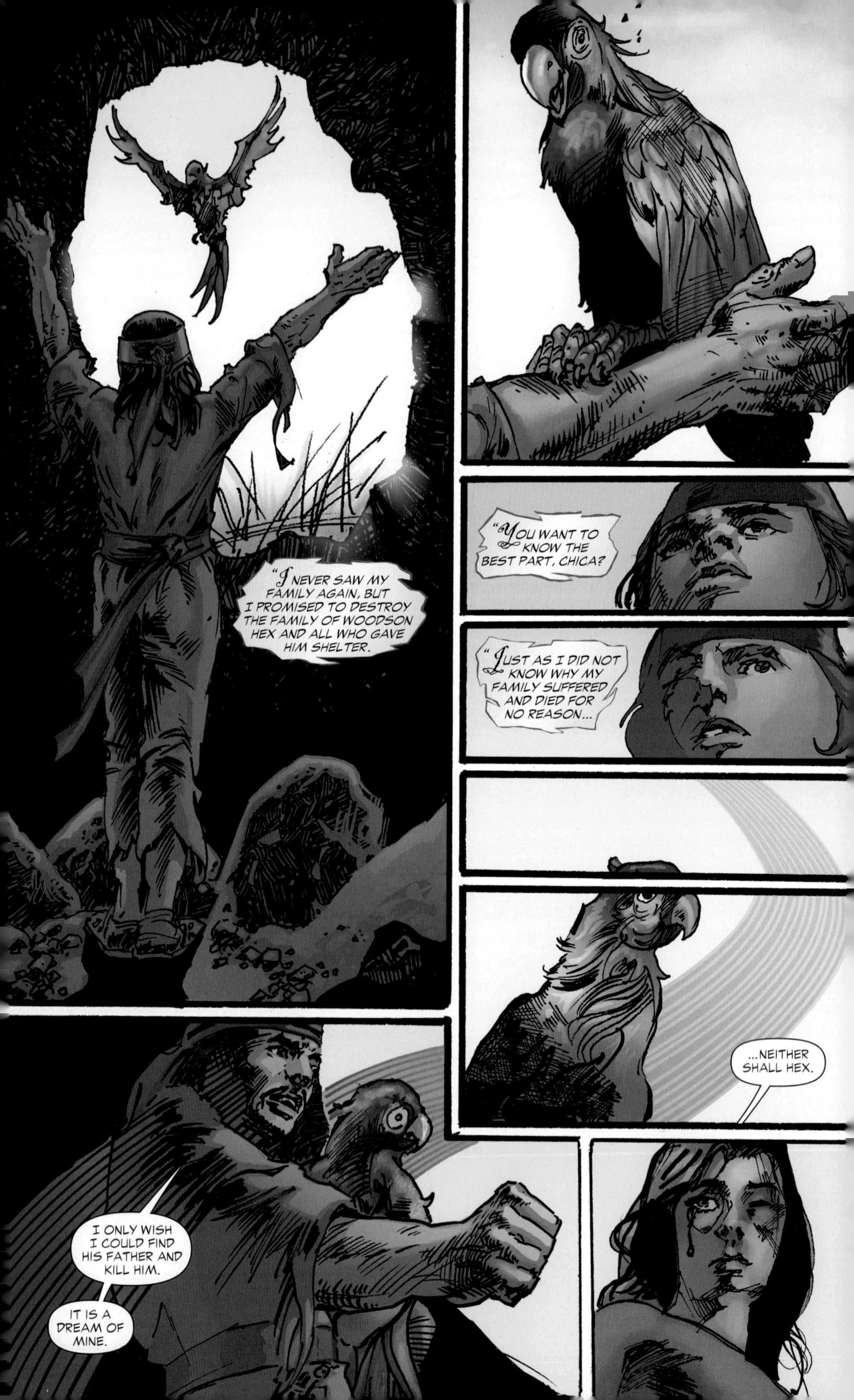
"I NEVER SAW MY FAMILY AGAIN, BUT I PROMISED TO DESTROY THE FAMILY OF WOODSON HEX AND ALL WHO GAVE HIM SHELTER.
"YOU WANT TO KNOW THE BEST PART, CHICA?
"JUST AS I DID NOT KNOW WHY MY FAMILY SUFFERED AND DIED FOR NO REASON...
...NEITHER SHALL HEX.
I ONLY WISH I COULD FIND HIS FATHER AND KILL HIM.
IT IS A DREAM OF MINE.

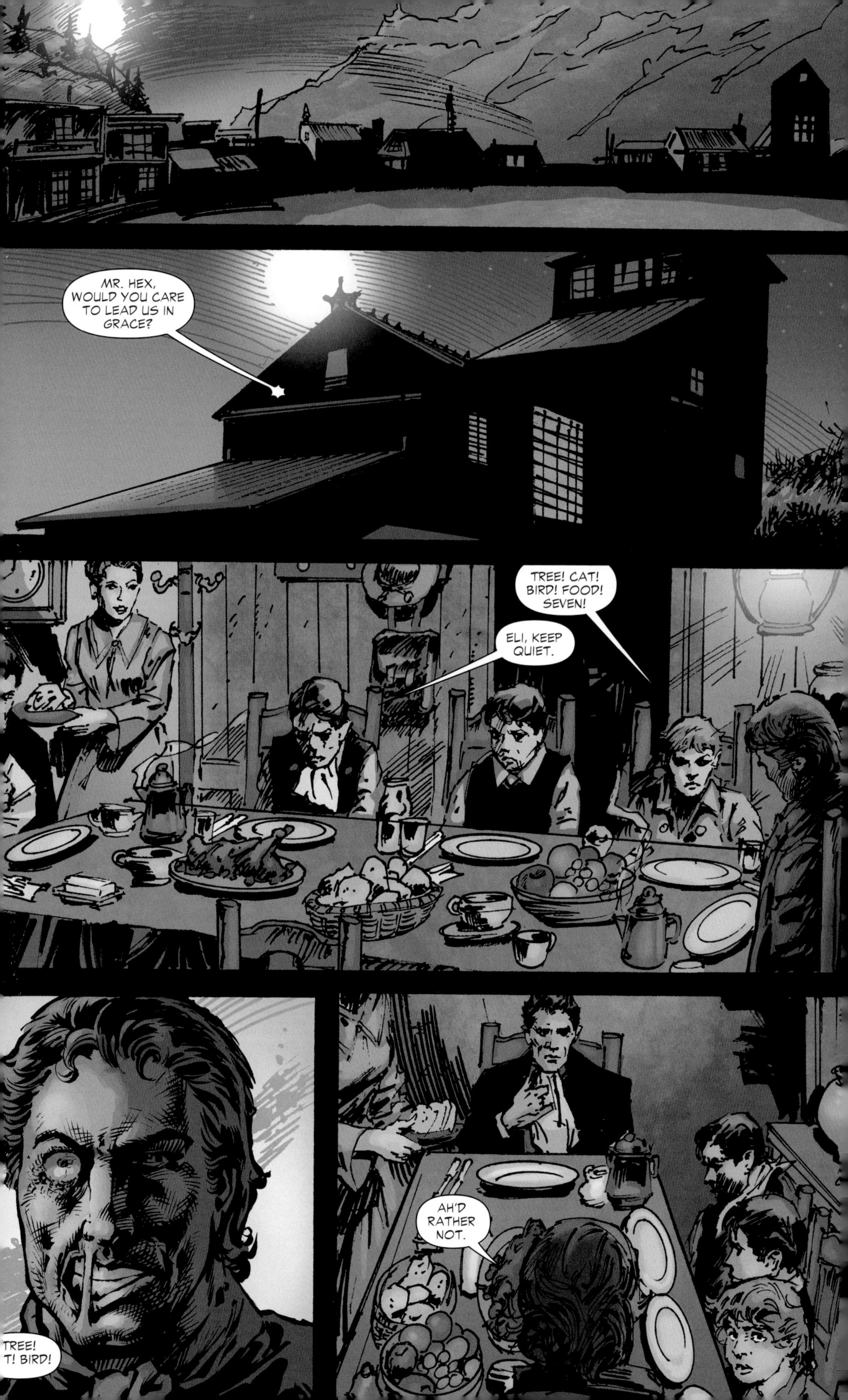
MR. HEX, WOULD YOU CARE TO LEAD US IN GRACE?
TREE! CAT! BIRD! FOOD! SEVEN!
ELI, KEEP QUIET.
TREE! T! BIRD!
AH'D RATHER NOT.

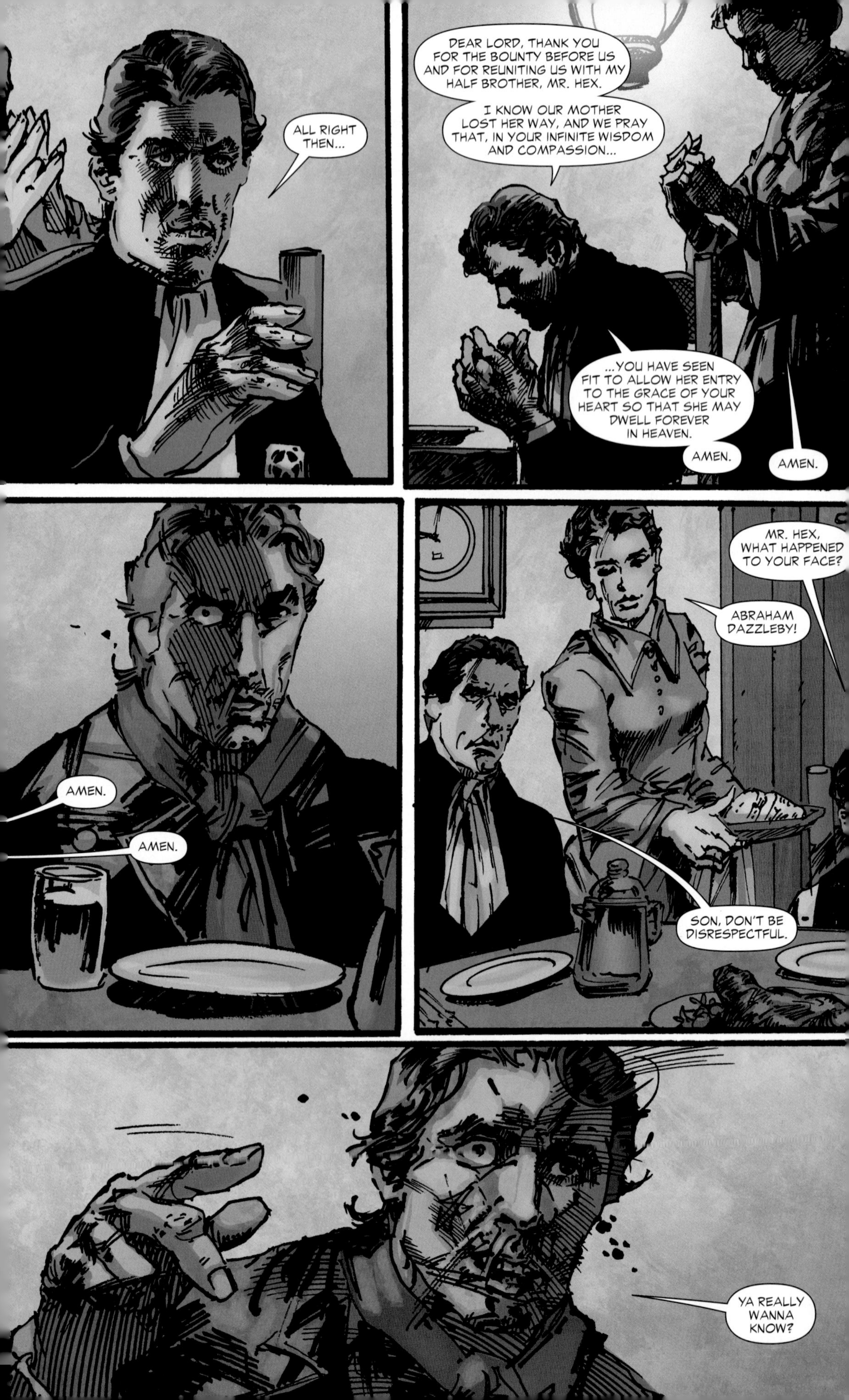
ALL RIGHT THEN...
DEAR LORD, THANK YOU FOR THE BOUNTY BEFORE US AND FOR REUNITING US WITH MY HALF BROTHER, MR. HEX.
I KNOW OUR MOTHER LOST HER WAY, AND WE PRAY THAT, IN YOUR INFINITE WISDOM AND COMPASSION...
...YOU HAVE SEEN FIT TO ALLOW HER ENTRY TO THE GRACE OF YOUR HEART SO THAT SHE MAY DWELL FOREVER IN HEAVEN.
AMEN.
AMEN.
AMEN.
AMEN.
MR. HEX, WHAT HAPPENED TO YOUR FACE?
ABRAHAM DAZZLEBY!
SON, DON'T BE DISRESPECTFUL.
YA REALLY WANNA KNOW?

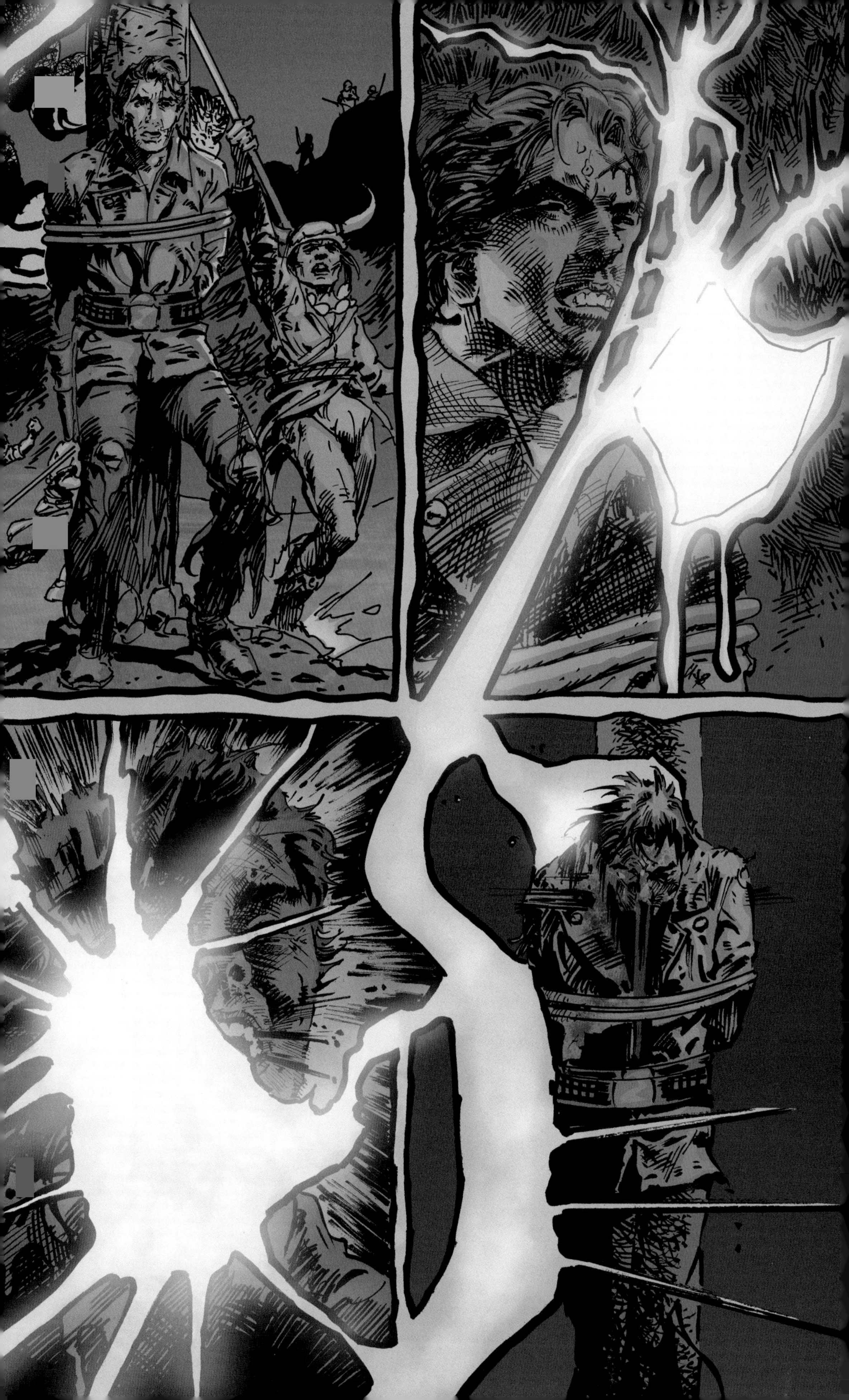

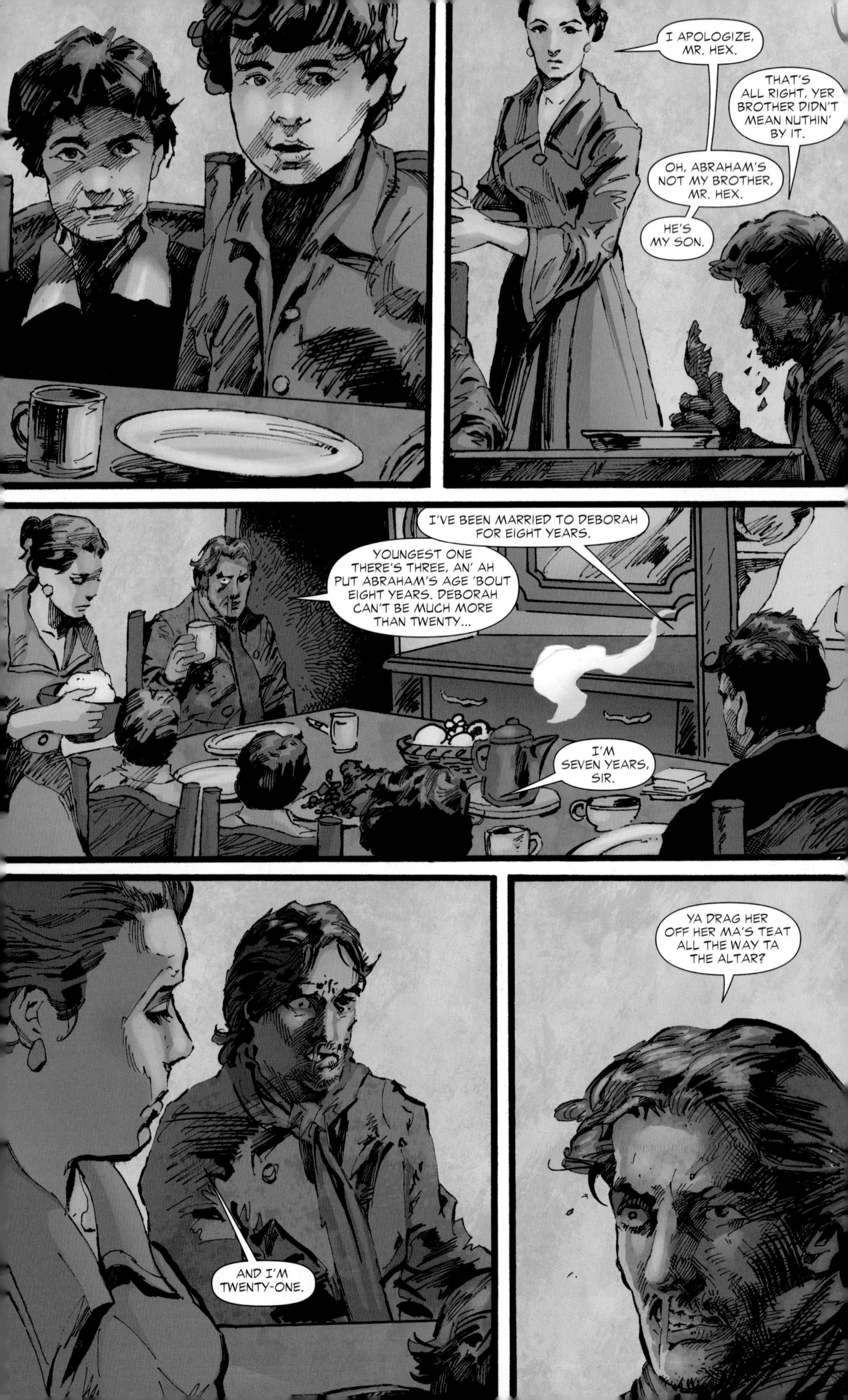
I APOLOGIZE, MR. HEX.
THAT'S ALL RIGHT, YER BROTHER DIDN'T MEAN NUTHIN' BY IT.
OH, ABRAHAM'S NOT MY BROTHER, MR. HEX.
HE'S MY SON.
I'VE BEEN MARRIED TO DEBORAH FOR EIGHT YEARS.
YOUNGEST ONE THERE'S THREE, AN' AH PUT ABRAHAM'S AGE 'BOUT EIGHT YEARS. DEBORAH CAN'T BE MUCH MORE THAN TWENTY...
I'M SEVEN YEARS, SIR.
AND I'M TWENTY-ONE.
YA DRAG HER OFF HER MA'S TEAT ALL THE WAY TA THE ALTAR?

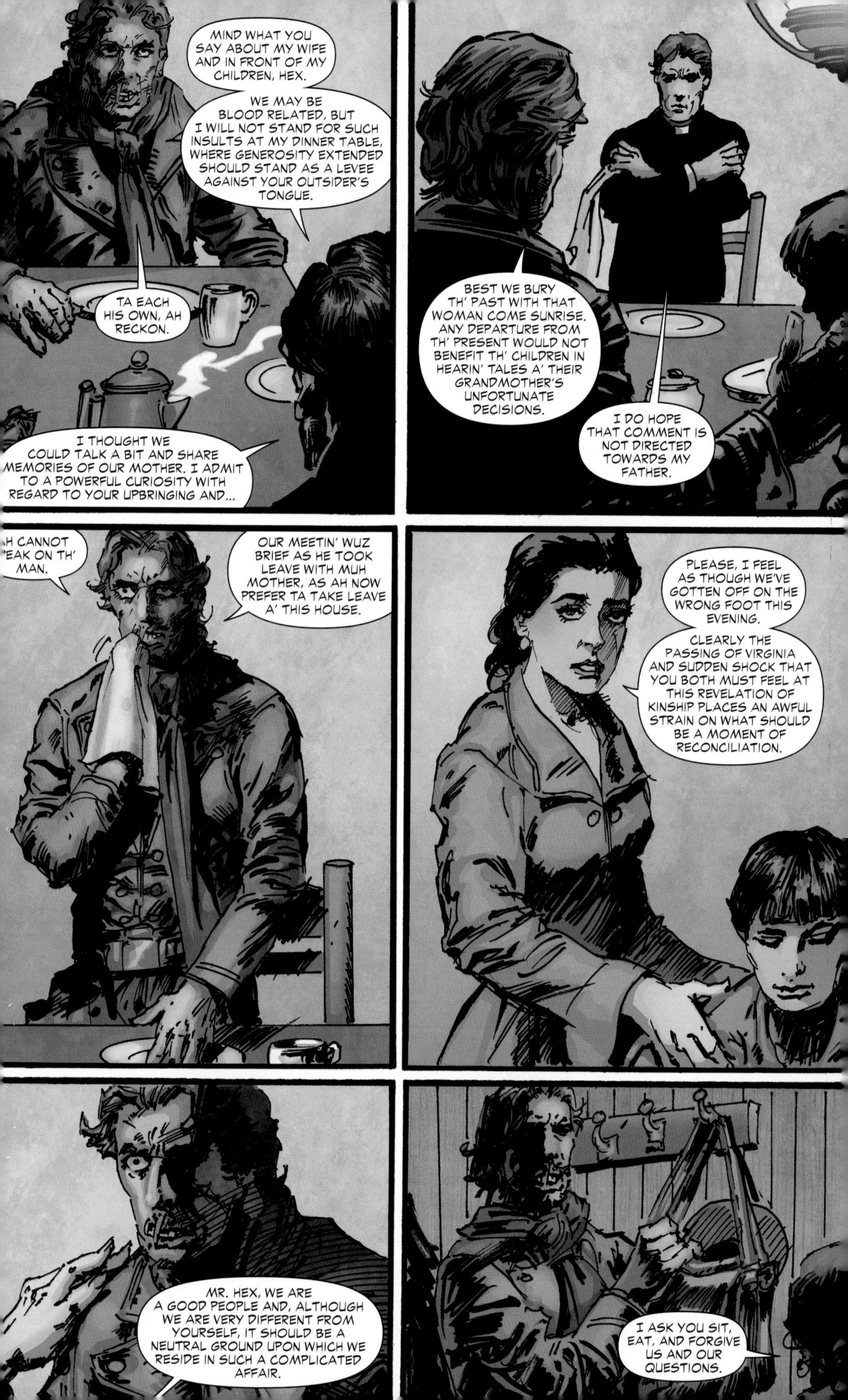
MIND WHAT YOU SAY ABOUT MY WIFE AND IN FRONT OF MY CHILDREN, HEX.
WE MAY BE BLOOD RELATED, BUT I WILL NOT STAND FOR SUCH INSULTS AT MY DINNER TABLE, WHERE GENEROSITY EXTENDED SHOULD STAND AS A LEVEE AGAINST YOUR OUTSIDER'S TONGUE.
TA EACH HIS OWN, AH RECKON.
I THOUGHT WE COULD TALK A BIT AND SHARE MEMORIES OF OUR MOTHER. I ADMIT TO A POWERFUL CURIOSITY WITH REGARD TO YOUR UPBRINGING AND...
BEST WE BURY TH' PAST WITH THAT WOMAN COME SUNRISE. ANY DEPARTURE FROM TH' PRESENT WOULD NOT BENEFIT TH' CHILDREN IN HEARIN' TALES A' THEIR GRANDMOTHER'S UNFORTUNATE DECISIONS.
I DO HOPE THAT COMMENT IS NOT DIRECTED TOWARDS MY FATHER.
H CANNOT EAK ON TH' MAN.
OUR MEETIN' WUZ BRIEF AS HE TOOK LEAVE WITH MUH MOTHER, AS AH NOW PREFER TA TAKE LEAVE A' THIS HOUSE.
PLEASE, I FEEL AS THOUGH WE'VE GOTTEN OFF ON THE WRONG FOOT THIS EVENING.
CLEARLY THE PASSING OF VIRGINIA AND SUDDEN SHOCK THAT YOU BOTH MUST FEEL AT THIS REVELATION OF KINSHIP PLACES AN AWFUL STRAIN ON WHAT SHOULD BE A MOMENT OF RECONCILIATION.
MR. HEX, WE ARE A GOOD PEOPLE AND, ALTHOUGH WE ARE VERY DIFFERENT FROM YOURSELF, IT SHOULD BE A NEUTRAL GROUND UPON WHICH WE RESIDE IN SUCH A COMPLICATED AFFAIR.
I ASK YOU SIT, EAT, AND FORGIVE US AND OUR QUESTIONS.

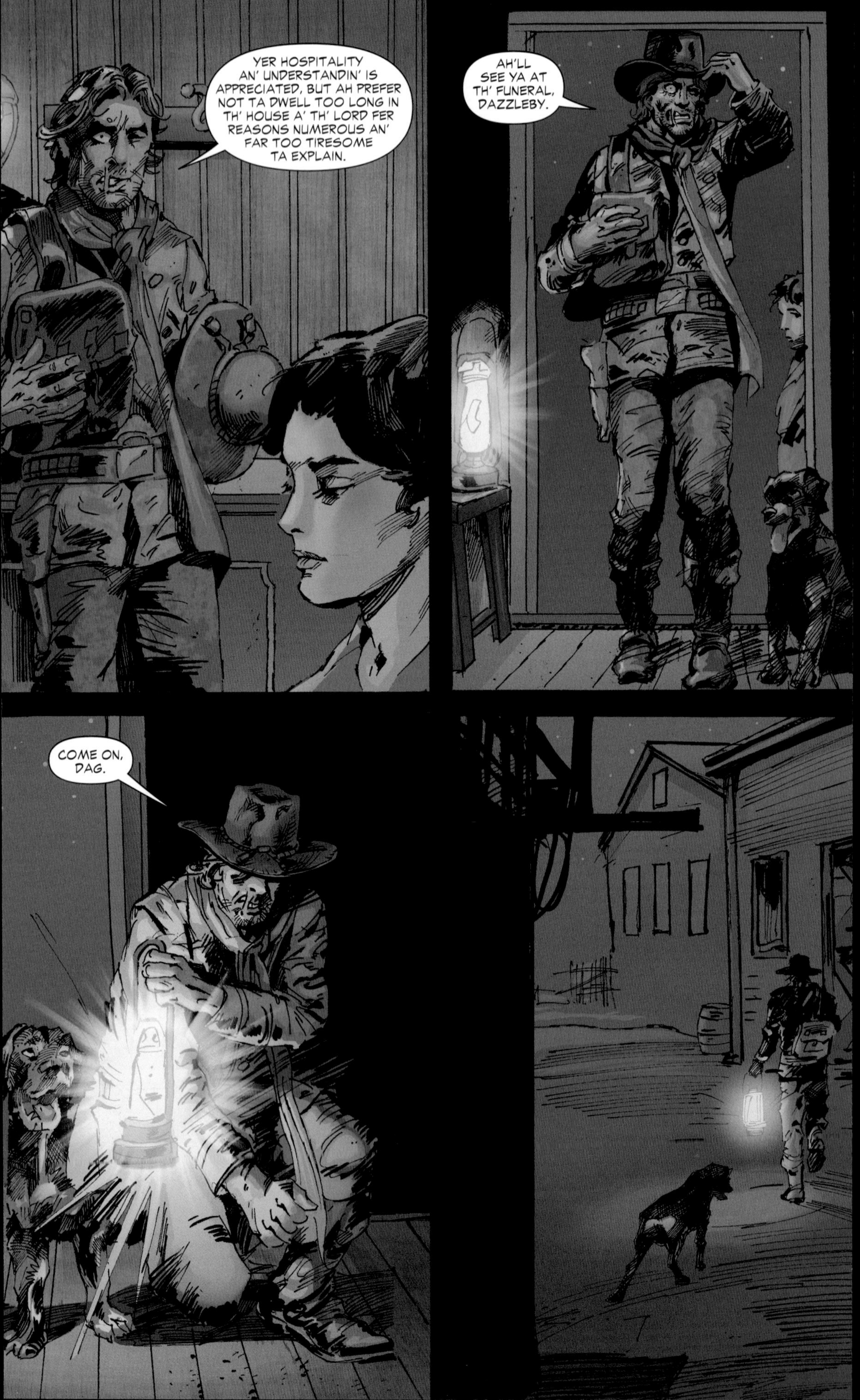
YER HOSPITALITY AN' UNDERSTANDIN' IS APPRECIATED, BUT AH PREFER NOT TA DWELL TOO LONG IN TH' HOUSE A' TH' LORD FER REASONS NUMEROUS AN' FAR TOO TIRESOME TA EXPLAIN.
AH'LL SEE YA AT TH' FUNERAL, DAZZLEBY.
COME ON, DAG.

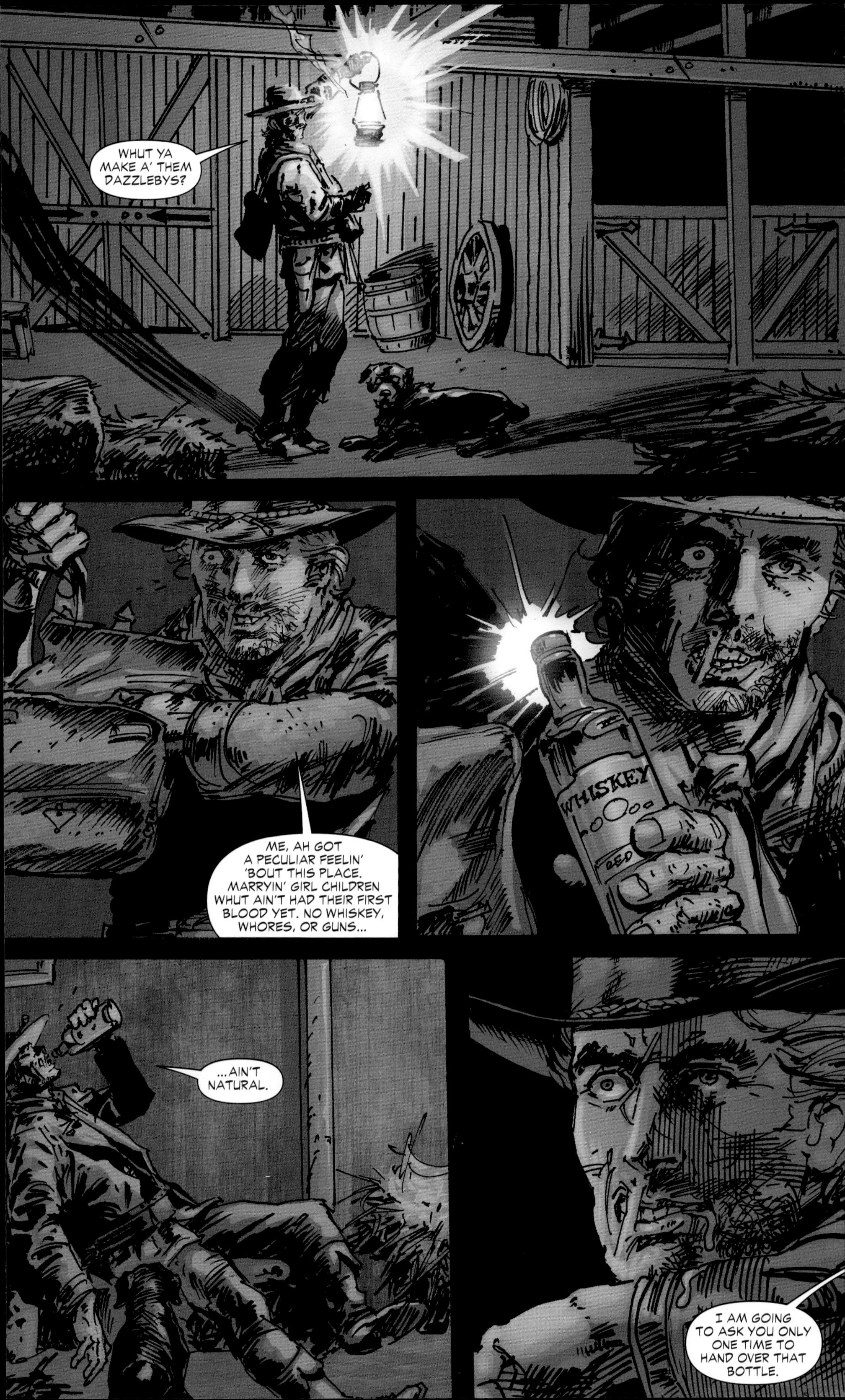
WHUT YA MAKE A' THEM DAZZLEBYS?
ME, AH GOT A PECULIAR FEELIN' 'BOUT THIS PLACE. MARRYIN' GIRL CHILDREN WHUT AIN'T HAD THEIR FIRST BLOOD YET. NO WHISKEY, WHORES, OR GUNS...
WHISKEY
...AIN'T NATURAL.
I AM GOING TO ASK YOU ONLY ONE TIME TO HAND OVER THAT BOTTLE.

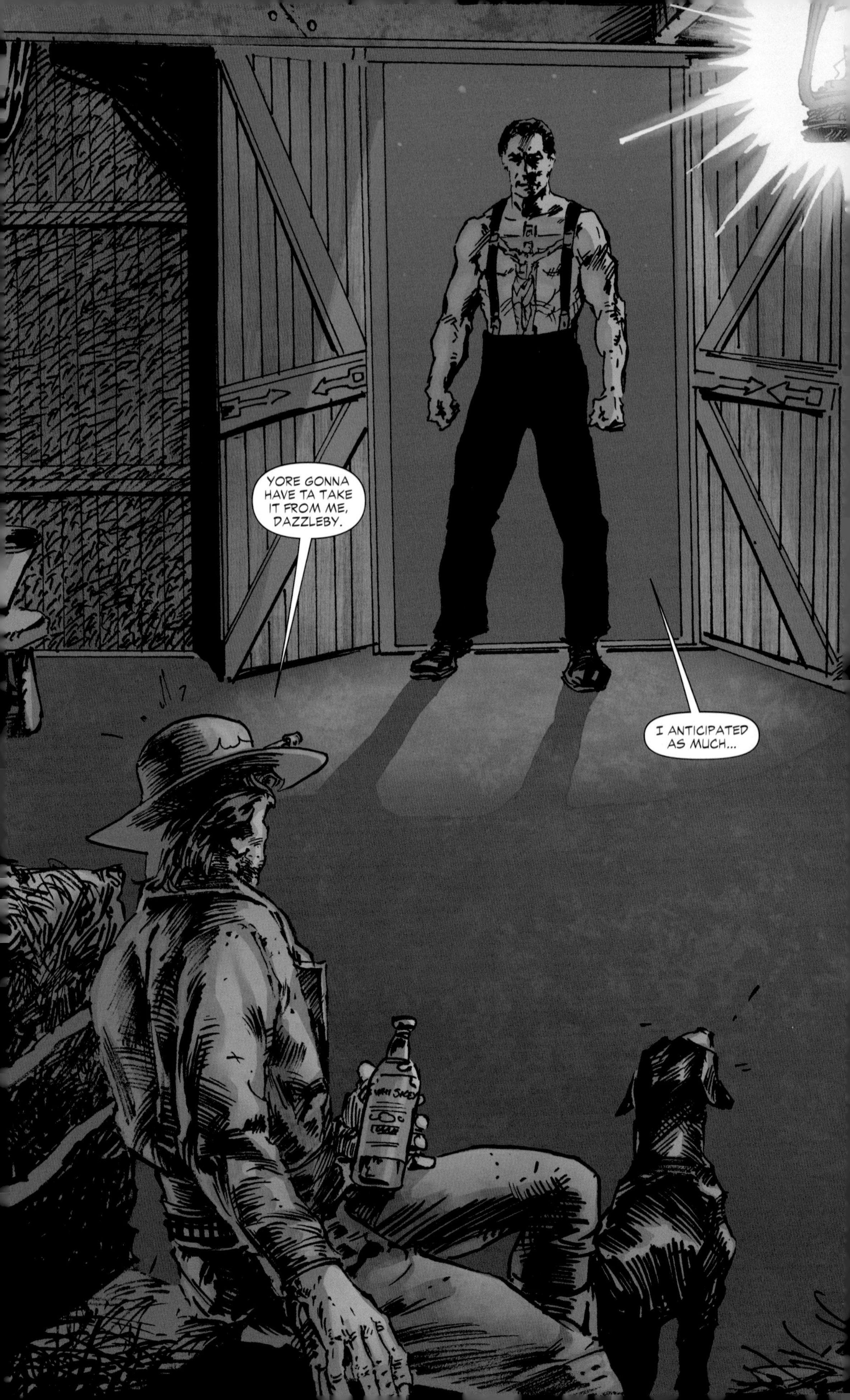
YORE GONNA HAVE TA TAKE IT FROM ME, DAZZLEBY.
I ANTICIPATED AS MUCH...

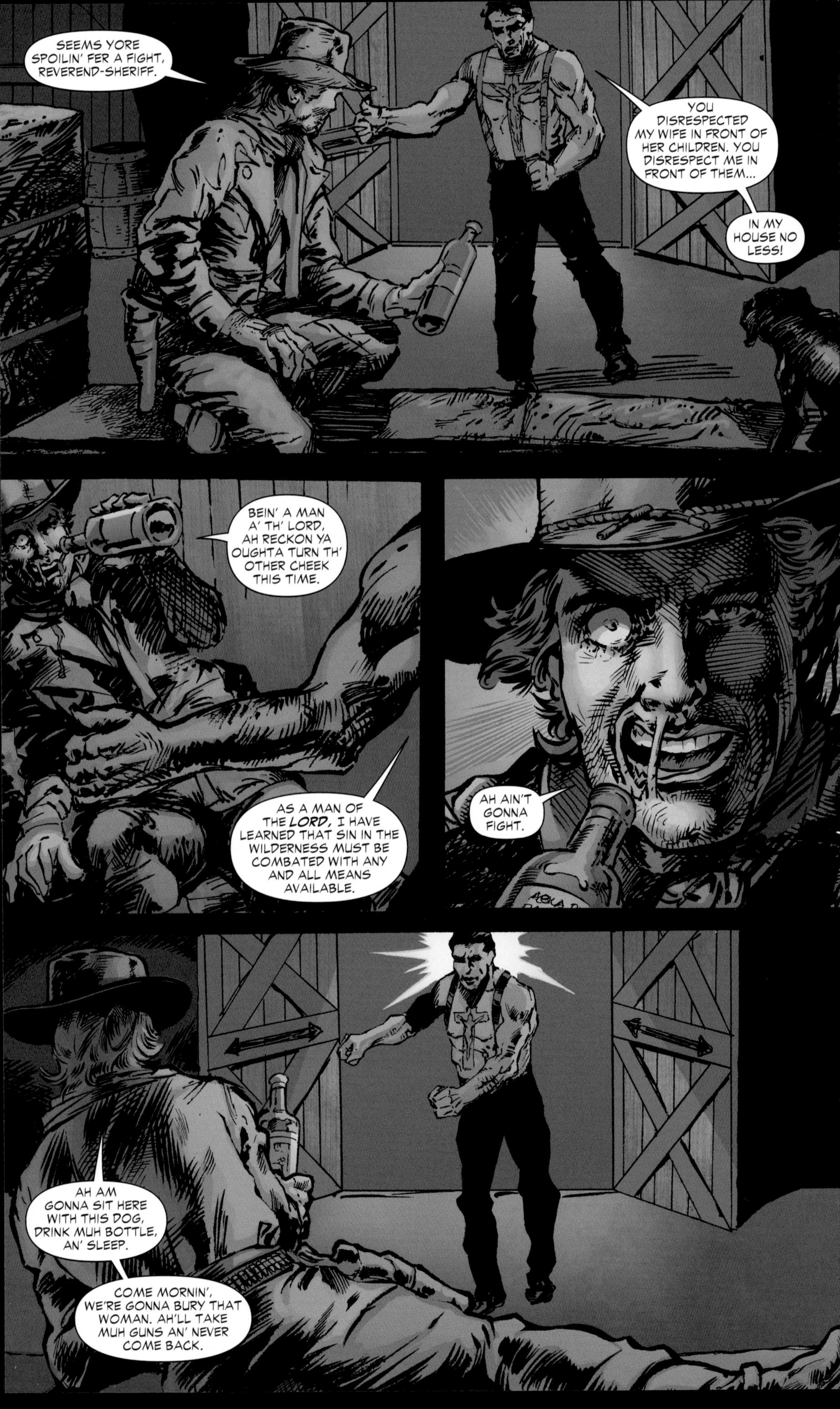
SEEMS YORE SPOILIN' FER A FIGHT, REVEREND-SHERIFF.
YOU DISRESPECTED MY WIFE IN FRONT OF HER CHILDREN. YOU DISRESPECT ME IN FRONT OF THEM...
IN MY HOUSE NO LESS!
BEIN' A MAN A' TH' LORD, AH RECKON YA OUGHTA TURN TH' OTHER CHEEK THIS TIME.
AS A MAN OF THE LORD, I HAVE LEARNED THAT SIN IN THE WILDERNESS MUST BE COMBATED WITH ANY AND ALL MEANS AVAILABLE.
AH AIN'T GONNA FIGHT.
AH AM GONNA SIT HERE WITH THIS DOG, DRINK MUH BOTTLE, AN' SLEEP.
COME MORNIN', WE'RE GONNA BURY THAT WOMAN. AH'LL TAKE MUH GUNS AN' NEVER COME BACK.

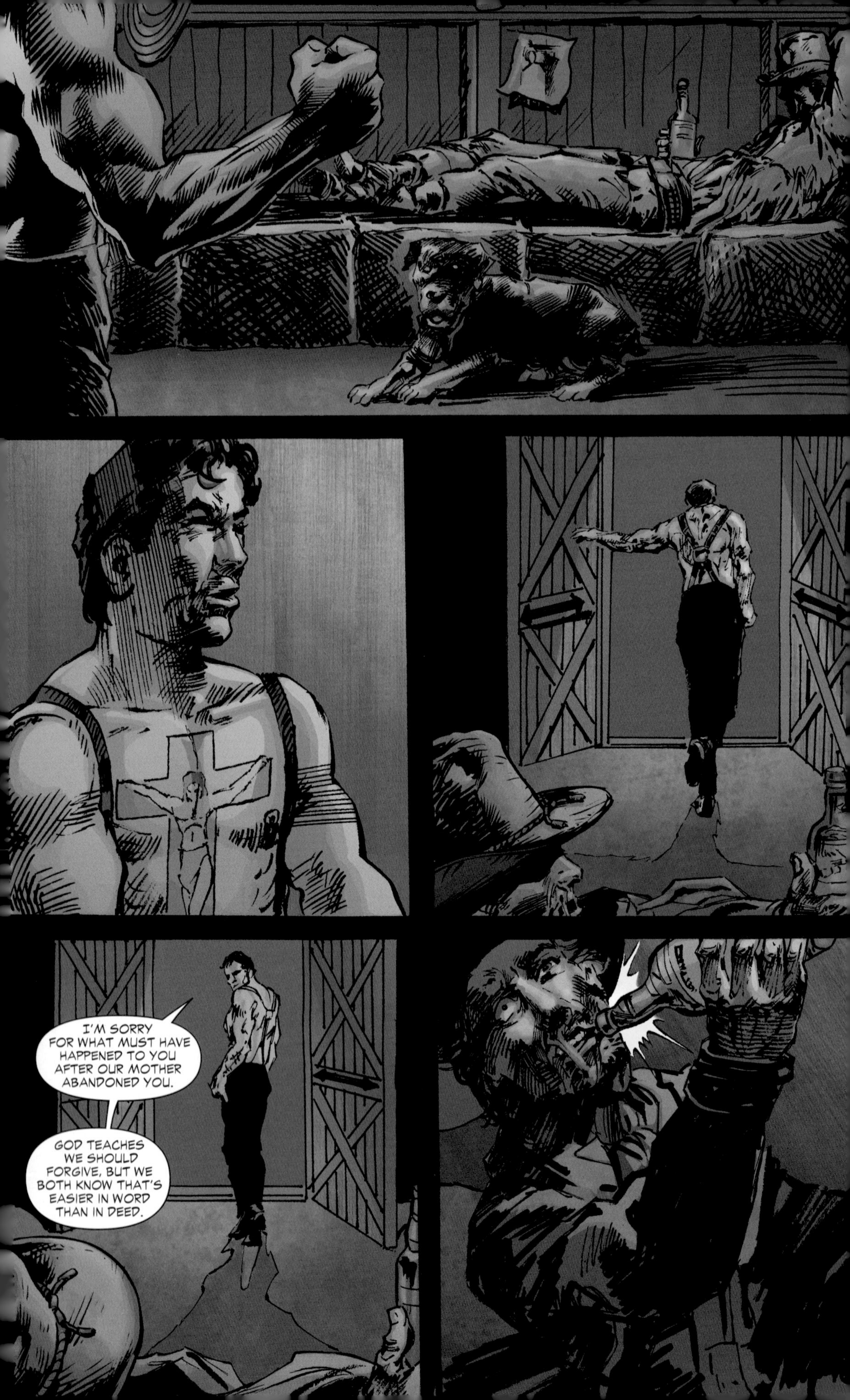
I'M SORRY FOR WHAT MUST HAVE HAPPENED TO YOU AFTER OUR MOTHER ABANDONED YOU.
GOD TEACHES WE SHOULD FORGIVE, BUT WE BOTH KNOW THAT'S EASIER IN WORD THAN IN DEED.

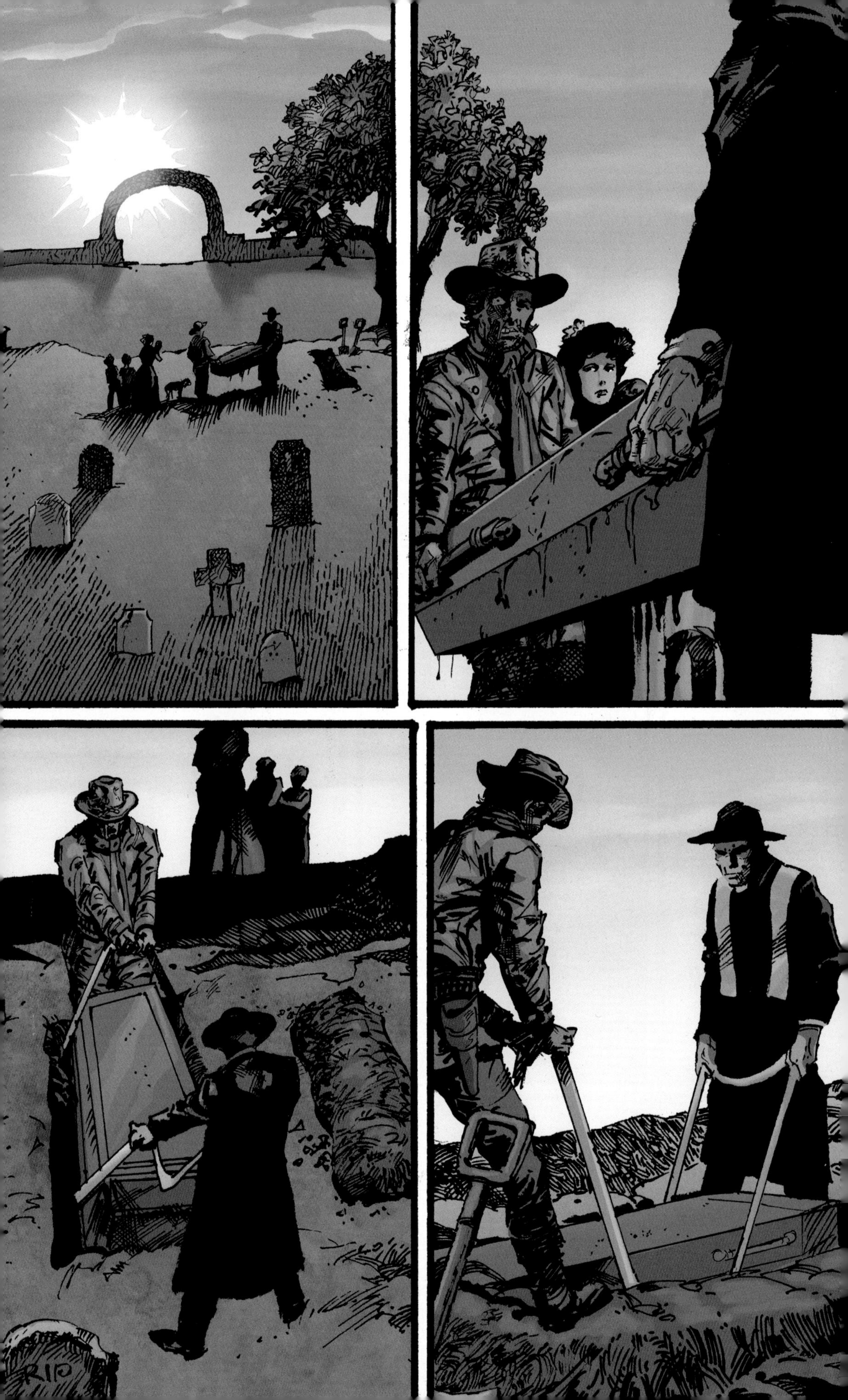
RIP

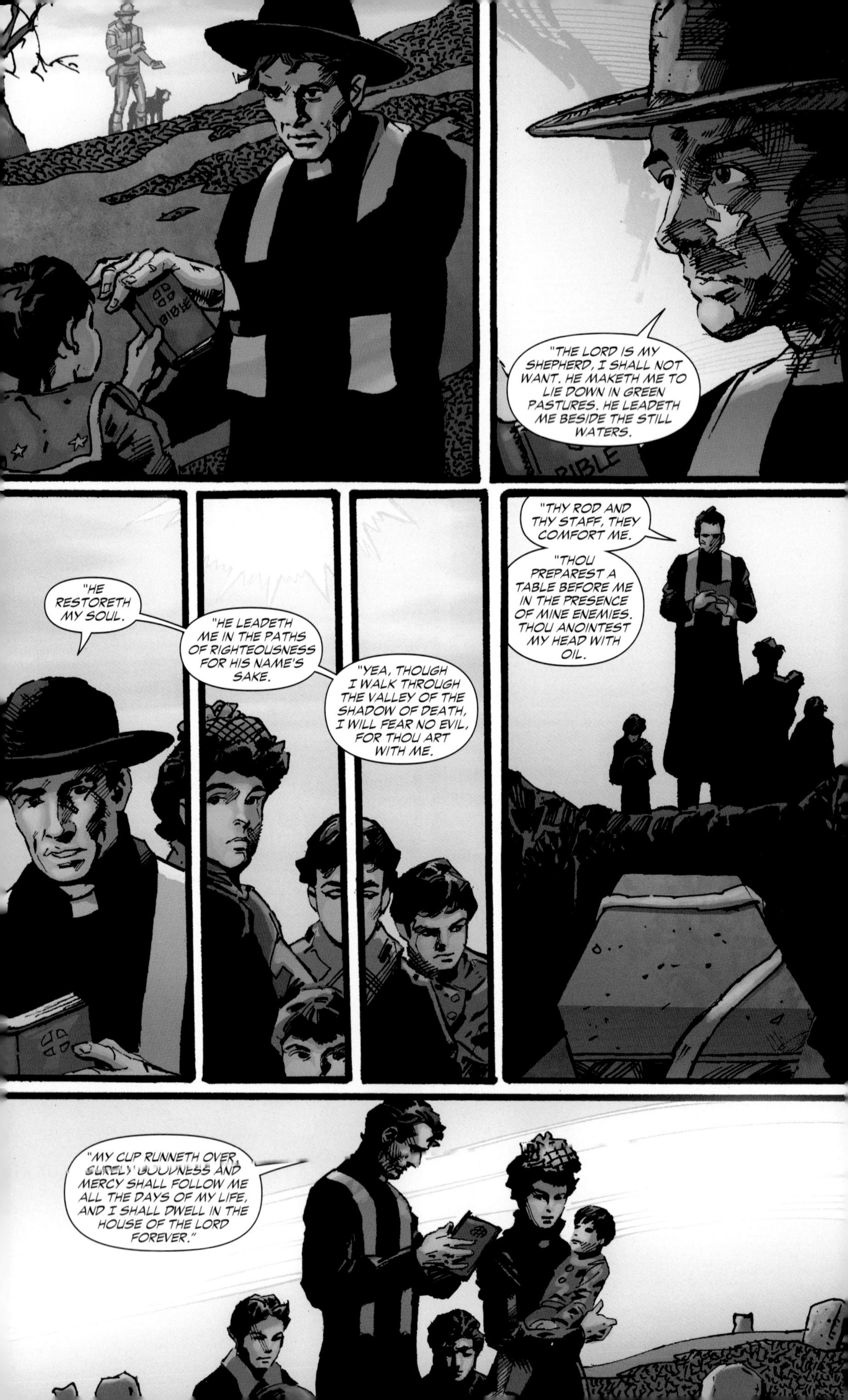
"THE LORD IS MY SHEPHERD, I SHALL NOT WANT. HE MAKETH ME TO LIE DOWN IN GREEN PASTURES. HE LEADETH ME BESIDE THE STILL WATERS.
"HE RESTORETH MY SOUL.
"HE LEADETH ME IN THE PATHS OF RIGHTEOUSNESS FOR HIS NAME'S SAKE.
"YEA, THOUGH I WALK THROUGH THE VALLEY OF THE SHADOW OF DEATH, I WILL FEAR NO EVIL, FOR THOU ART WITH ME.
"THY ROD AND THY STAFF, THEY COMFORT ME.
"THOU PREPAREST A TABLE BEFORE ME IN THE PRESENCE OF MINE ENEMIES. THOU ANOINTEST MY HEAD WITH OIL.
"MY CUP RUNNETH OVER, SURELY GOODNESS AND MERCY SHALL FOLLOW ME ALL THE DAYS OF MY LIFE, AND I SHALL DWELL IN THE HOUSE OF THE LORD FOREVER."

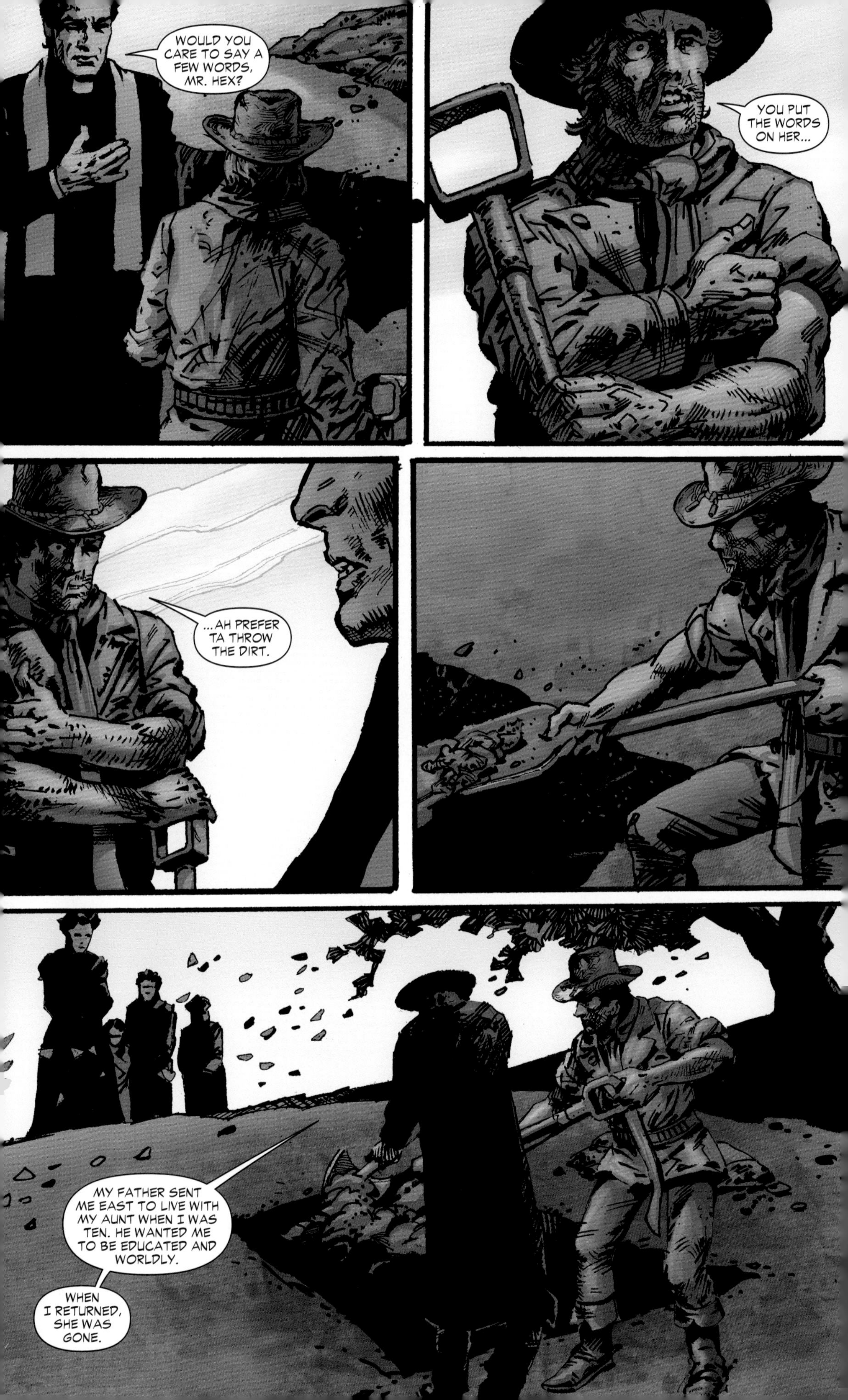
WOULD YOU CARE TO SAY A FEW WORDS, MR. HEX?
YOU PUT THE WORDS ON HER...
...AH PREFER TA THROW THE DIRT.
MY FATHER SENT ME EAST TO LIVE WITH MY AUNT WHEN I WAS TEN. HE WANTED ME TO BE EDUCATED AND WORLDLY.
WHEN I RETURNED, SHE WAS GONE.

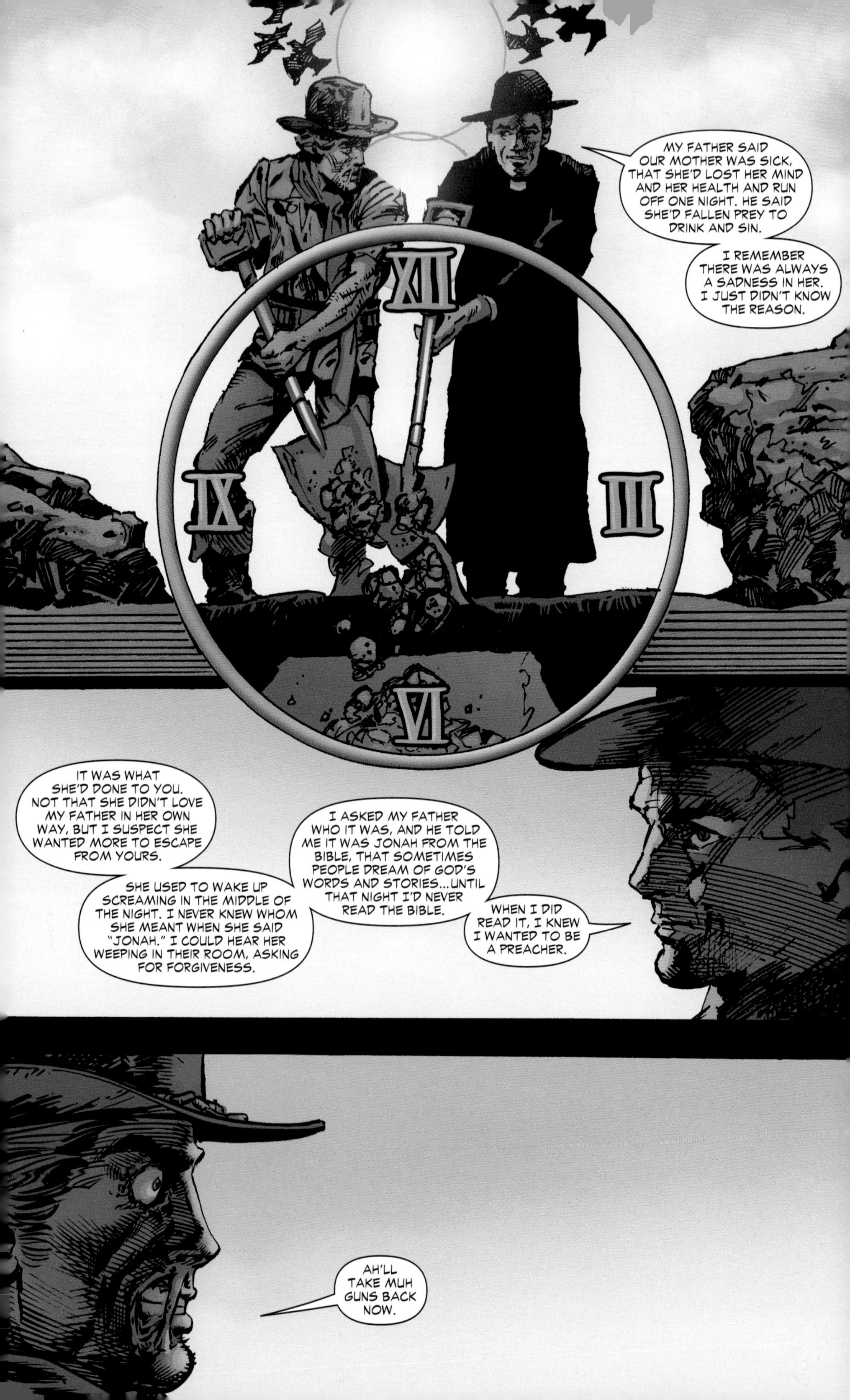
MY FATHER SAID OUR MOTHER WAS SICK, THAT SHE'D LOST HER MIND AND HER HEALTH AND RUN OFF ONE NIGHT. HE SAID SHE'D FALLEN PREY TO DRINK AND SIN.
I REMEMBER THERE WAS ALWAYS A SADNESS IN HER. I JUST DIDN'T KNOW THE REASON.
XII
IX
III
VI
IT WAS WHAT SHE'D DONE TO YOU. NOT THAT SHE DIDN'T LOVE MY FATHER IN HER OWN WAY, BUT I SUSPECT SHE WANTED MORE TO ESCAPE FROM YOURS.
SHE USED TO WAKE UP SCREAMING IN THE MIDDLE OF THE NIGHT. I NEVER KNEW WHOM SHE MEANT WHEN SHE SAID "JONAH." I COULD HEAR HER WEEPING IN THEIR ROOM, ASKING FOR FORGIVENESS.
I ASKED MY FATHER WHO IT WAS, AND HE TOLD ME IT WAS JONAH FROM THE BIBLE, THAT SOMETIMES PEOPLE DREAM OF GOD'S WORDS AND STORIES...UNTIL THAT NIGHT I'D NEVER READ THE BIBLE.
WHEN I DID READ IT, I KNEW I WANTED TO BE A PREACHER.
AH'LL TAKE MUH GUNS BACK NOW.

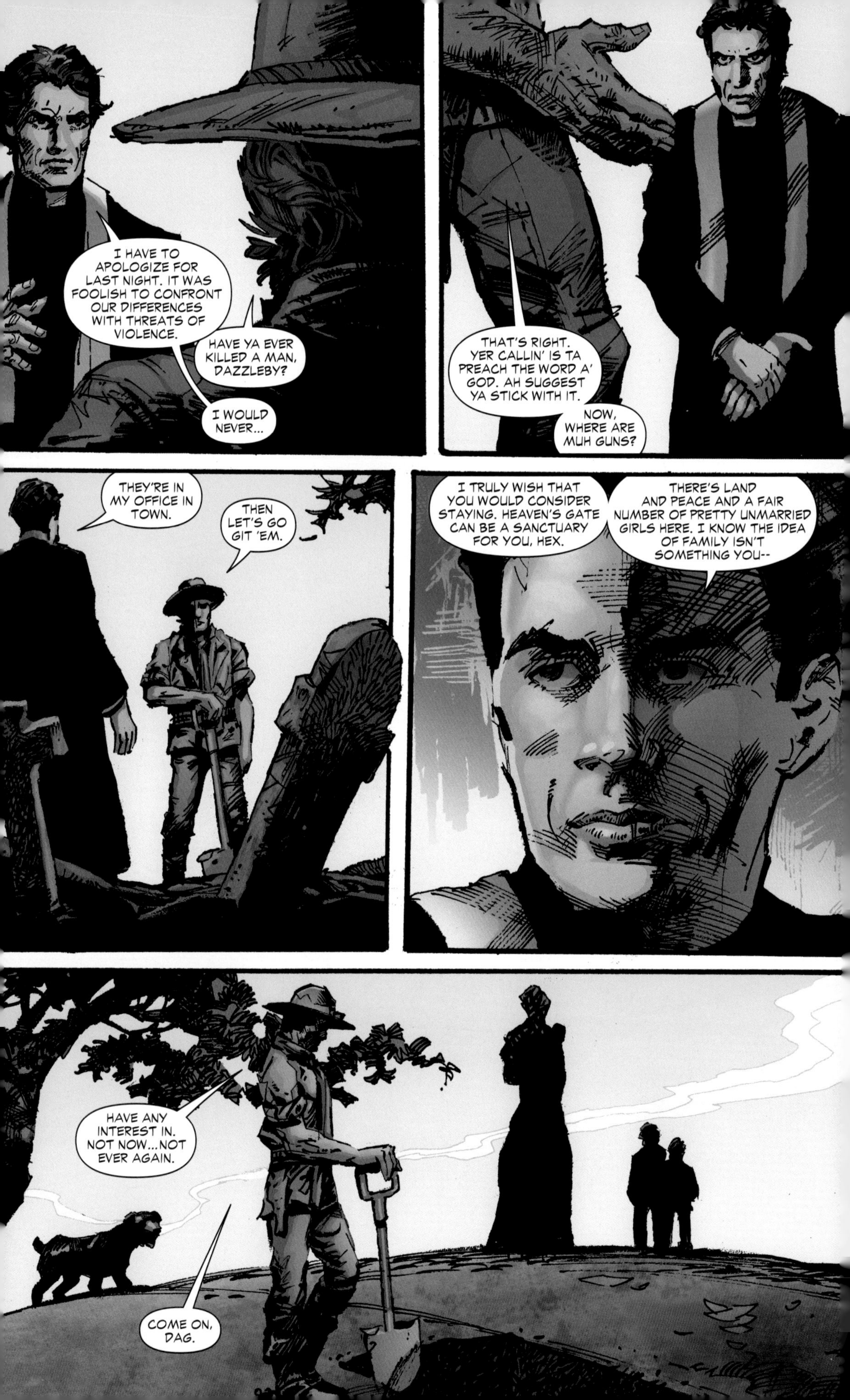
I HAVE TO APOLOGIZE FOR LAST NIGHT. IT WAS FOOLISH TO CONFRONT OUR DIFFERENCES WITH THREATS OF VIOLENCE.
HAVE YA EVER KILLED A MAN, DAZZLEBY?
I WOULD NEVER...
THAT'S RIGHT. YER CALLIN' IS TA PREACH THE WORD A' GOD. AH SUGGEST YA STICK WITH IT.
NOW, WHERE ARE MUH GUNS?
THEY'RE IN MY OFFICE IN TOWN.
THEN LET'S GO GIT 'EM.
I TRULY WISH THAT YOU WOULD CONSIDER STAYING. HEAVEN'S GATE CAN BE A SANCTUARY FOR YOU, HEX.
THERE'S LAND AND PEACE AND A FAIR NUMBER OF PRETTY UNMARRIED GIRLS HERE. I KNOW THE IDEA OF FAMILY ISN'T SOMETHING YOU--
HAVE ANY INTEREST IN. NOT NOW...NOT EVER AGAIN.
COME ON, DAG.

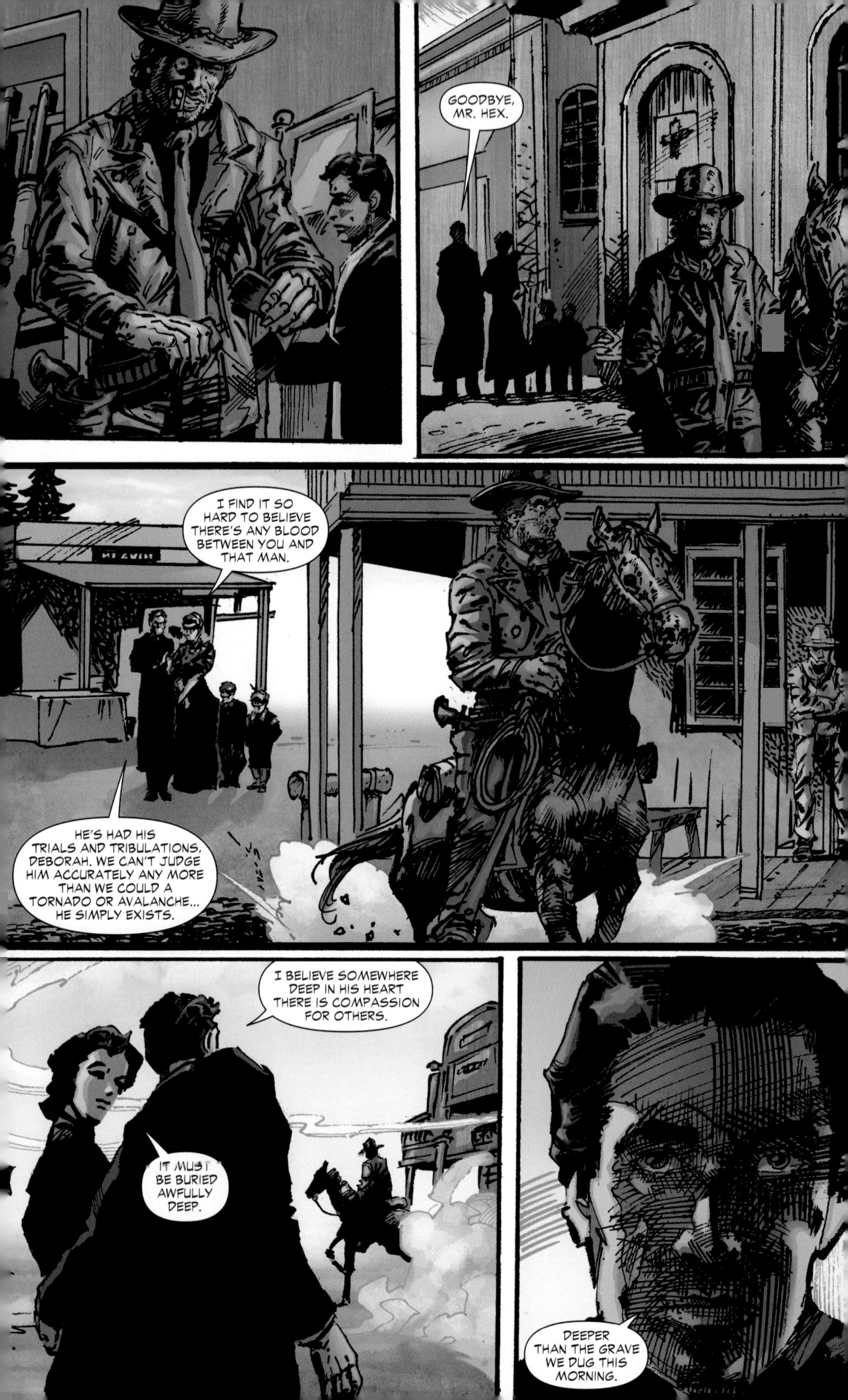
GOODBYE, MR. HEX.
I FIND IT SO HARD TO BELIEVE THERE'S ANY BLOOD BETWEEN YOU AND THAT MAN.
HE'S HAD HIS TRIALS AND TRIBULATIONS, DEBORAH. WE CAN'T JUDGE HIM ACCURATELY ANY MORE THAN WE COULD A TORNADO OR AVALANCHE... HE SIMPLY EXISTS.
I BELIEVE SOMEWHERE DEEP IN HIS HEART THERE IS COMPASSION FOR OTHERS.
IT MUST BE BURIED AWFULLY DEEP.
DEEPER THAN THE GRAVE WE DUG THIS MORNING.

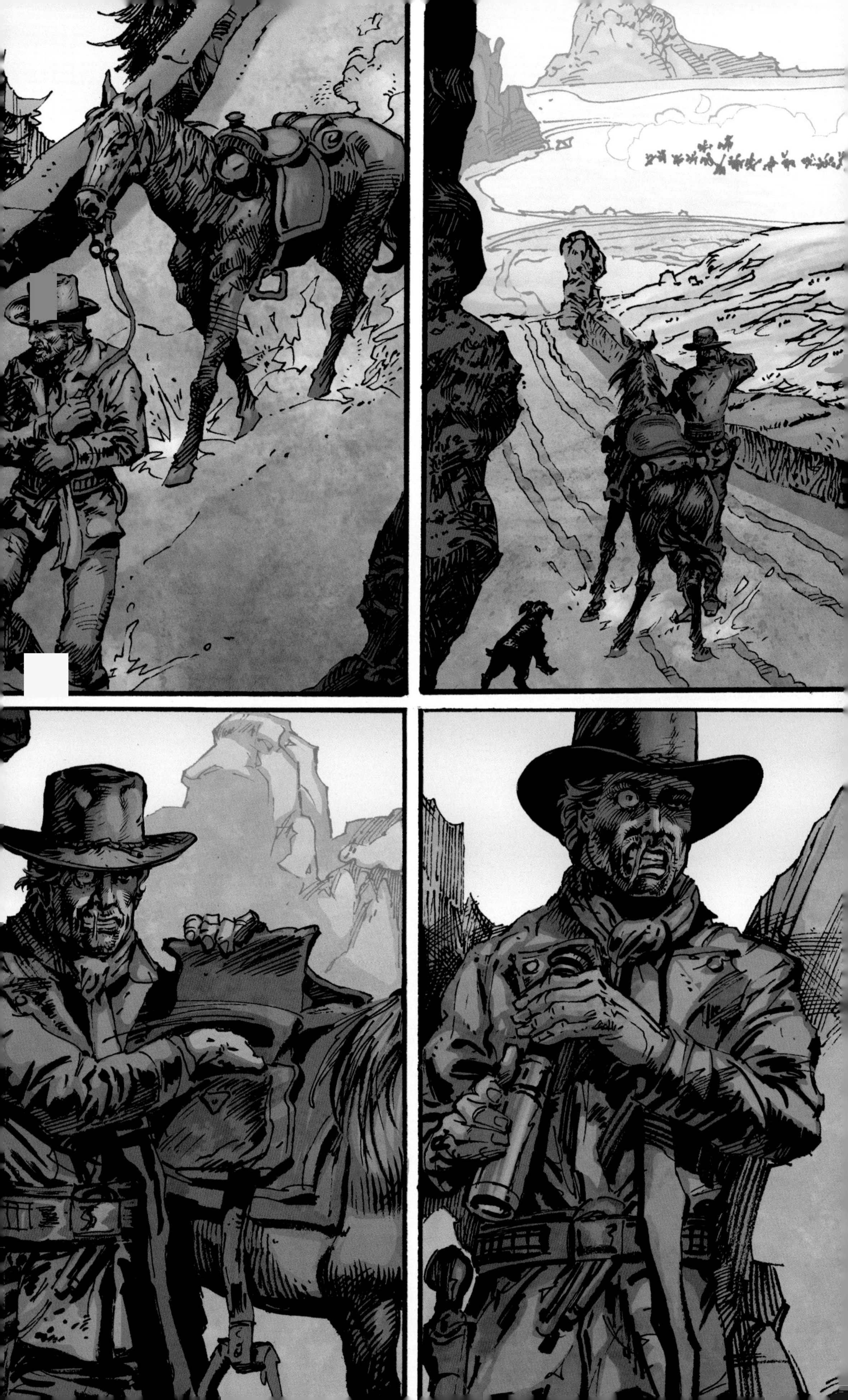

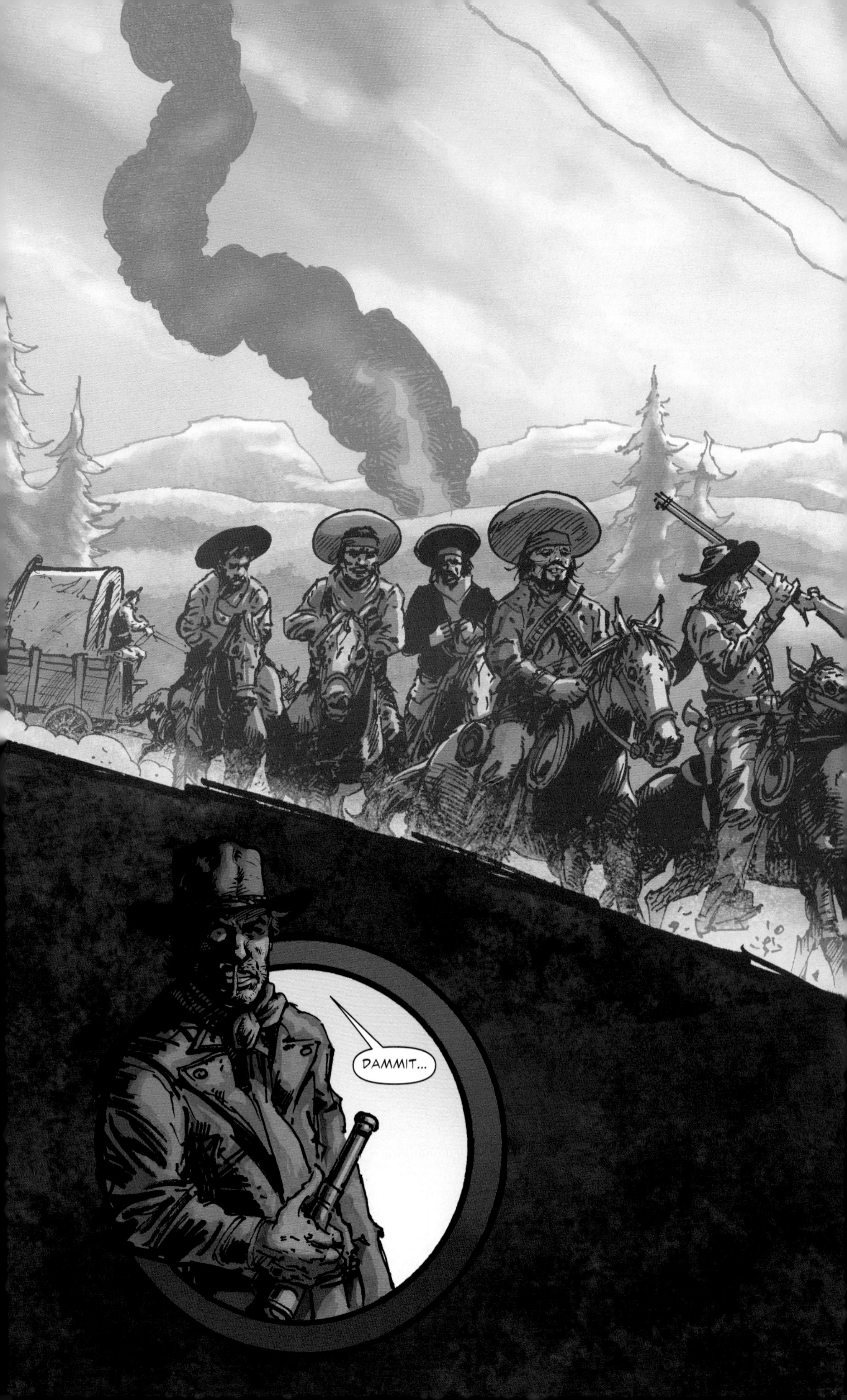
DAMMIT...

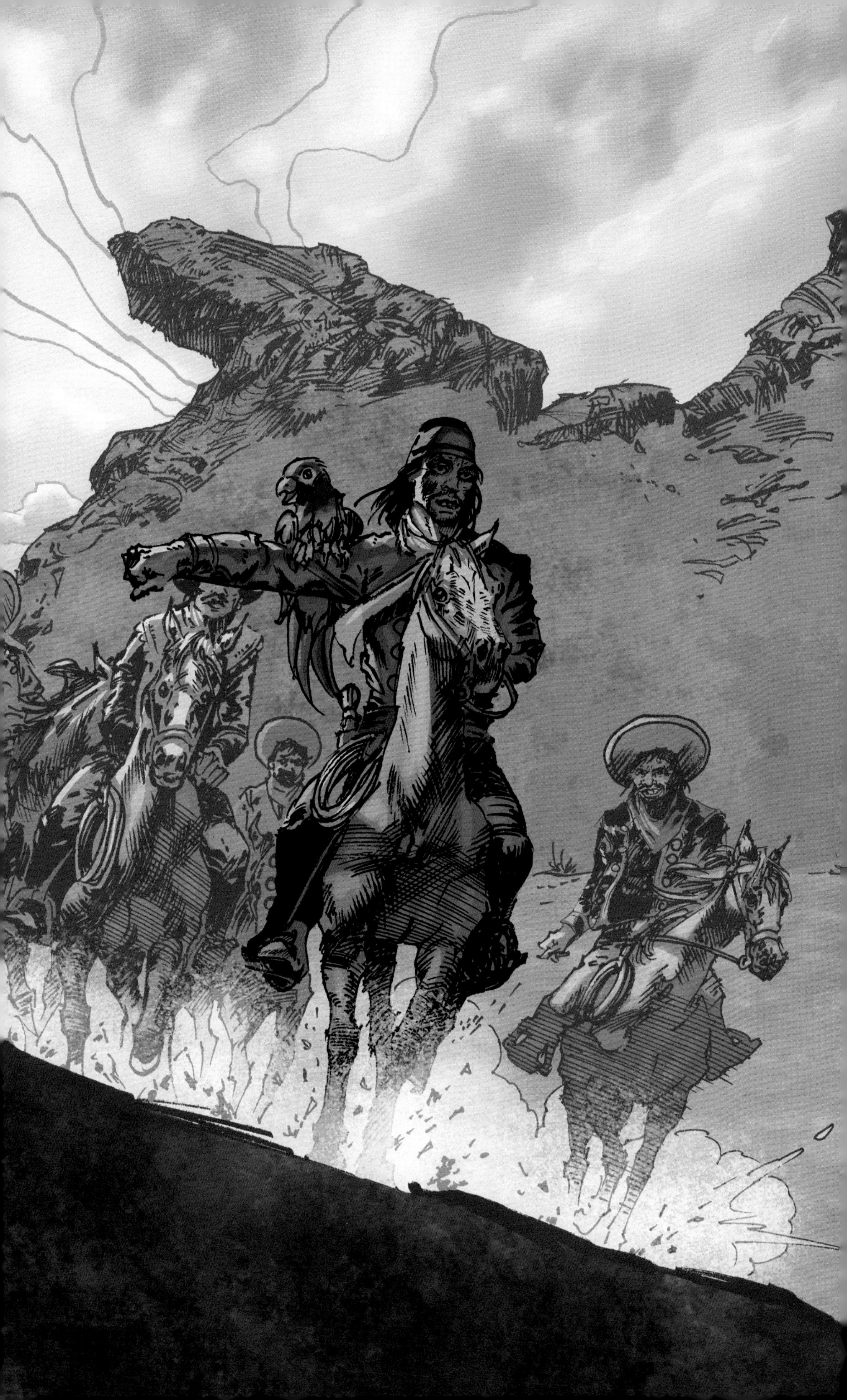

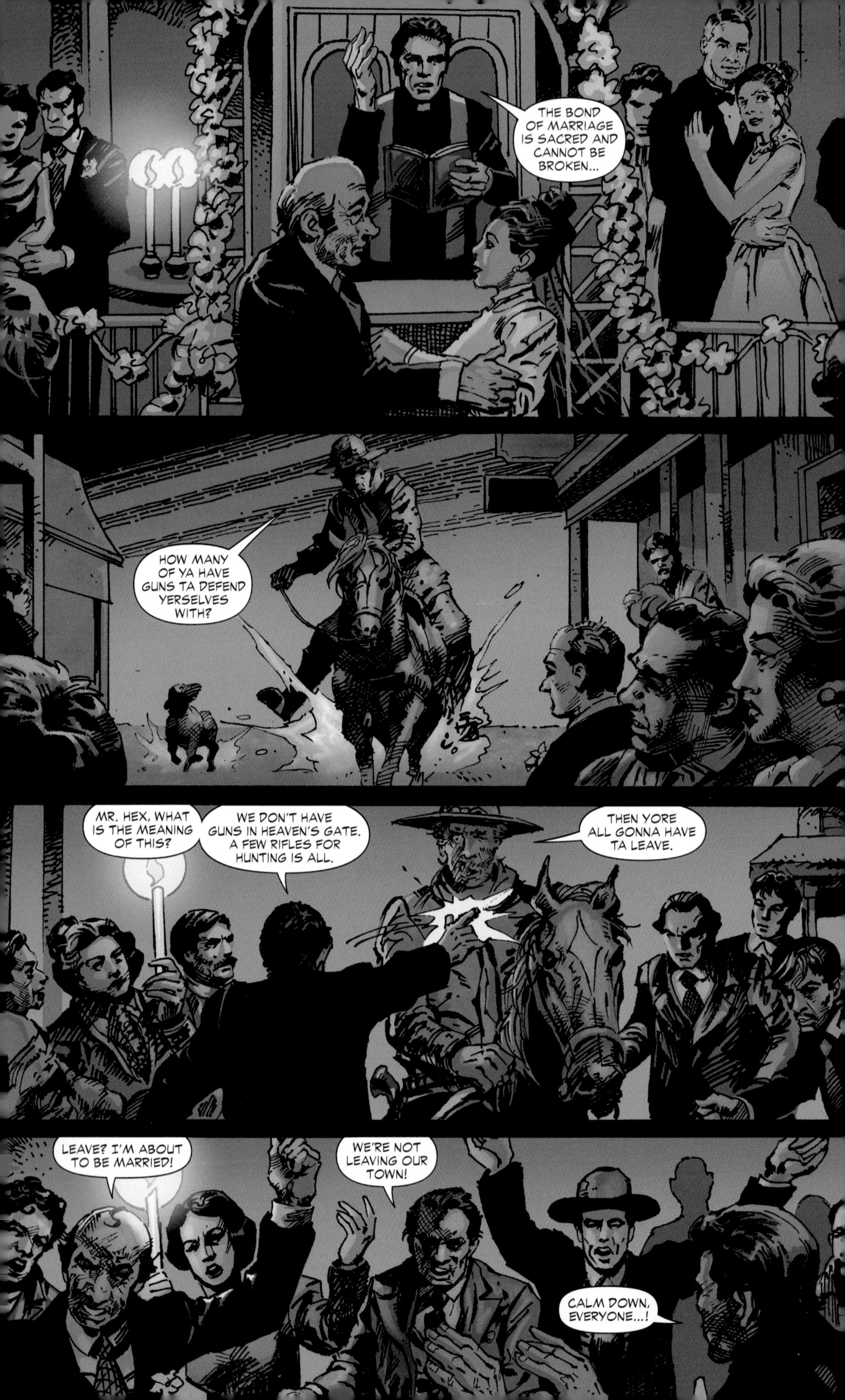
THE BOND OF MARRIAGE IS SACRED AND CANNOT BE BROKEN...
HOW MANY OF YA HAVE GUNS TA DEFEND YERSELVES WITH?
MR. HEX, WHAT IS THE MEANING OF THIS?
WE DON'T HAVE GUNS IN HEAVEN'S GATE. A FEW RIFLES FOR HUNTING IS ALL.
THEN YORE ALL GONNA HAVE TA LEAVE.
LEAVE? I'M ABOUT TO BE MARRIED!
WE'RE NOT LEAVING OUR TOWN!
CALM DOWN, EVERYONE...!

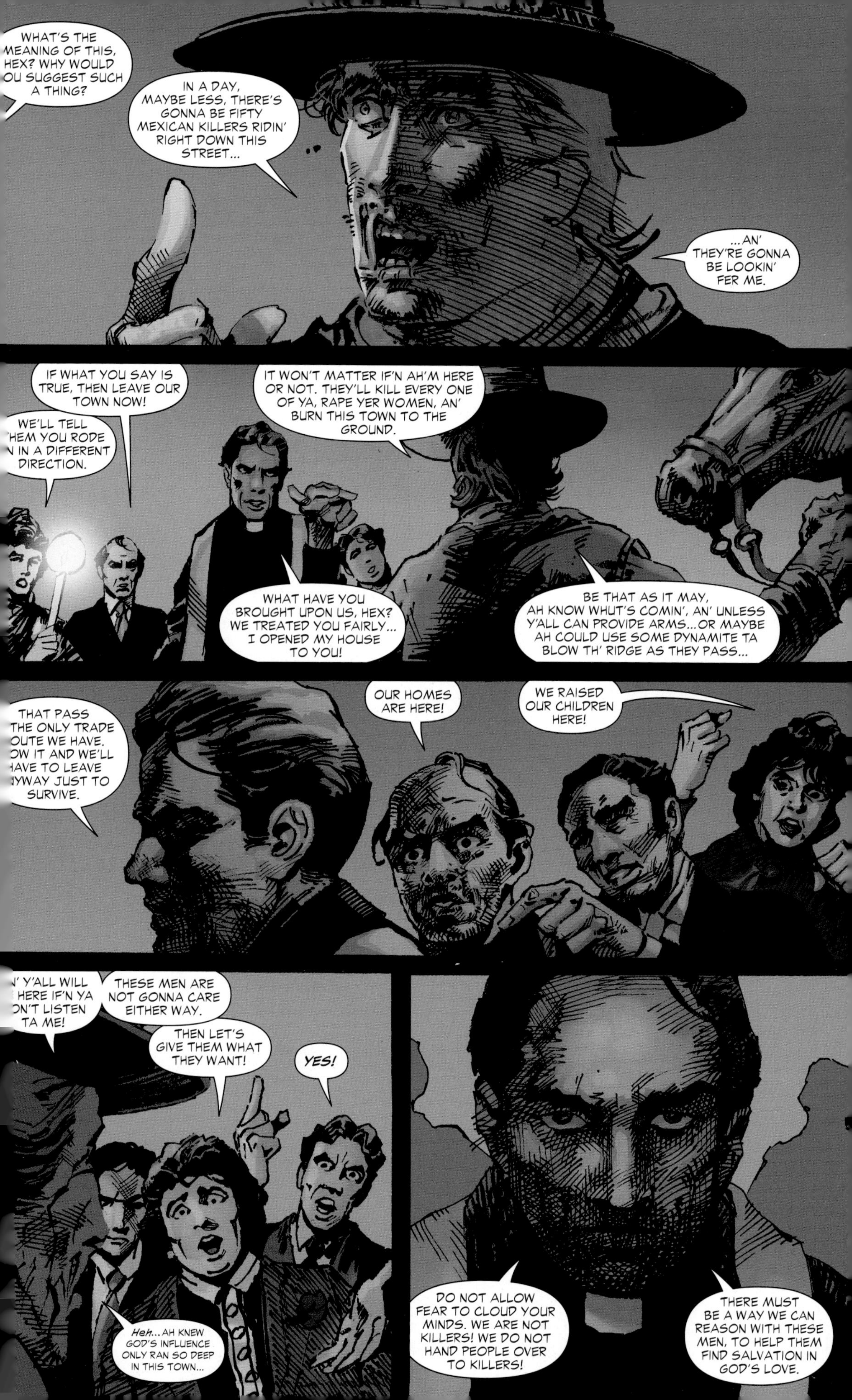
WHAT'S THE MEANING OF THIS, HEX? WHY WOULD OU SUGGEST SUCH A THING?
IN A DAY, MAYBE LESS, THERE'S GONNA BE FIFTY MEXICAN KILLERS RIDIN' RIGHT DOWN THIS STREET...
...AN' THEY'RE GONNA BE LOOKIN' FER ME.
IF WHAT YOU SAY IS TRUE, THEN LEAVE OUR TOWN NOW!
WE'LL TELL HEM YOU RODE N IN A DIFFERENT DIRECTION.
IT WON'T MATTER IF'N AH'M HERE OR NOT. THEY'LL KILL EVERY ONE OF YA, RAPE YER WOMEN, AN' BURN THIS TOWN TO THE GROUND.
WHAT HAVE YOU BROUGHT UPON US, HEX? WE TREATED YOU FAIRLY... I OPENED MY HOUSE TO YOU!
BE THAT AS IT MAY, AH KNOW WHUT'S COMIN', AN' UNLESS Y'ALL CAN PROVIDE ARMS...OR MAYBE AH COULD USE SOME DYNAMITE TA BLOW TH' RIDGE AS THEY PASS...
THAT PASS THE ONLY TRADE OUTE WE HAVE. OW IT AND WE'LL HAVE TO LEAVE NYWAY JUST TO SURVIVE.
OUR HOMES ARE HERE!
WE RAISED OUR CHILDREN HERE!
N' Y'ALL WILL HERE IF'N YA ON'T LISTEN TA ME!
THESE MEN ARE NOT GONNA CARE EITHER WAY.
THEN LET'S GIVE THEM WHAT THEY WANT!
YES!
Heh... AH KNEW GOD'S INFLUENCE ONLY RAN SO DEEP IN THIS TOWN...
DO NOT ALLOW FEAR TO CLOUD YOUR MINDS. WE ARE NOT KILLERS! WE DO NOT HAND PEOPLE OVER TO KILLERS!
THERE MUST BE A WAY WE CAN REASON WITH THESE MEN, TO HELP THEM FIND SALVATION IN GOD'S LOVE.

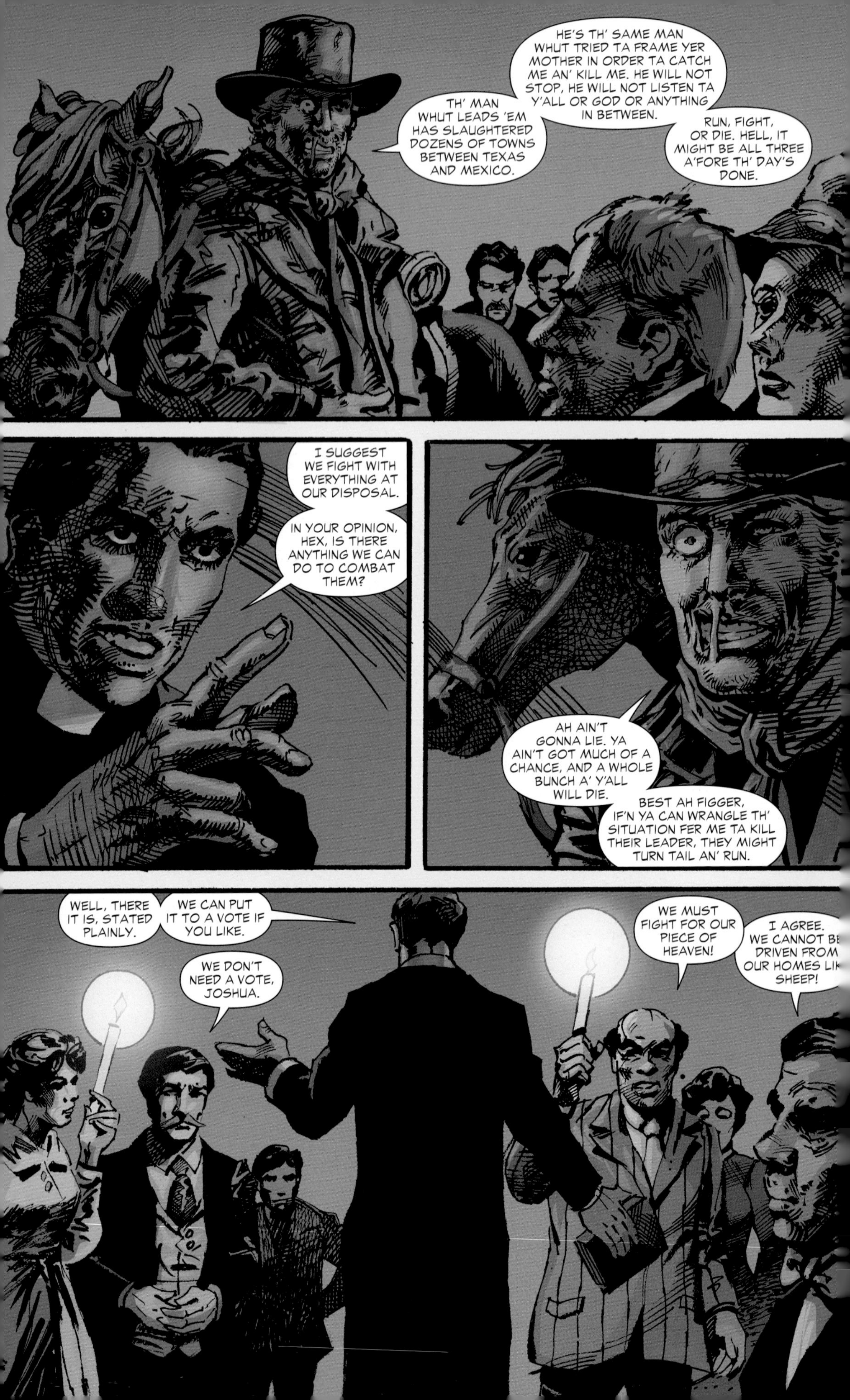
TH' MAN WHUT LEADS 'EM HAS SLAUGHTERED DOZENS OF TOWNS BETWEEN TEXAS AND MEXICO.
HE'S TH' SAME MAN WHUT TRIED TA FRAME YER MOTHER IN ORDER TA CATCH ME AN' KILL ME. HE WILL NOT STOP, HE WILL NOT LISTEN TA Y'ALL OR GOD OR ANYTHING IN BETWEEN.
RUN, FIGHT, OR DIE. HELL, IT MIGHT BE ALL THREE A'FORE TH' DAY'S DONE.
I SUGGEST WE FIGHT WITH EVERYTHING AT OUR DISPOSAL.
IN YOUR OPINION, HEX, IS THERE ANYTHING WE CAN DO TO COMBAT THEM?
AH AIN'T GONNA LIE. YA AIN'T GOT MUCH OF A CHANCE, AND A WHOLE BUNCH A' Y'ALL WILL DIE.
BEST AH FIGGER, IF'N YA CAN WRANGLE TH' SITUATION FER ME TA KILL THEIR LEADER, THEY MIGHT TURN TAIL AN' RUN.
WELL, THERE IT IS, STATED PLAINLY.
WE CAN PUT IT TO A VOTE IF YOU LIKE.
WE DON'T NEED A VOTE, JOSHUA.
WE MUST FIGHT FOR OUR PIECE OF HEAVEN!
I AGREE. WE CANNOT BE DRIVEN FROM OUR HOMES LIKE SHEEP!

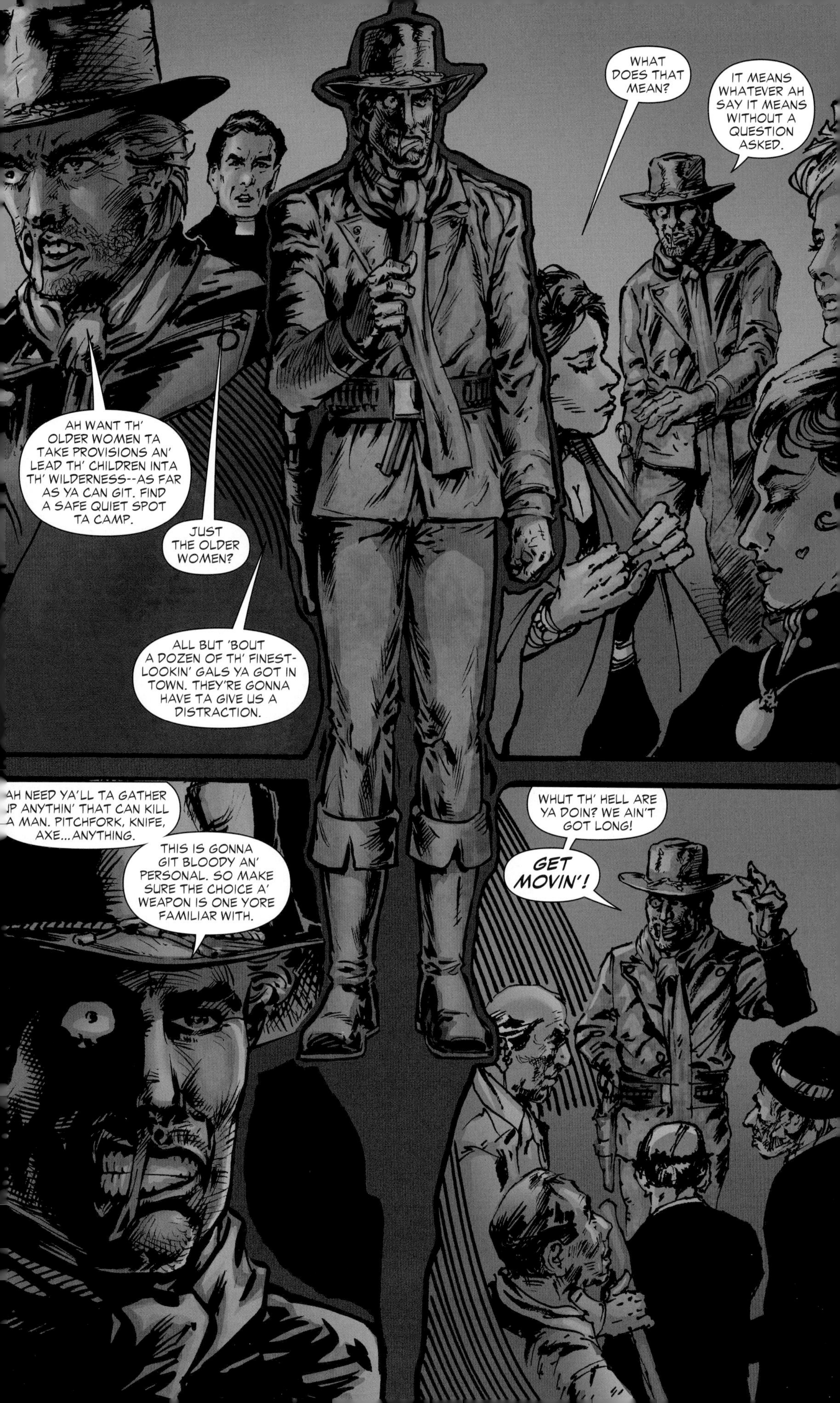
AH WANT TH' OLDER WOMEN TA TAKE PROVISIONS AN' LEAD TH' CHILDREN INTA TH' WILDERNESS--AS FAR AS YA CAN GIT. FIND A SAFE QUIET SPOT TA CAMP.
JUST THE OLDER WOMEN?
ALL BUT 'BOUT A DOZEN OF TH' FINEST-LOOKIN' GALS YA GOT IN TOWN. THEY'RE GONNA HAVE TA GIVE US A DISTRACTION.
WHAT DOES THAT MEAN?
IT MEANS WHATEVER AH SAY IT MEANS WITHOUT A QUESTION ASKED.
AH NEED YA'LL TA GATHER UP ANYTHIN' THAT CAN KILL A MAN. PITCHFORK, KNIFE, AXE...ANYTHING.
THIS IS GONNA GIT BLOODY AN' PERSONAL. SO MAKE SURE THE CHOICE A' WEAPON IS ONE YORE FAMILIAR WITH.
WHUT TH' HELL ARE YA DOIN? WE AIN'T GOT LONG!
GET MOVIN'!

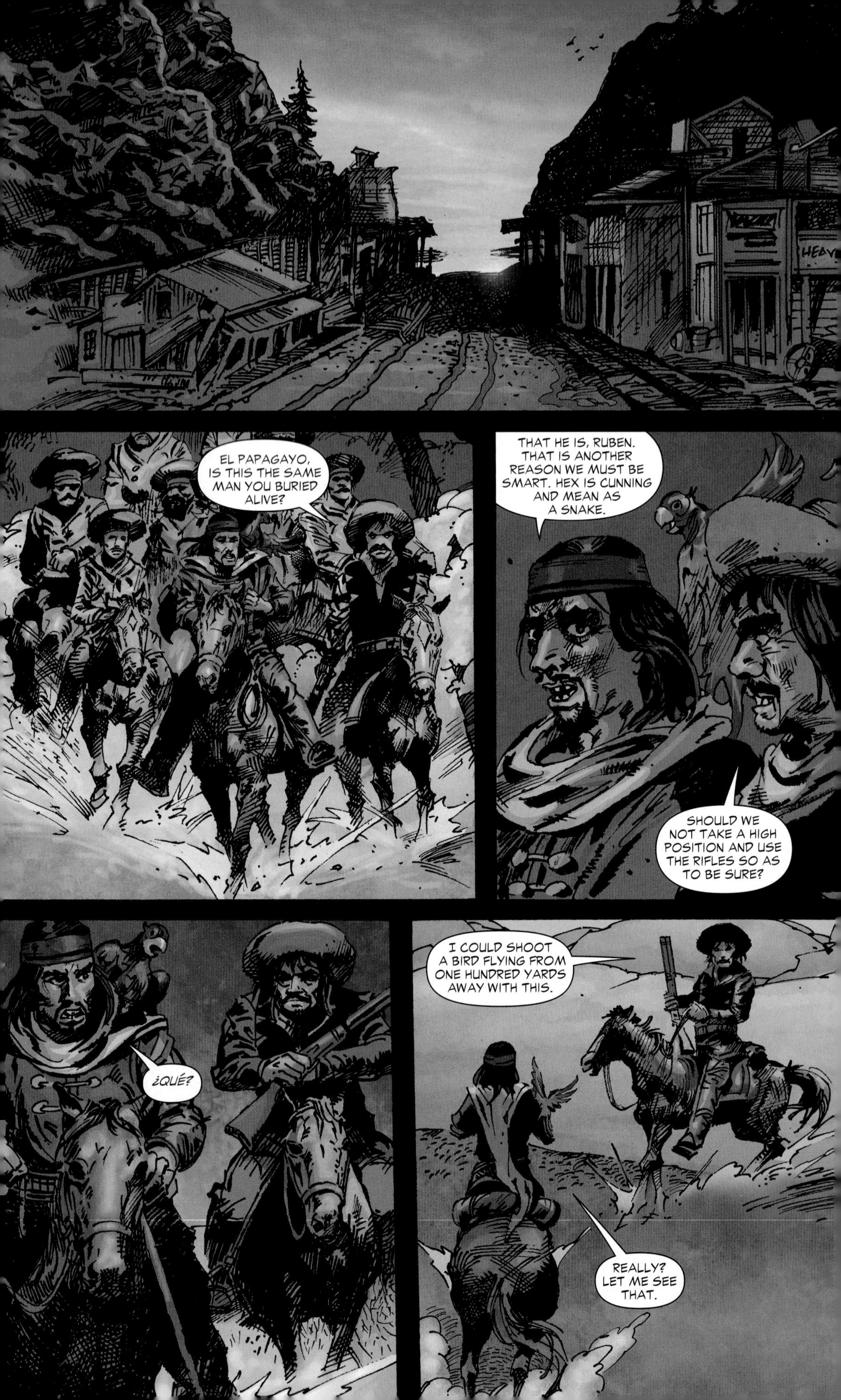
HEAV
EL PAPAGAYO, IS THIS THE SAME MAN YOU BURIED ALIVE?
THAT HE IS, RUBEN. THAT IS ANOTHER REASON WE MUST BE SMART. HEX IS CUNNING AND MEAN AS A SNAKE.
SHOULD WE NOT TAKE A HIGH POSITION AND USE THE RIFLES SO AS TO BE SURE?
¿QUÉ?
I COULD SHOOT A BIRD FLYING FROM ONE HUNDRED YARDS AWAY WITH THIS.
REALLY? LET ME SEE THAT.

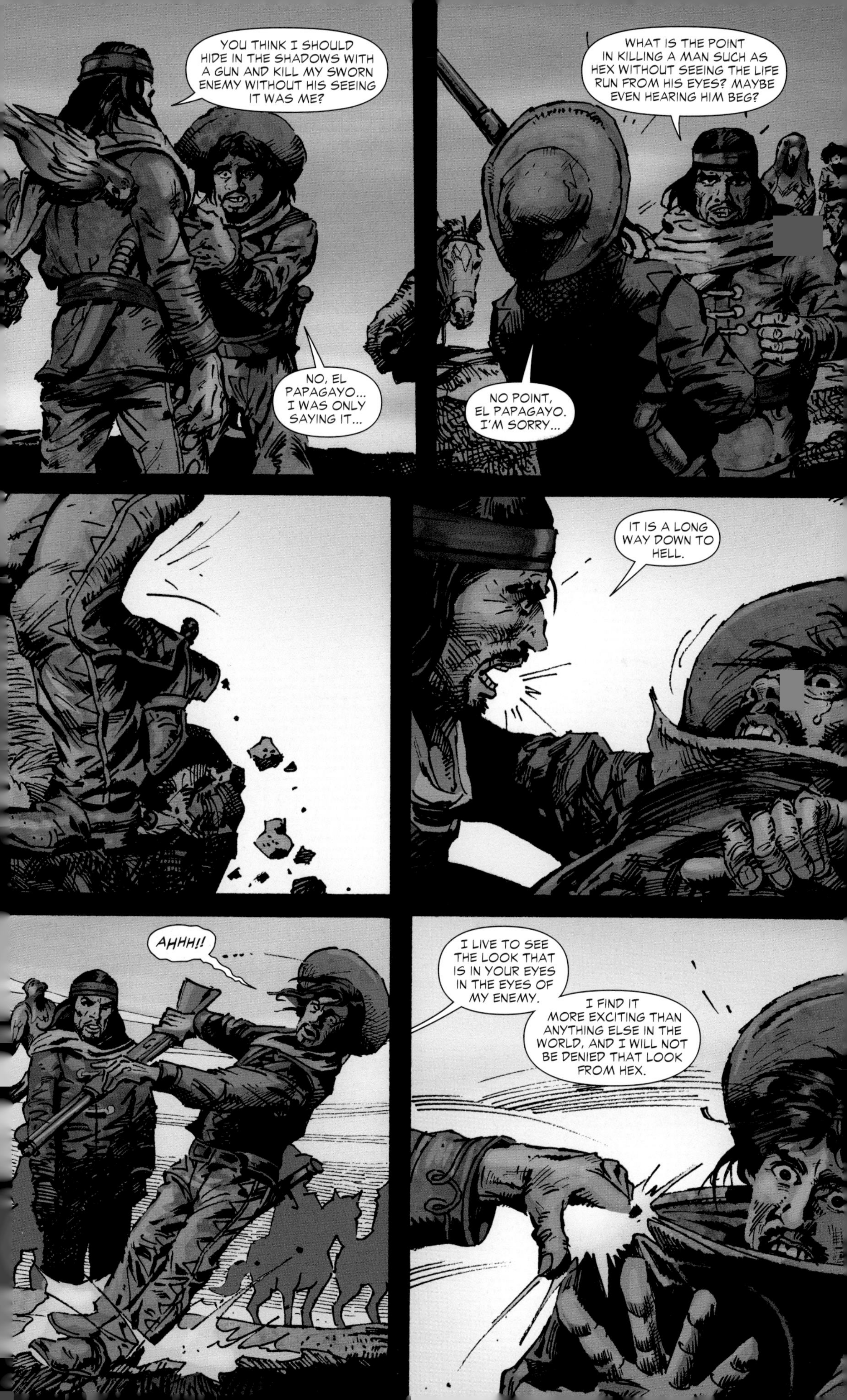
YOU THINK I SHOULD HIDE IN THE SHADOWS WITH A GUN AND KILL MY SWORN ENEMY WITHOUT HIS SEEING IT WAS ME?
NO, EL PAPAGAYO... I WAS ONLY SAYING IT...
WHAT IS THE POINT IN KILLING A MAN SUCH AS HEX WITHOUT SEEING THE LIFE RUN FROM HIS EYES? MAYBE EVEN HEARING HIM BEG?
NO POINT, EL PAPAGAYO. I'M SORRY...
IT IS A LONG WAY DOWN TO HELL.
AHHH!!
I LIVE TO SEE THE LOOK THAT IS IN YOUR EYES IN THE EYES OF MY ENEMY.
I FIND IT MORE EXCITING THAN ANYTHING ELSE IN THE WORLD, AND I WILL NOT BE DENIED THAT LOOK FROM HEX.

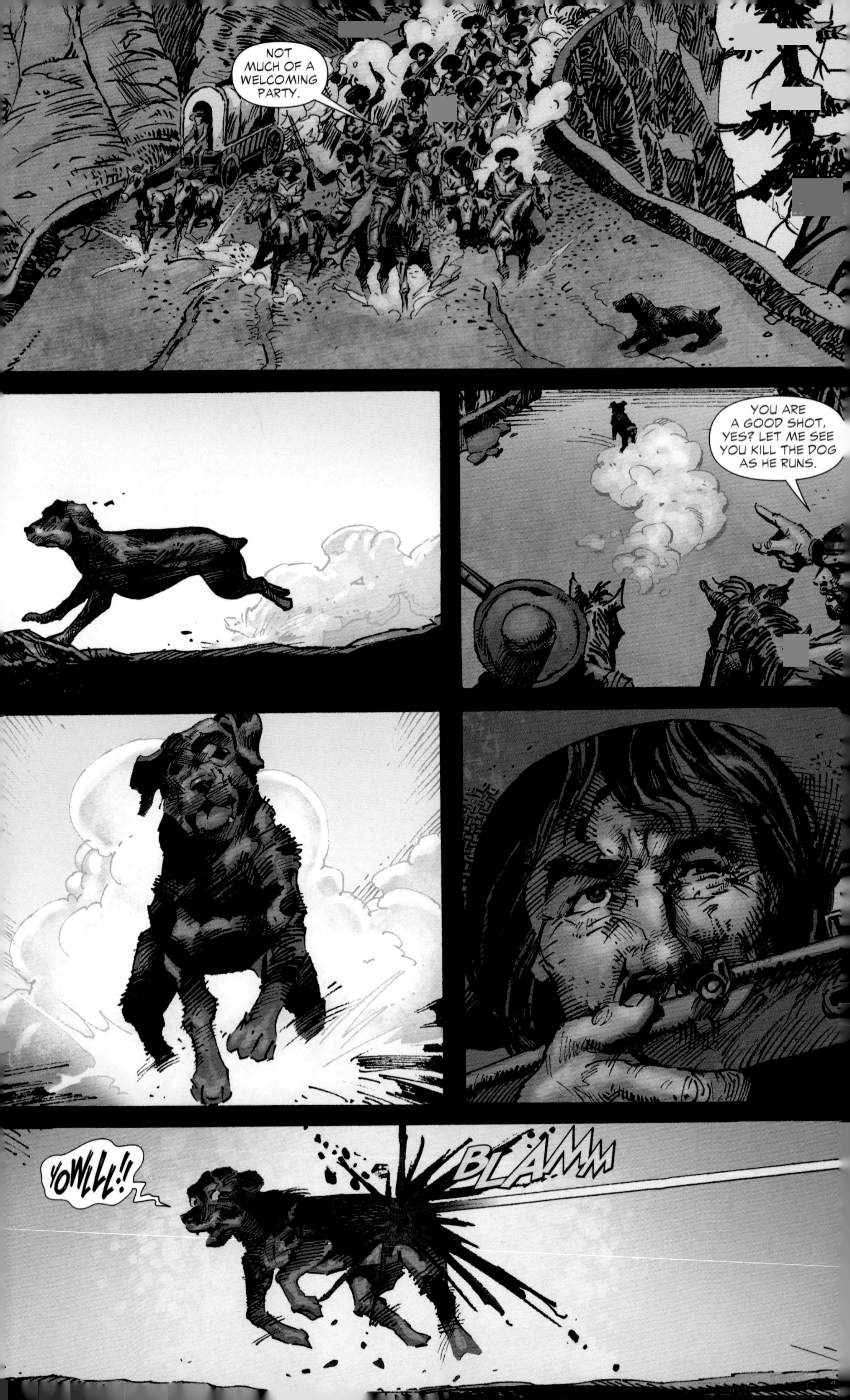
NOT MUCH OF A WELCOMING PARTY.
YOU ARE A GOOD SHOT, YES? LET ME SEE YOU KILL THE DOG AS HE RUNS.
YOWLLL!!
BLAMMM

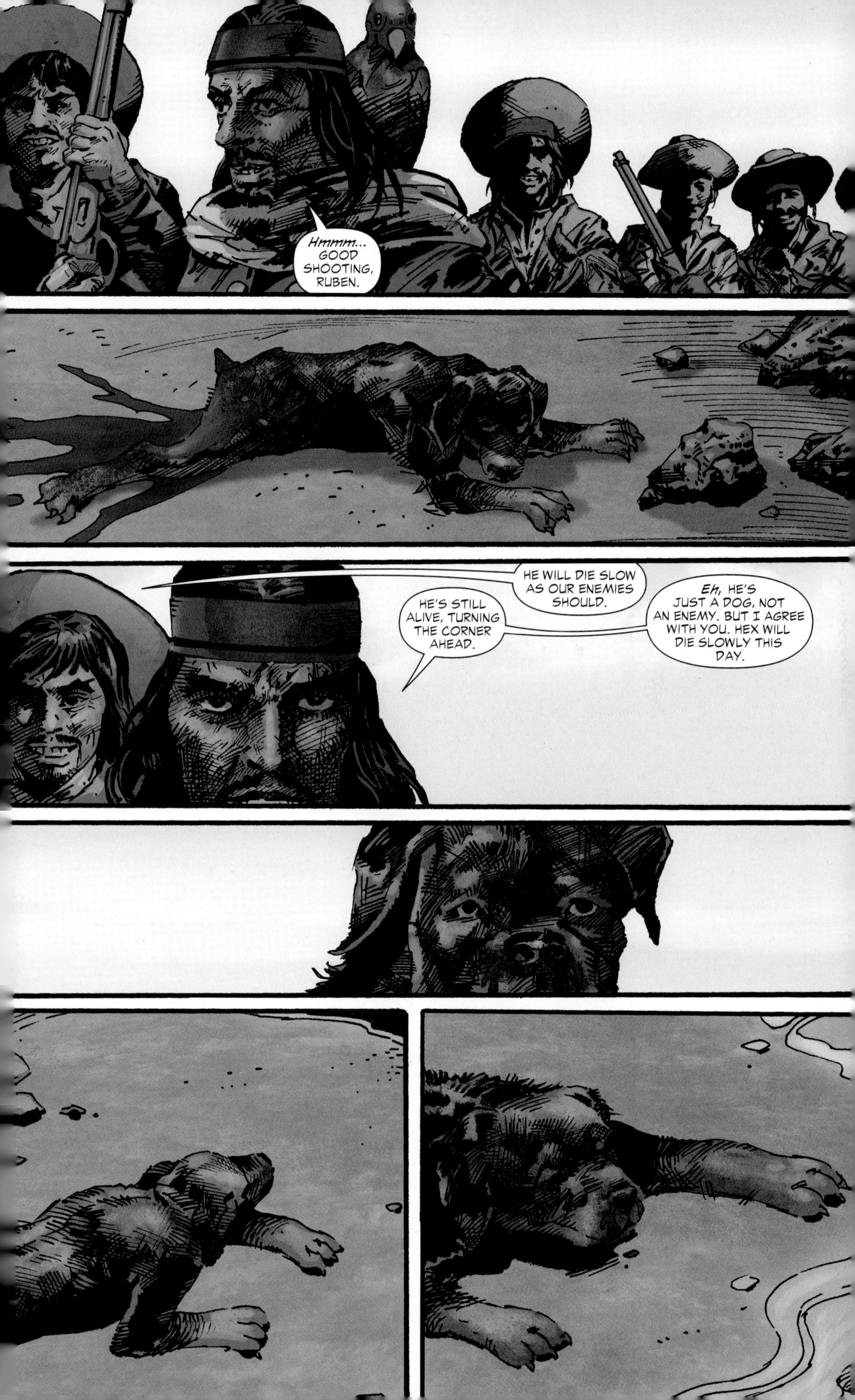
Hmmm... GOOD SHOOTING, RUBEN.
HE'S STILL ALIVE, TURNING THE CORNER AHEAD.
HE WILL DIE SLOW AS OUR ENEMIES SHOULD.
Eh, HE'S JUST A DOG, NOT AN ENEMY. BUT I AGREE WITH YOU. HEX WILL DIE SLOWLY THIS DAY.

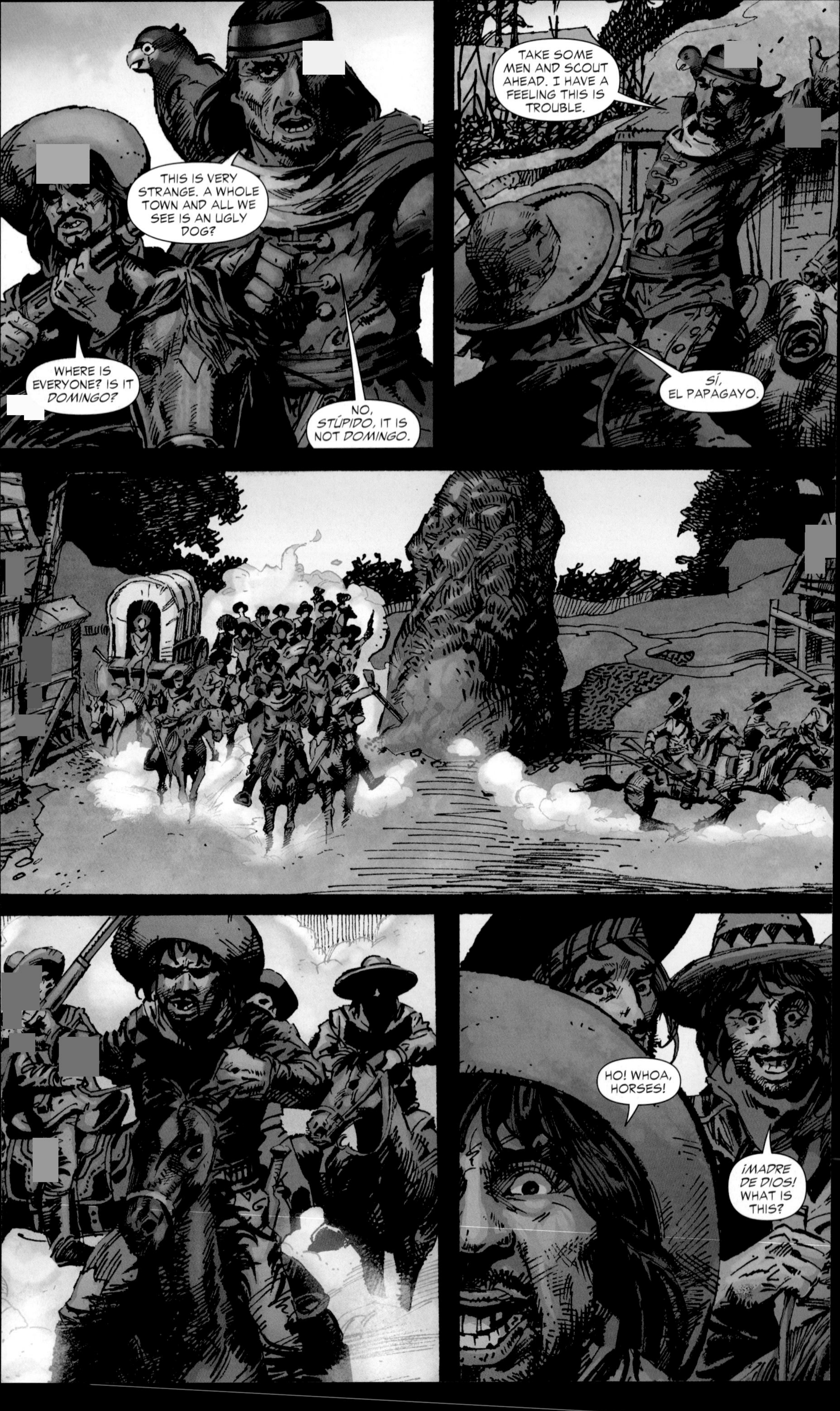
THIS IS VERY STRANGE. A WHOLE TOWN AND ALL WE SEE IS AN UGLY DOG?
WHERE IS EVERYONE? IS IT *DOMINGO?*
NO, *STÚPIDO,* IT IS NOT *DOMINGO.*
TAKE SOME MEN AND SCOUT AHEAD. I HAVE A FEELING THIS IS TROUBLE.
SÍ, EL PAPAGAYO.
HO! WHOA, HORSES!
¡MADRE DE DIOS! WHAT IS THIS?

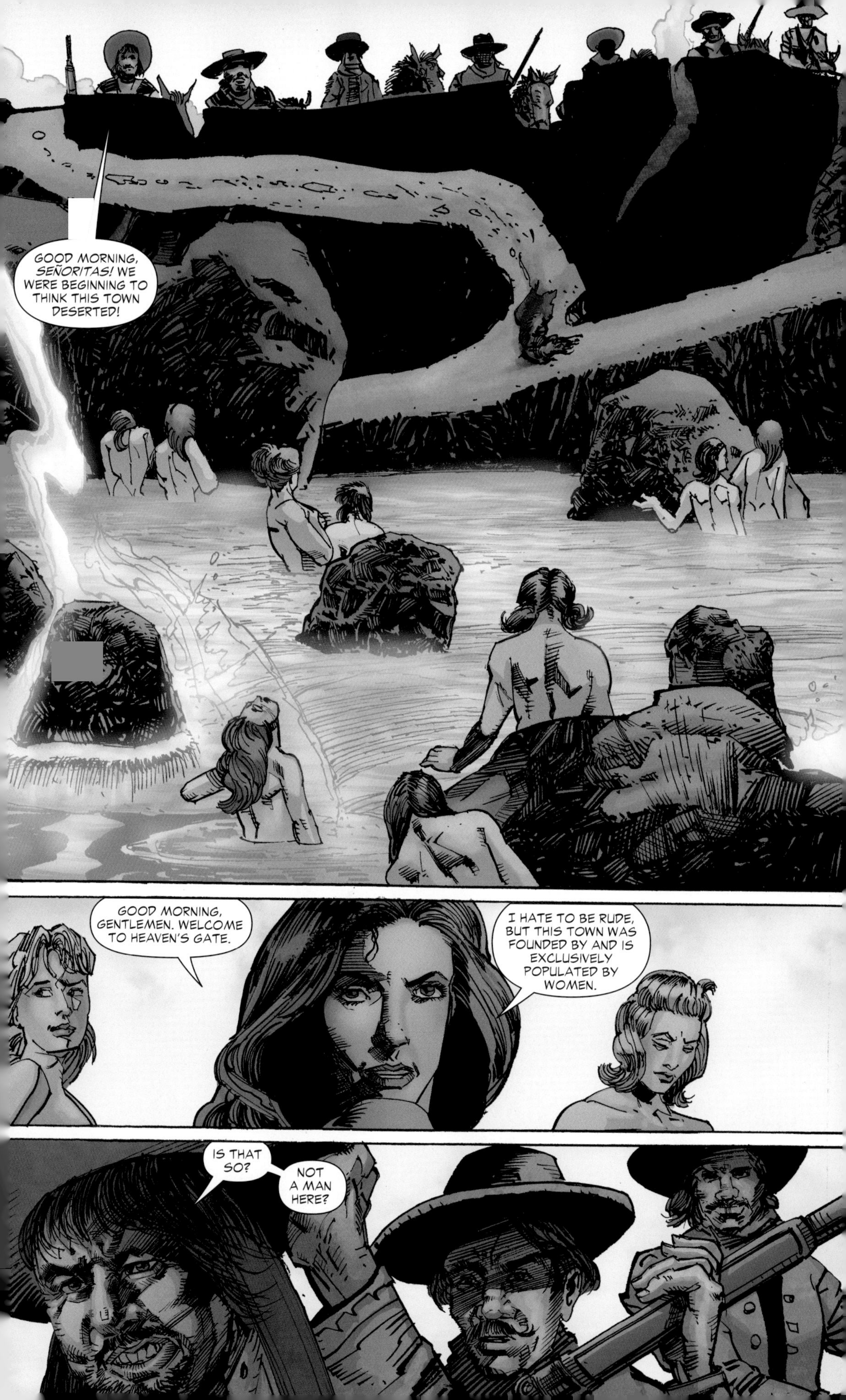
GOOD MORNING, SEÑORITAS! WE WERE BEGINNING TO THINK THIS TOWN DESERTED!
GOOD MORNING, GENTLEMEN. WELCOME TO HEAVEN'S GATE.
I HATE TO BE RUDE, BUT THIS TOWN WAS FOUNDED BY AND IS EXCLUSIVELY POPULATED BY WOMEN.
IS THAT SO?
NOT A MAN HERE?

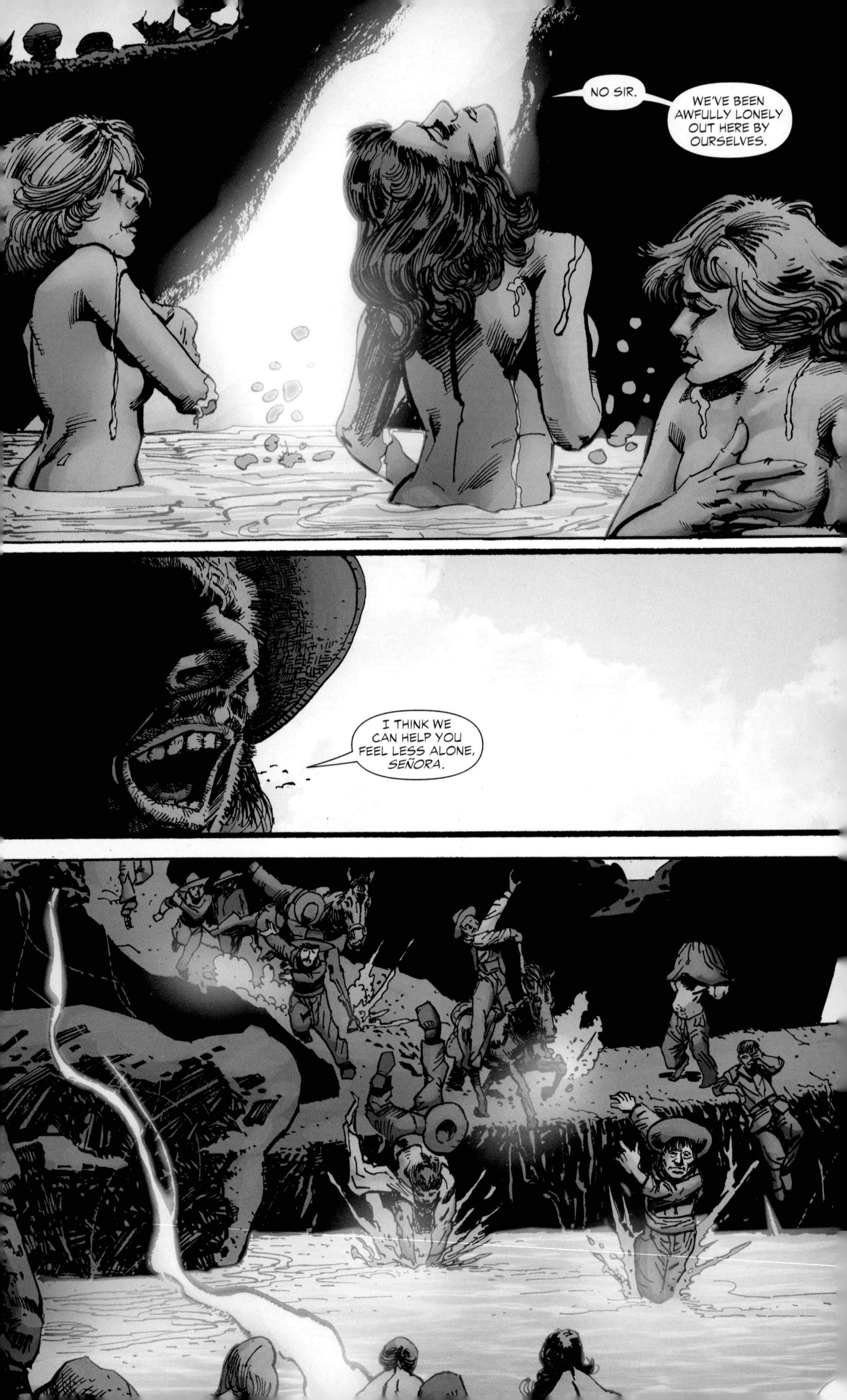
NO SIR.
WE'VE BEEN AWFULLY LONELY OUT HERE BY OURSELVES.
I THINK WE CAN HELP YOU FEEL LESS ALONE, SEÑORA.

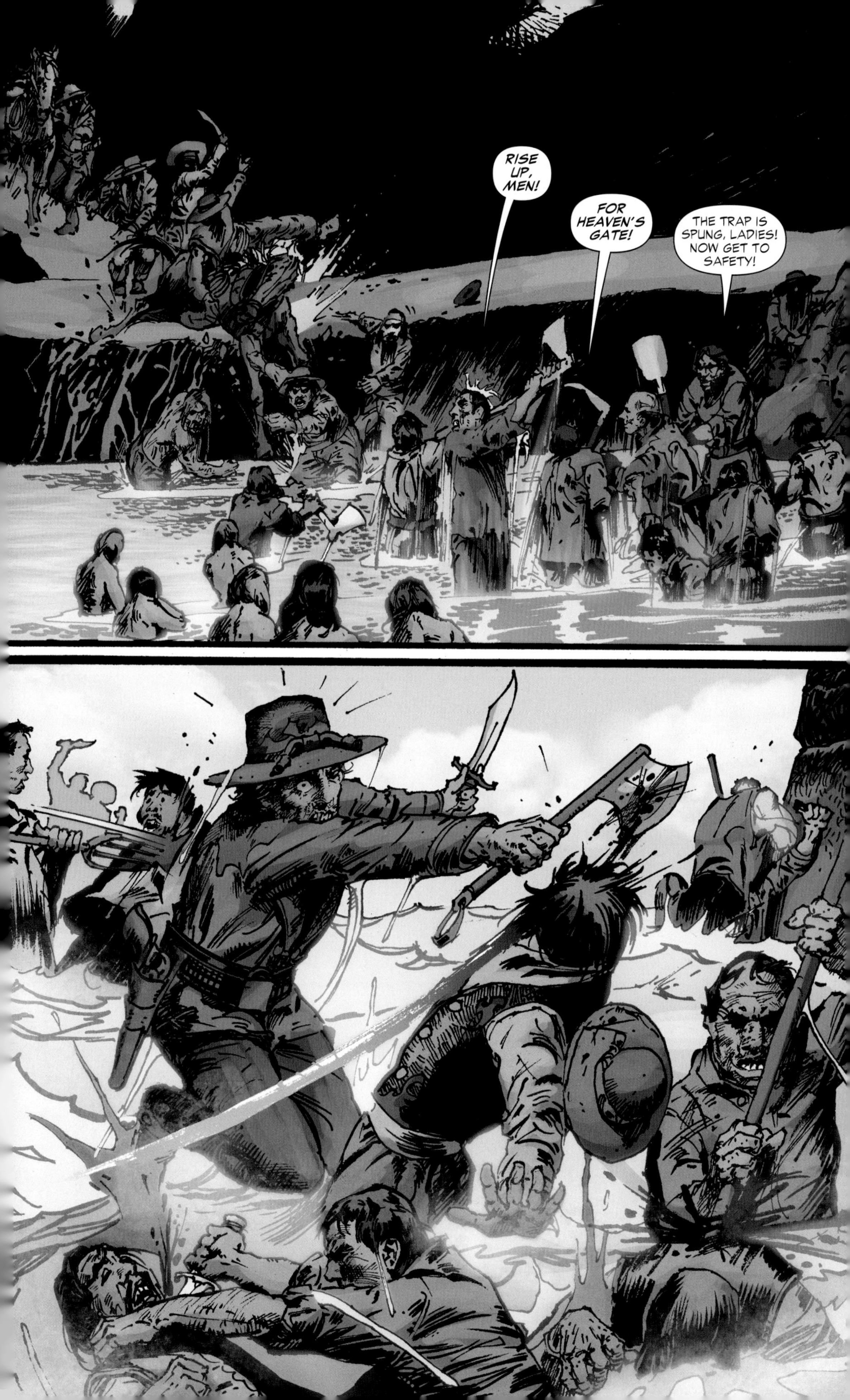
RISE UP, MEN!
FOR HEAVEN'S GATE!
THE TRAP IS SPUNG, LADIES! NOW GET TO SAFETY!

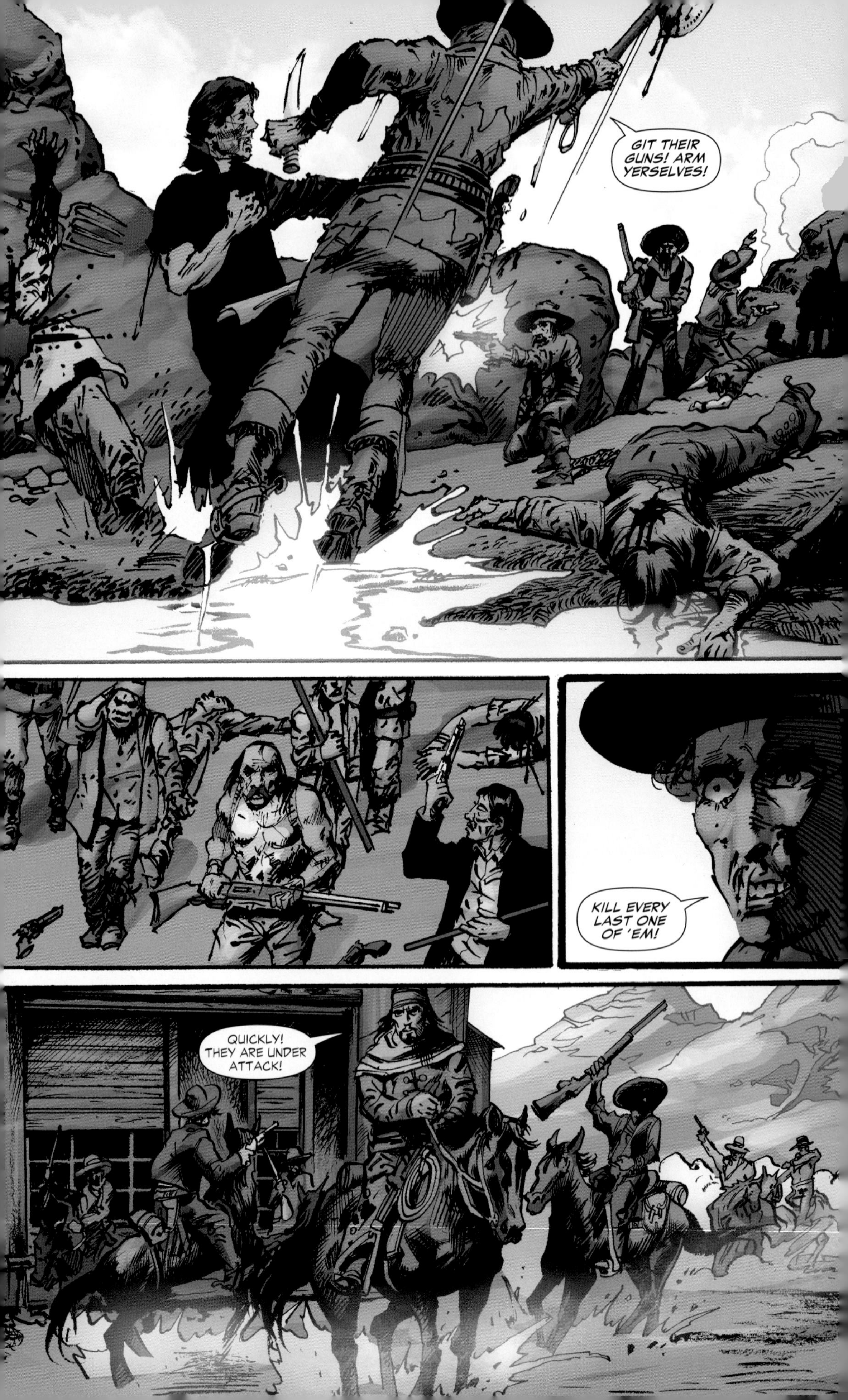
GIT THEIR GUNS! ARM YERSELVES!
KILL EVERY LAST ONE OF 'EM!
QUICKLY! THEY ARE UNDER ATTACK!

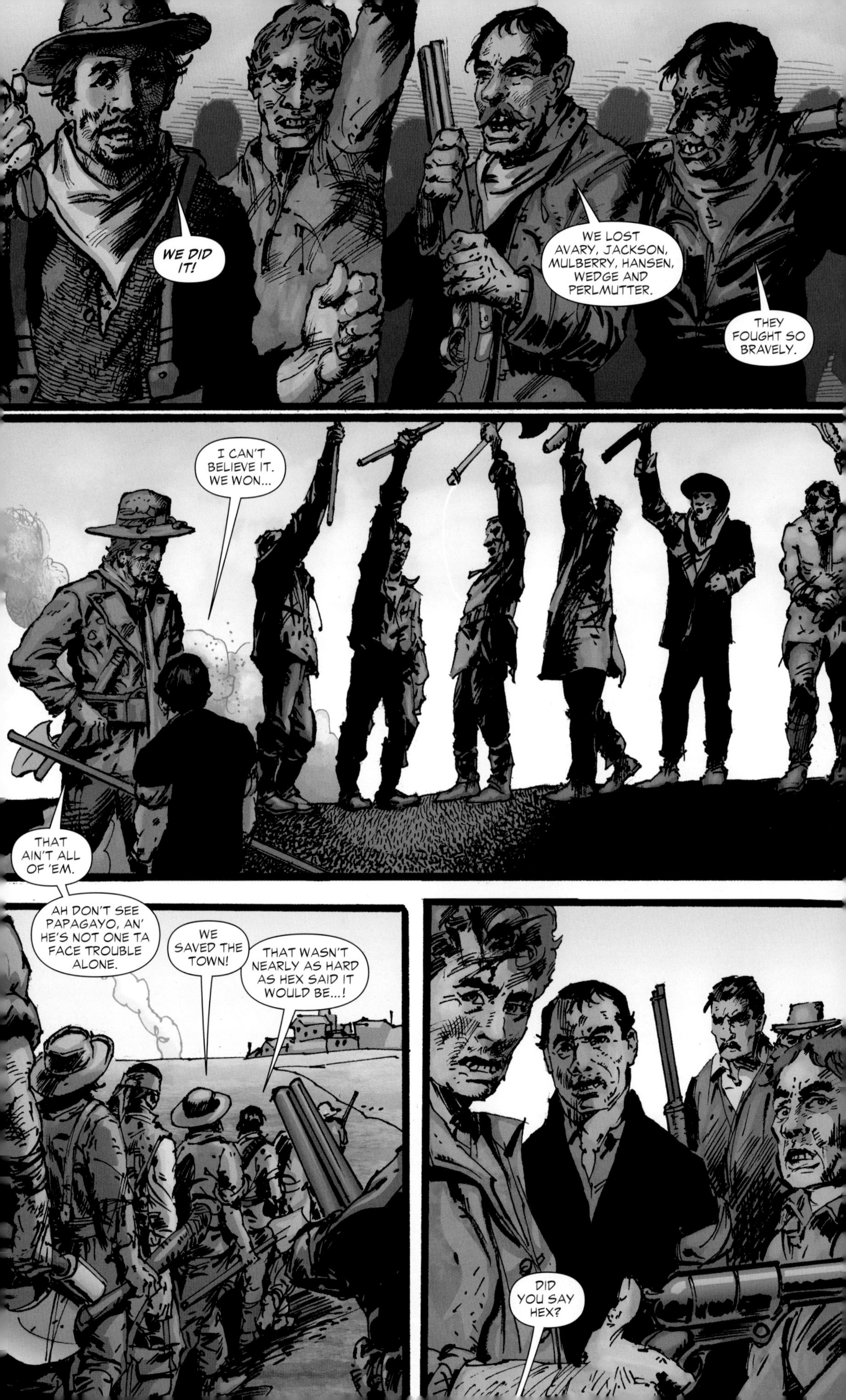
WE DID IT!
WE LOST AVARY, JACKSON, MULBERRY, HANSEN, WEDGE AND PERLMUTTER.
THEY FOUGHT SO BRAVELY.
I CAN'T BELIEVE IT. WE WON...
THAT AIN'T ALL OF 'EM.
AH DON'T SEE PAPAGAYO, AN' HE'S NOT ONE TA FACE TROUBLE ALONE.
WE SAVED THE TOWN!
THAT WASN'T NEARLY AS HARD AS HEX SAID IT WOULD BE...!
DID YOU SAY HEX?

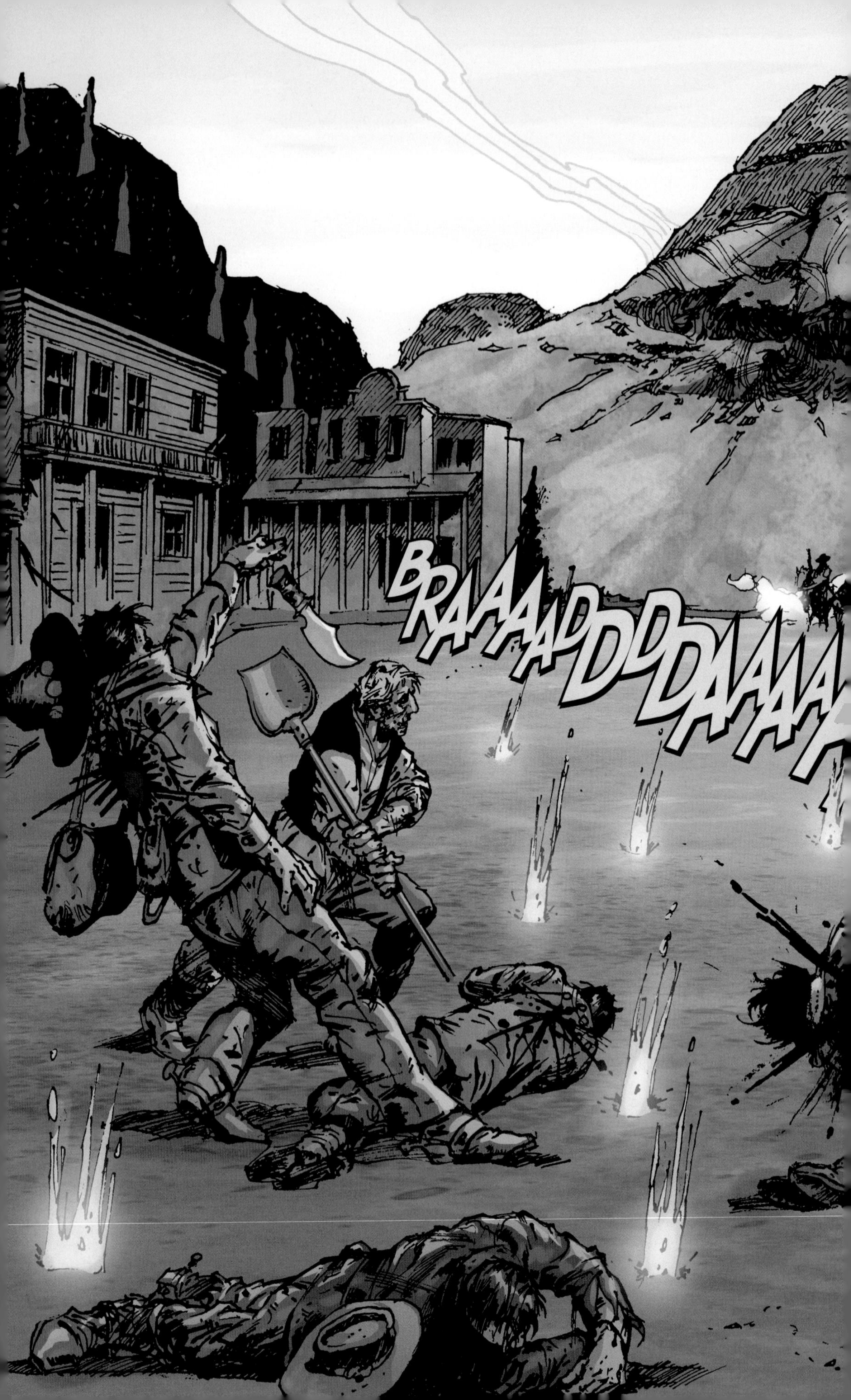
BRAAADDDDAAAA

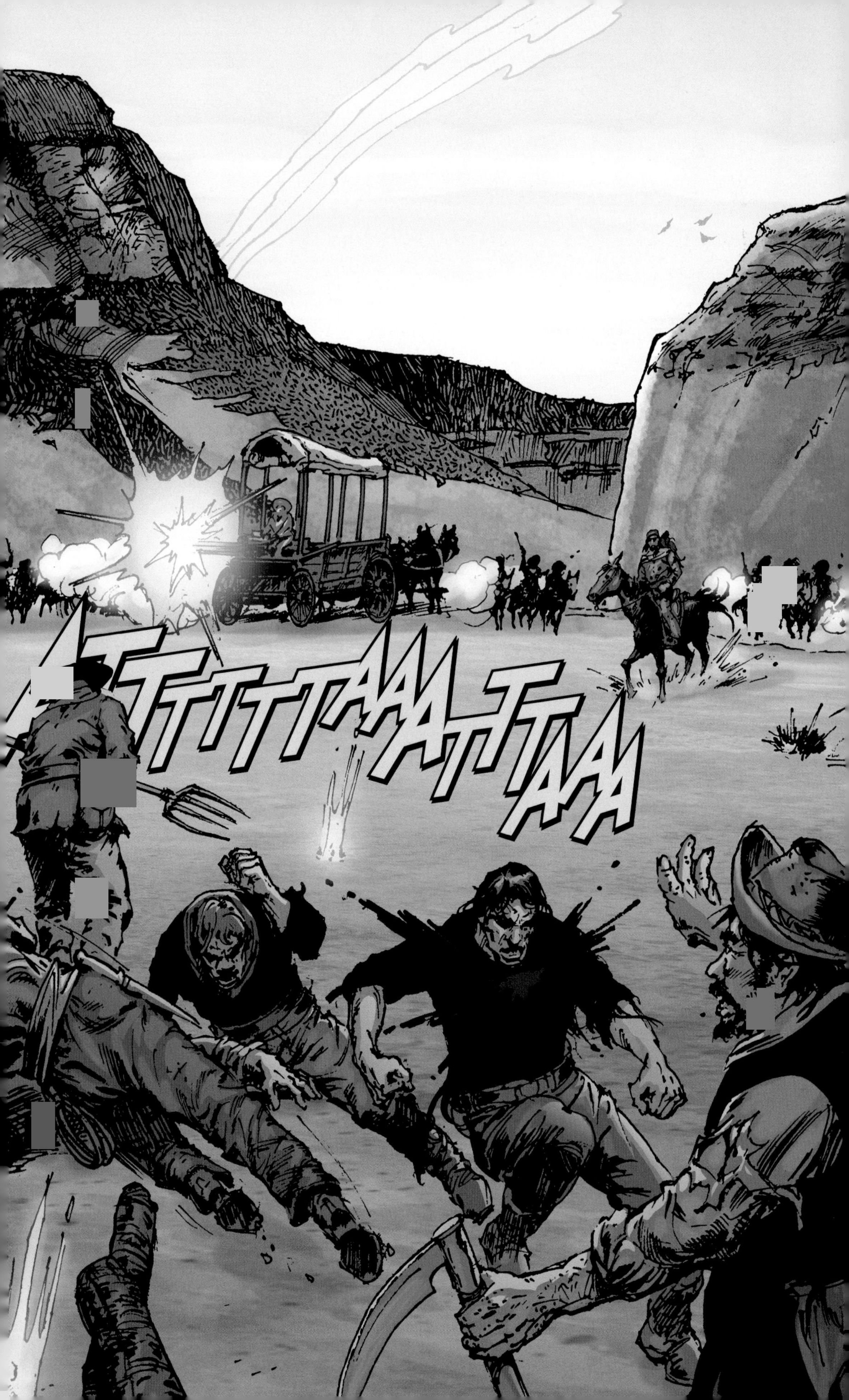
ATTTTTTAAATTAAA

HEX!

COME OUT AND FACE ME, *YOU COWARD!*

OR DO YOU HAVE MORE PEOPLE FOR ME TO KILL?

BRING ME HEX AND I WILL SPARE THE REST OF YOUR TOWN!

I SWEAR IT!

THAT SOUND.

A GATLING GUN FER SURE.

I SWEAR ON MY CHILDREN, I WILL NOT HARM YOUR TOWN IF YOU GIVE ME HEX!

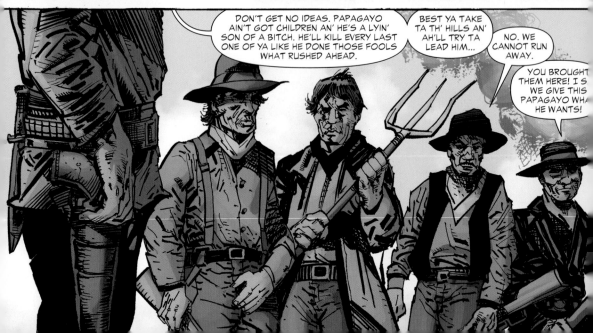

DON'T GET NO IDEAS. PAPAGAYO AIN'T GOT CHILDREN AN' HE'S A LYIN' SON OF A BITCH. HE'LL KILL EVERY LAST ONE OF YA LIKE HE DONE THOSE FOOLS WHAT RUSHED AHEAD.

BEST YA TAKE TA TH' HILLS AN' AH'LL TRY TA LEAD HIM...

NO. WE CANNOT RUN AWAY.

YOU BROUGHT THEM HERE! I S WE GIVE THIS PAPAGAYO WH HE WANTS!

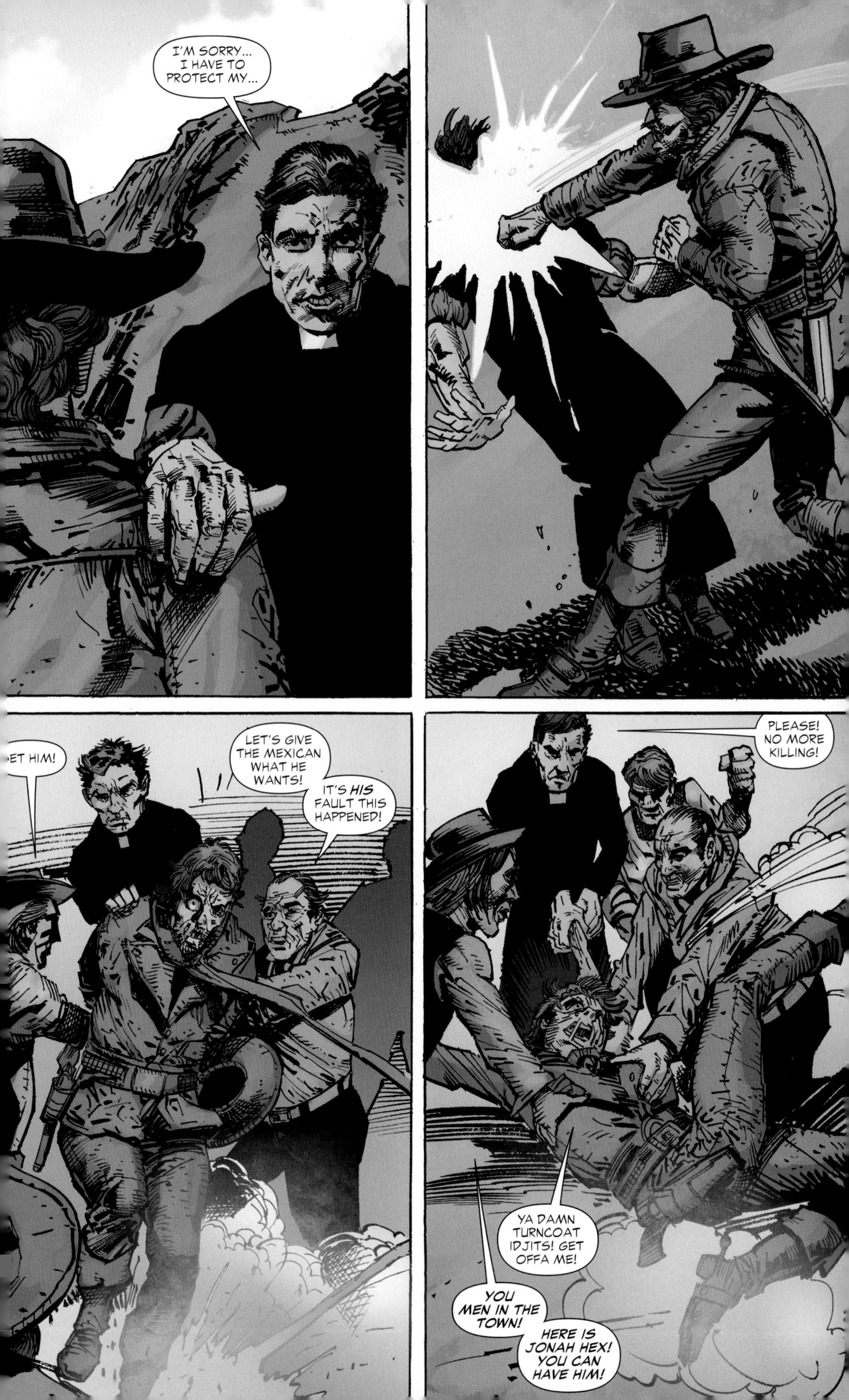
I'M SORRY... I HAVE TO PROTECT MY...
ET HIM!
LET'S GIVE THE MEXICAN WHAT HE WANTS!
IT'S *HIS* FAULT THIS HAPPENED!
PLEASE! NO MORE KILLING!
YA DAMN TURNCOAT IDJITS! GET OFFA ME!
YOU MEN IN THE TOWN!
HERE IS JONAH HEX! YOU CAN HAVE HIM!

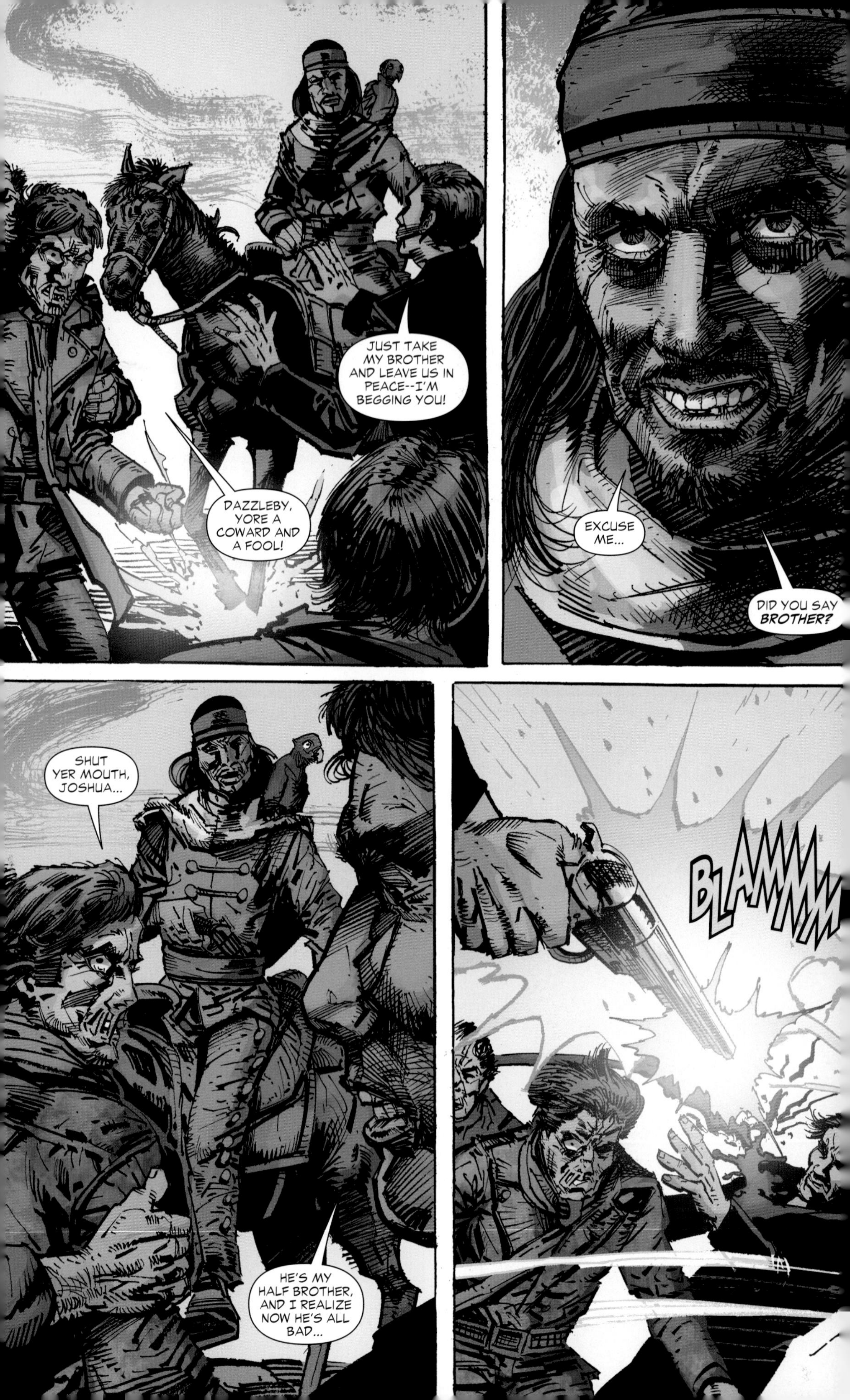
JUST TAKE MY BROTHER AND LEAVE US IN PEACE--I'M BEGGING YOU!
DAZZLEBY, YORE A COWARD AND A FOOL!
EXCUSE ME...
DID YOU SAY *BROTHER?*
SHUT YER MOUTH, JOSHUA...
HE'S MY HALF BROTHER, AND I REALIZE NOW HE'S ALL BAD...
BLAMMM

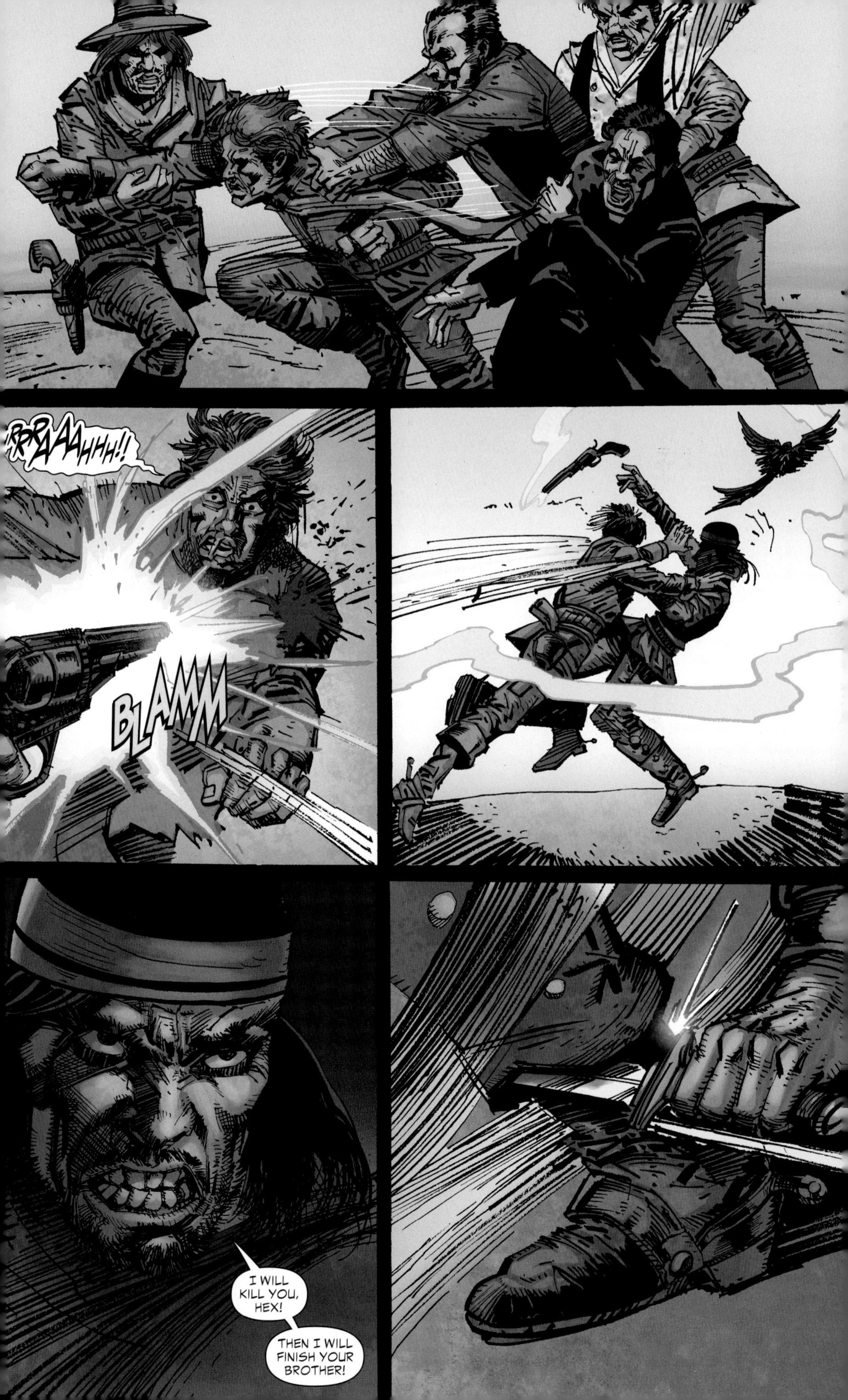
RRRAAAHHH!!
BLAMM
I WILL KILL YOU, HEX!
THEN I WILL FINISH YOUR BROTHER!

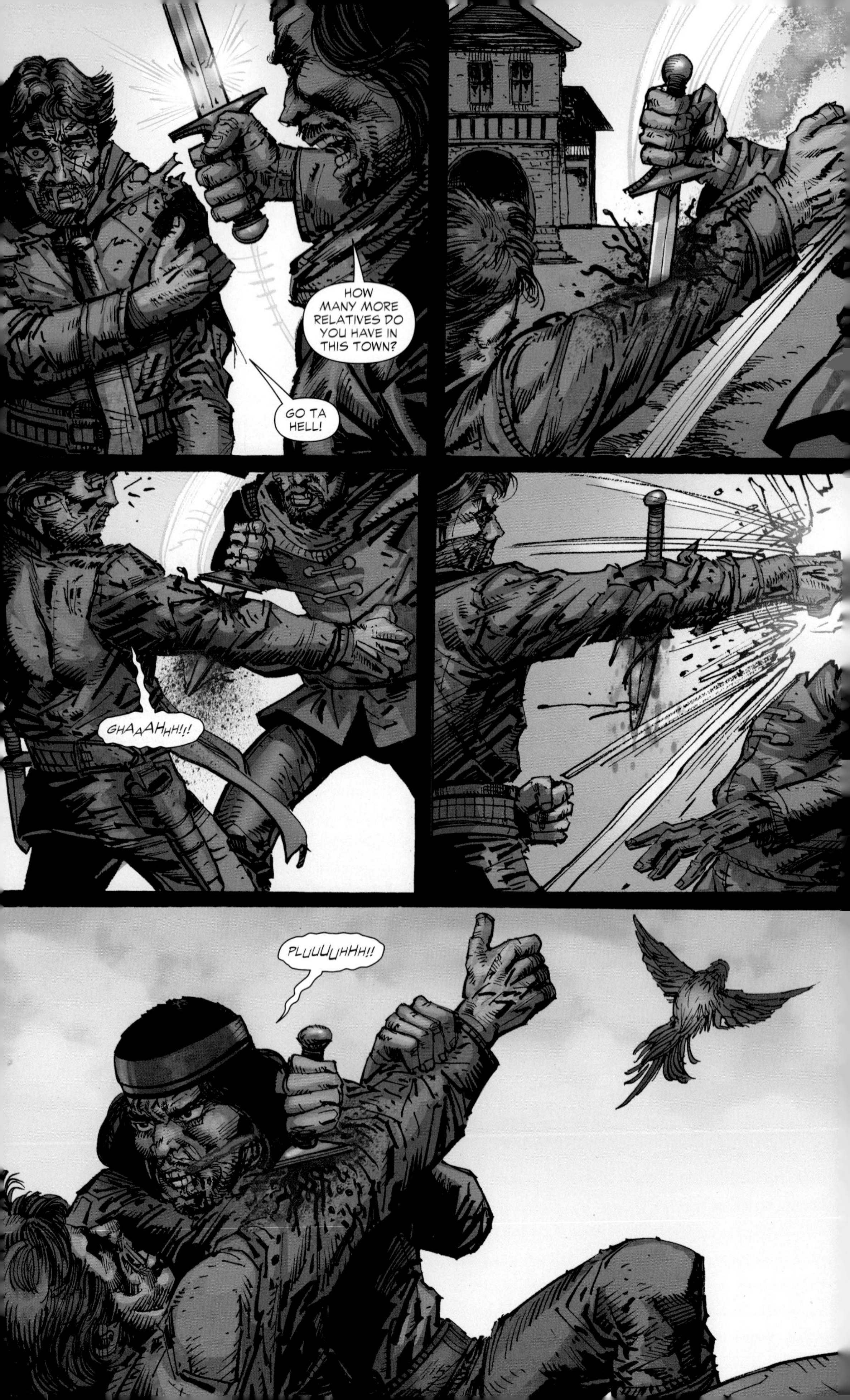
HOW MANY MORE RELATIVES DO YOU HAVE IN THIS TOWN?
GO TA HELL!
GHAAAHHH!!!
PLUUUUHHH!!

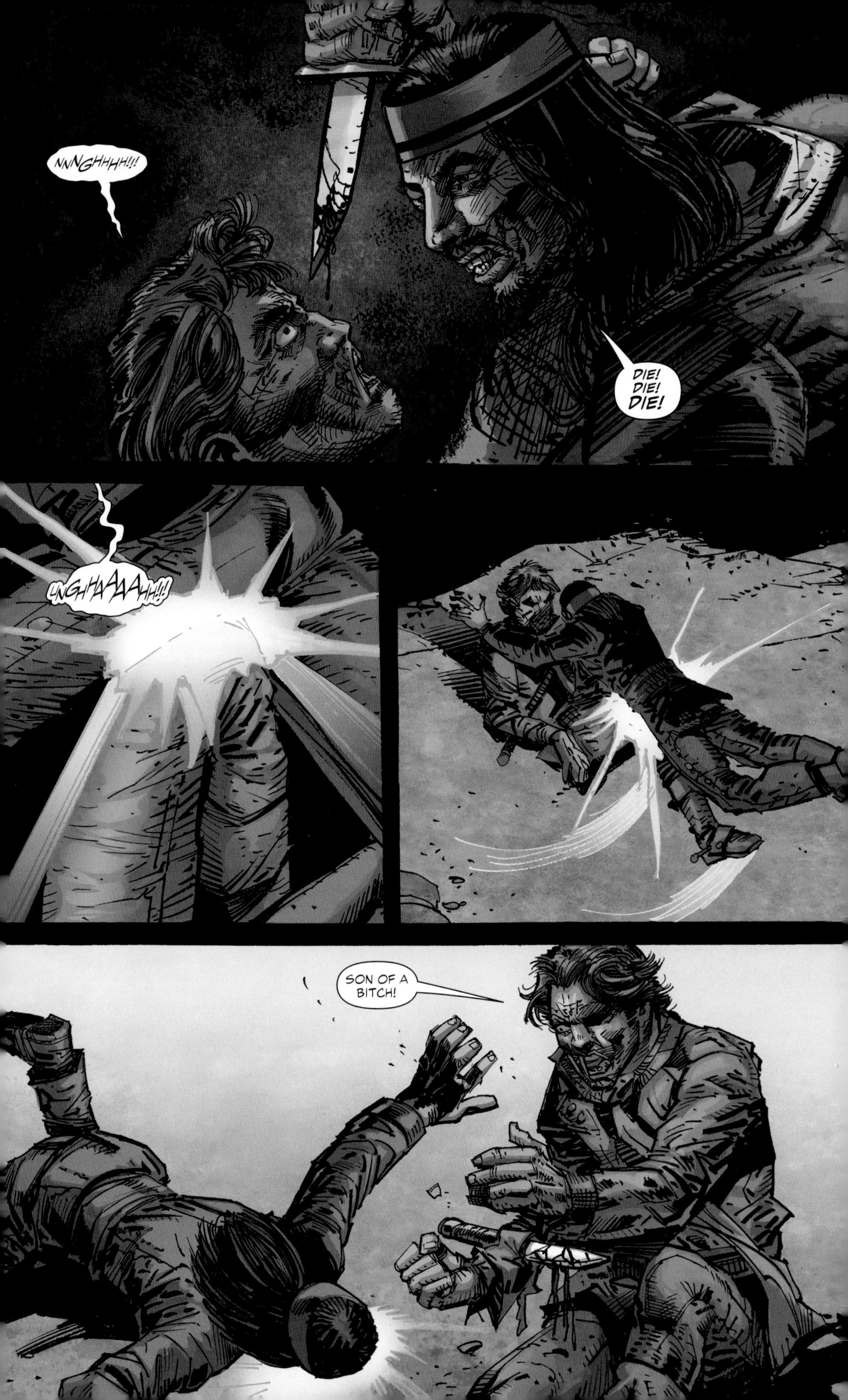
NNNGHHHH!!!
DIE! DIE! DIE!
UNGHHAAAAHH!!!
SON OF A BITCH!

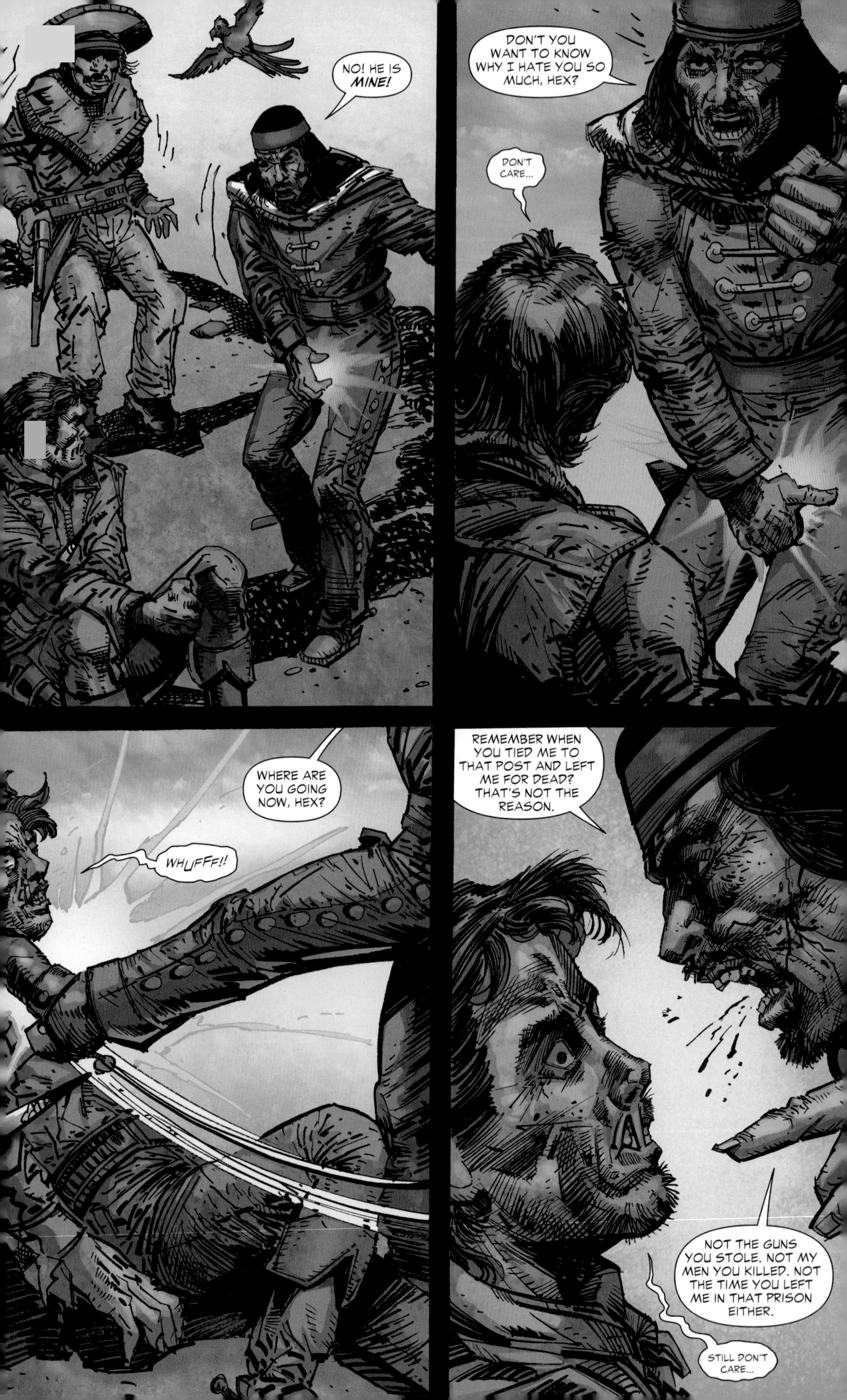
NO! HE IS *MINE!*
DON'T YOU WANT TO KNOW WHY I HATE YOU SO MUCH, HEX?
DON'T CARE...
WHERE ARE YOU GOING NOW, HEX?
WHUFFF!!
REMEMBER WHEN YOU TIED ME TO THAT POST AND LEFT ME FOR DEAD? THAT'S NOT THE REASON.
NOT THE GUNS YOU STOLE. NOT MY MEN YOU KILLED. NOT THE TIME YOU LEFT ME IN THAT PRISON EITHER.
STILL DON'T CARE...

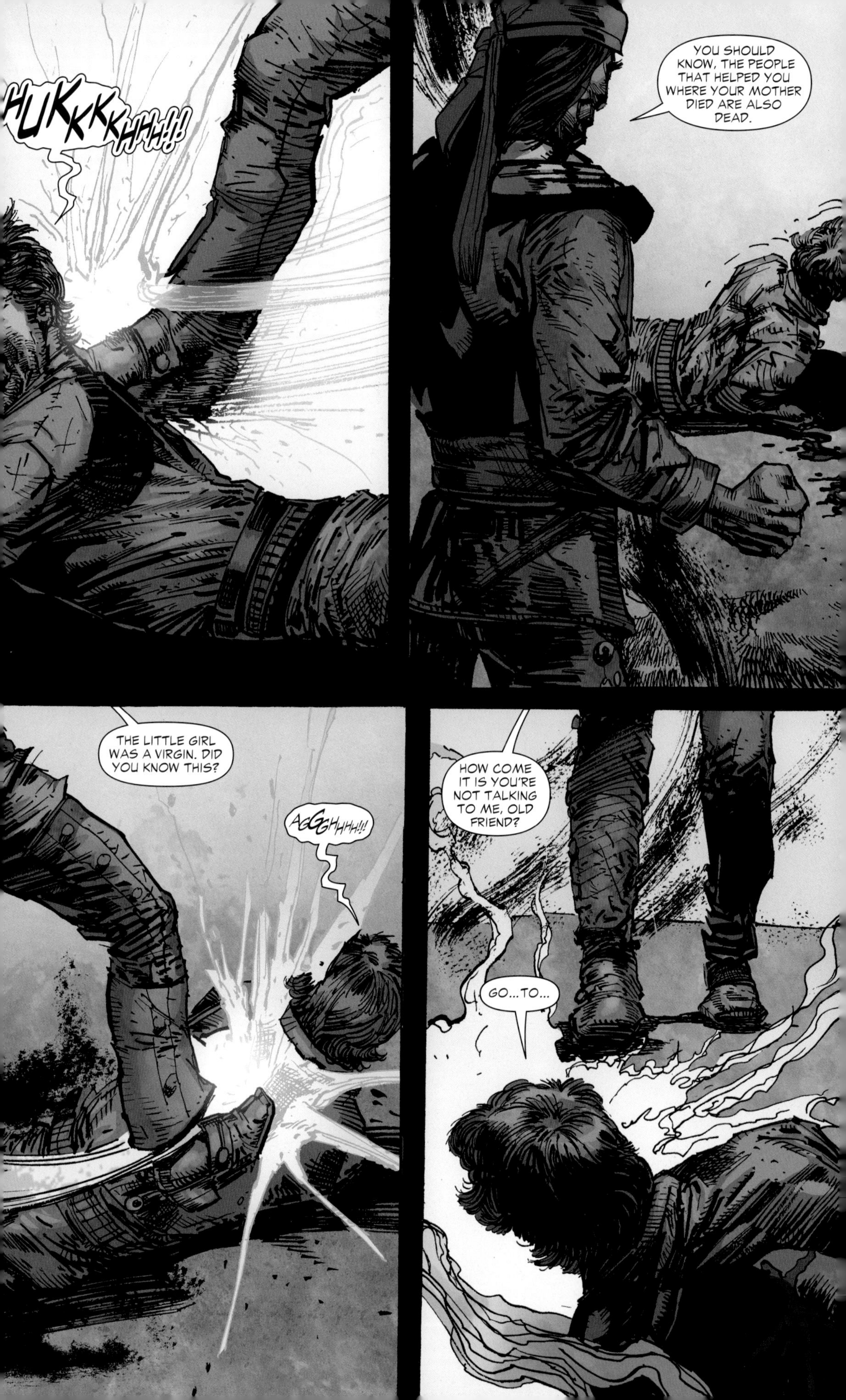
HUKKKKHHH!!!
YOU SHOULD KNOW, THE PEOPLE THAT HELPED YOU WHERE YOUR MOTHER DIED ARE ALSO DEAD.
THE LITTLE GIRL WAS A VIRGIN. DID YOU KNOW THIS?
AGGGHHHH!!!
HOW COME IT IS YOU'RE NOT TALKING TO ME, OLD FRIEND?
GO...TO...

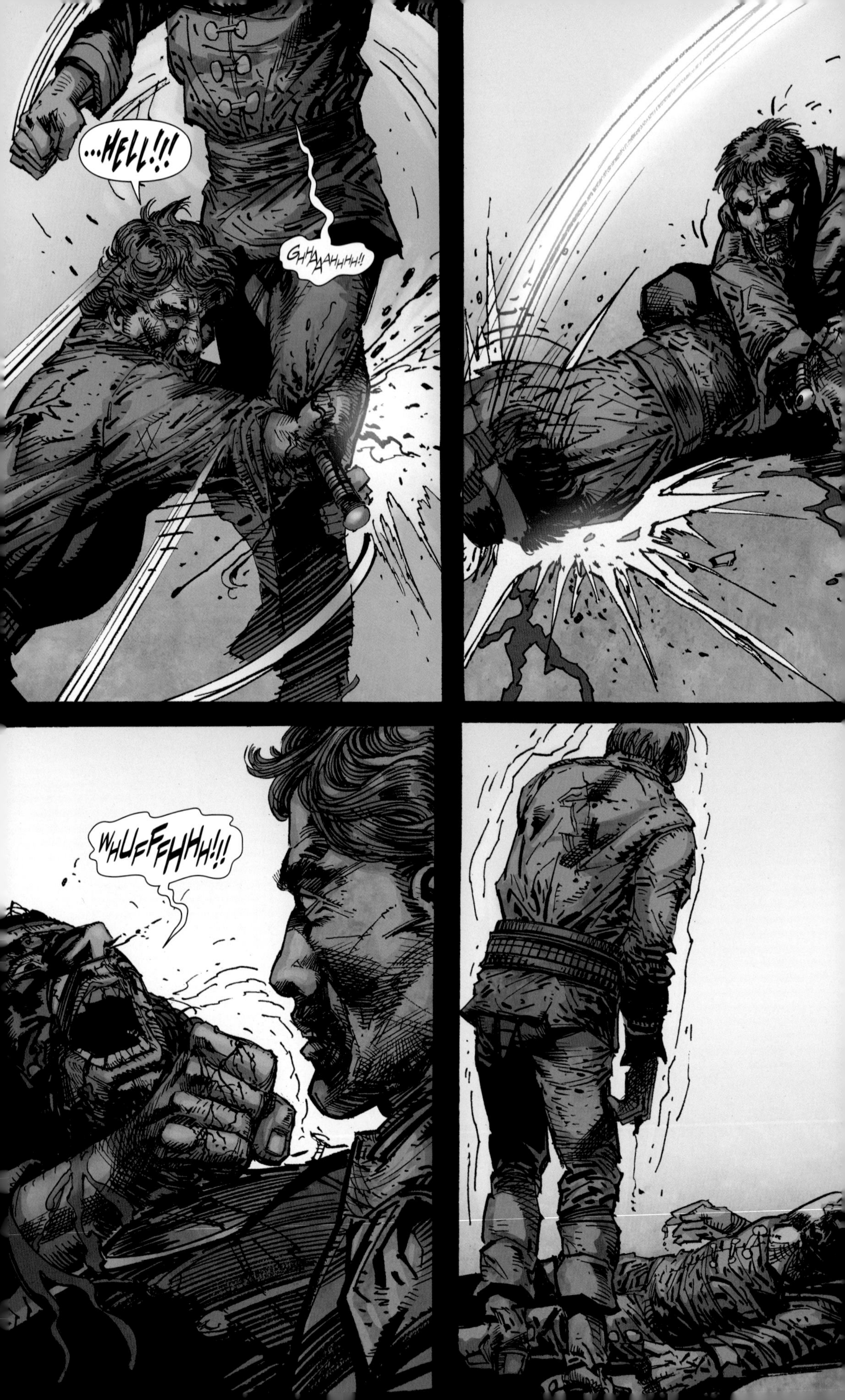
...HELL!!!
GHHAAAHHHH!!
WHUFFHHH!!!

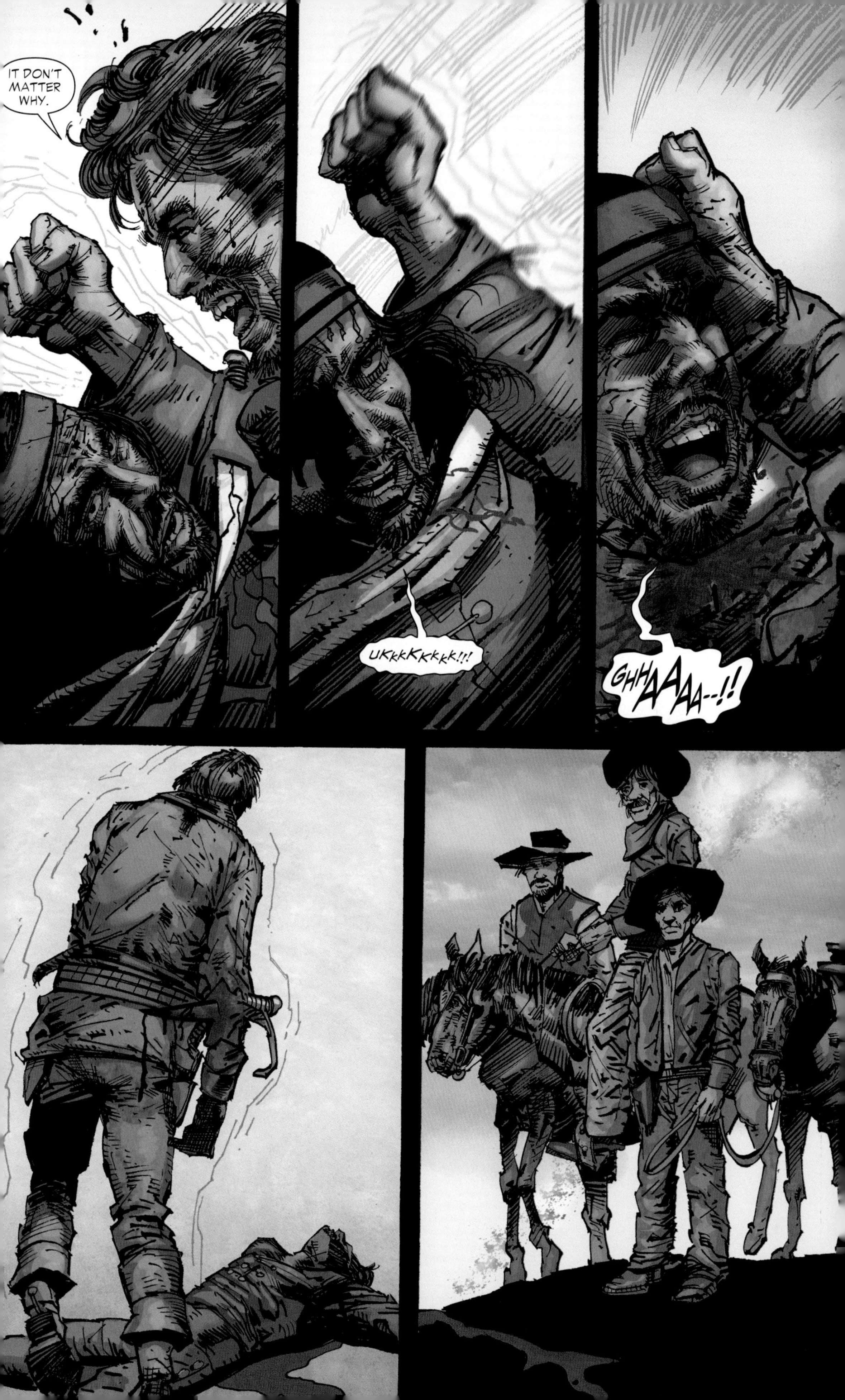
IT DON'T MATTER WHY.
UKKKKKKKK!!!
GHHAAAA--!!

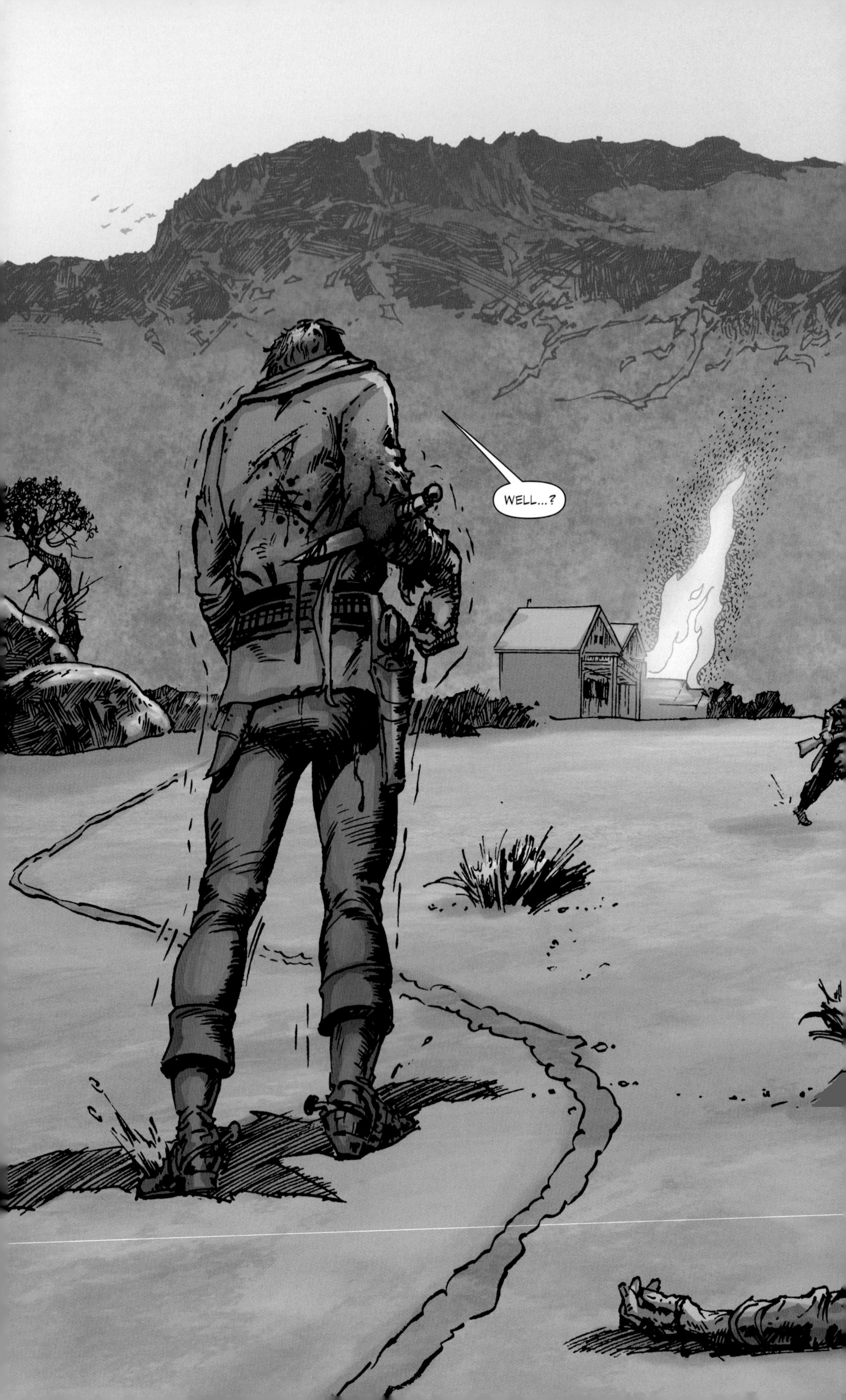
WELL...?

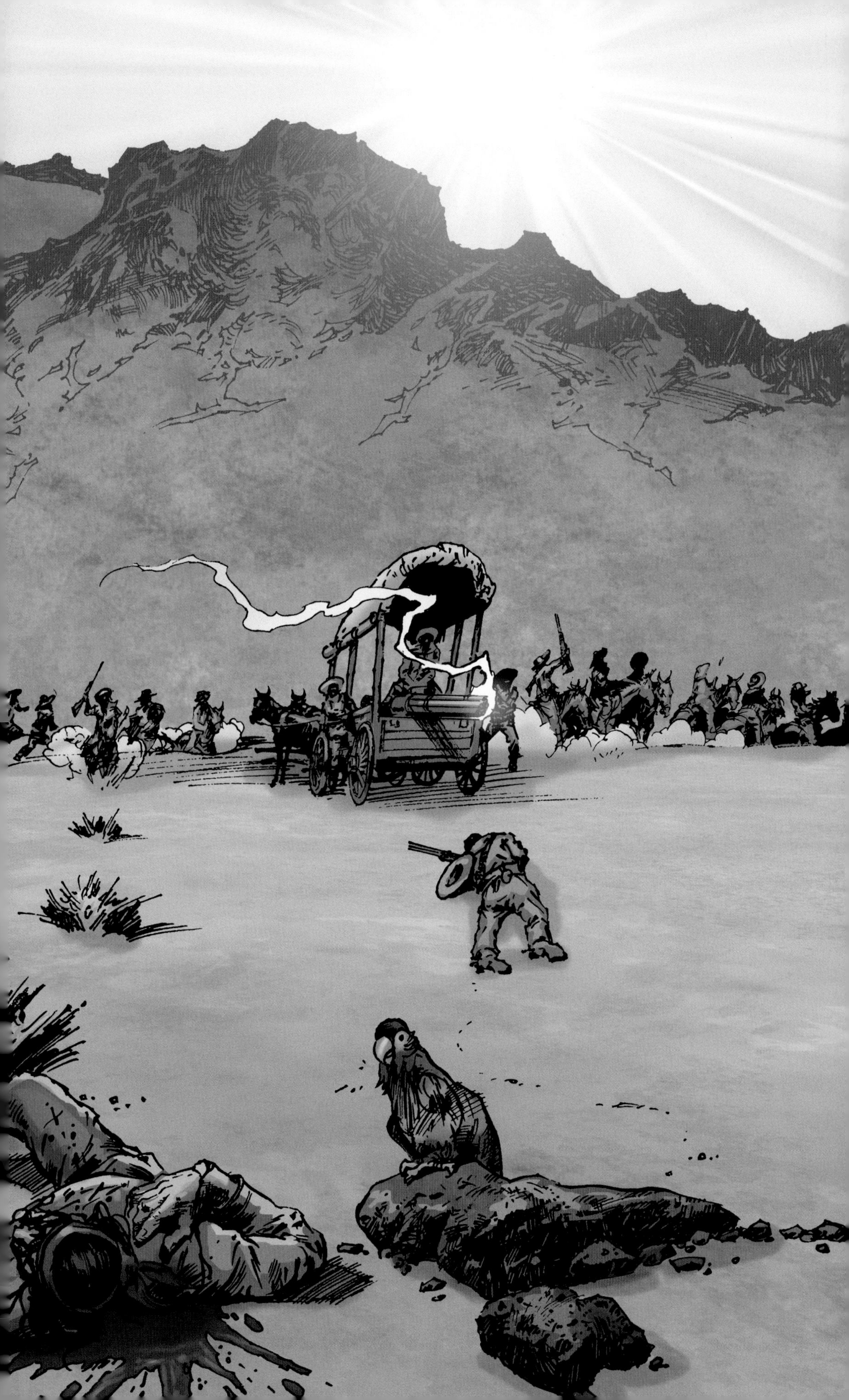

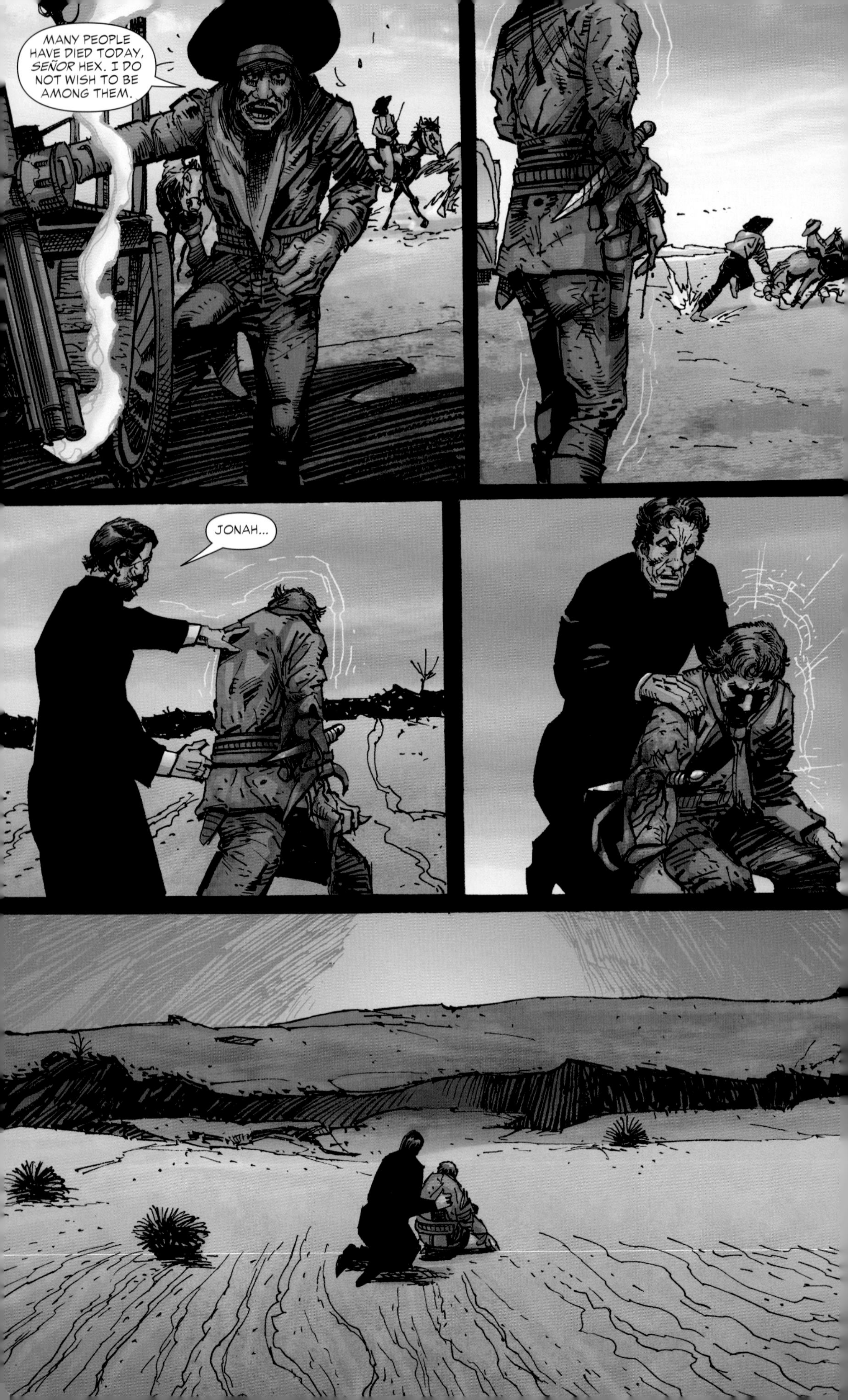
MANY PEOPLE HAVE DIED TODAY, SEÑOR HEX. I DO NOT WISH TO BE AMONG THEM.
JONAH...

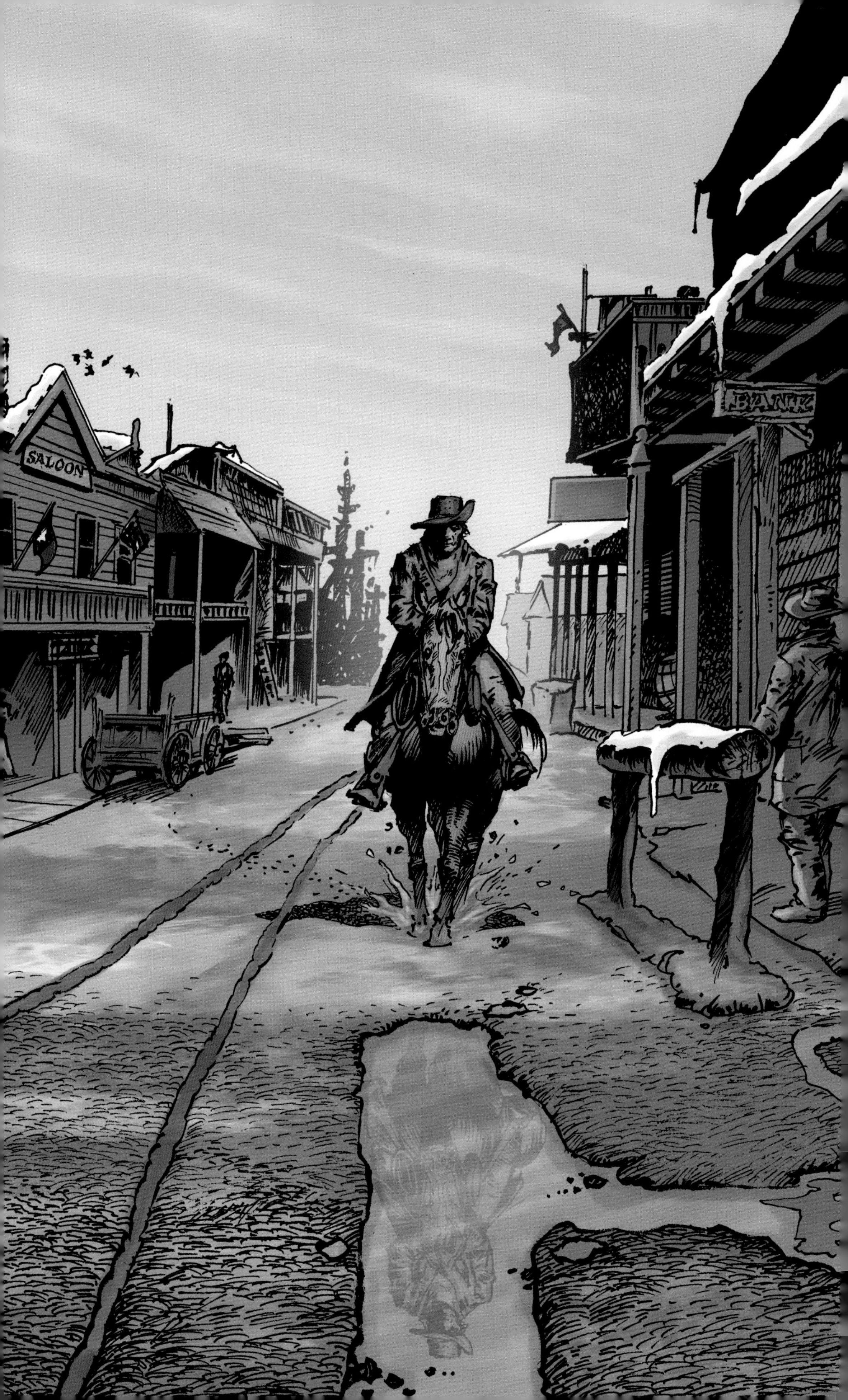
SALOON
BANK

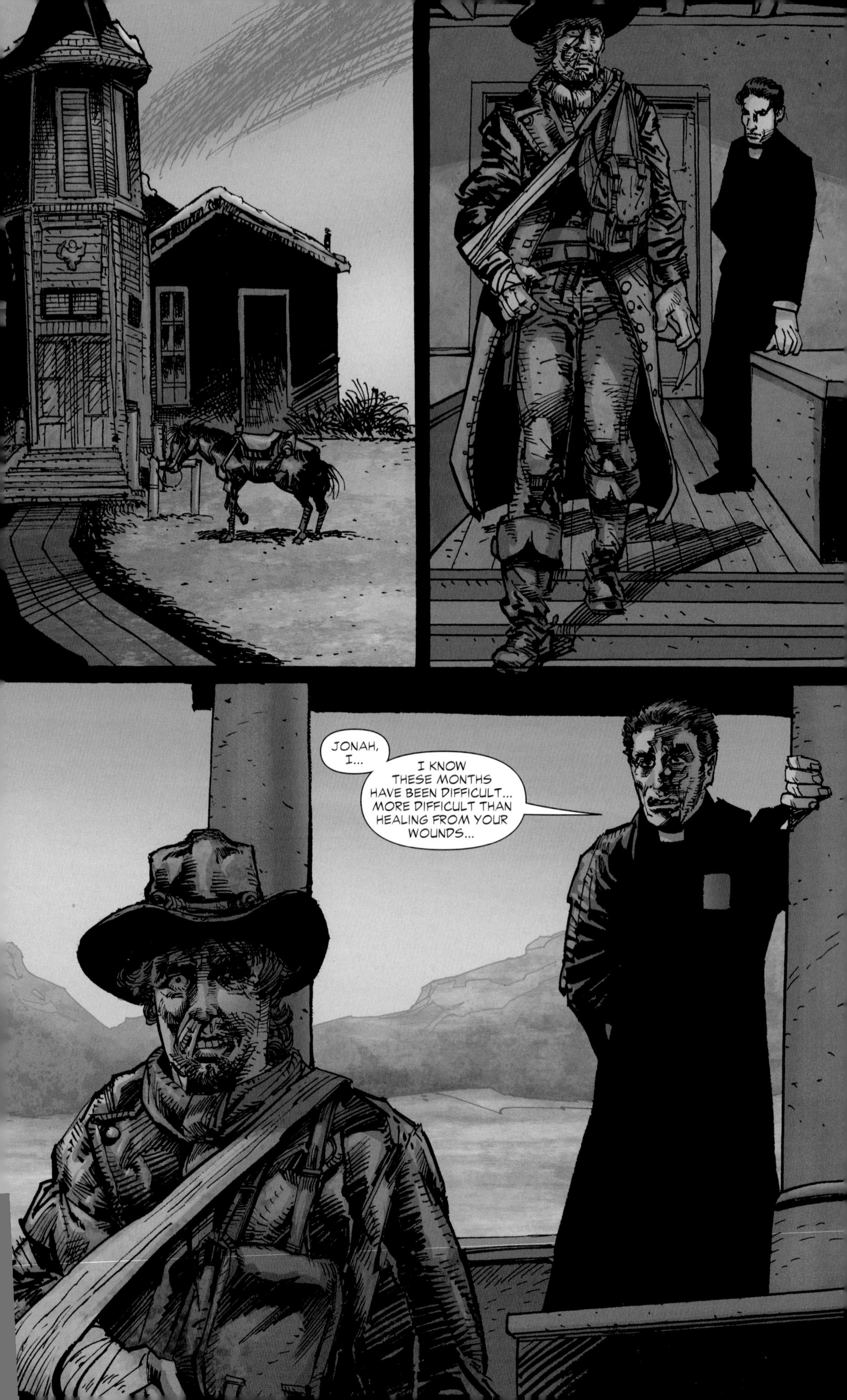
JONAH, I...
I KNOW THESE MONTHS HAVE BEEN DIFFICULT... MORE DIFFICULT THAN HEALING FROM YOUR WOUNDS...

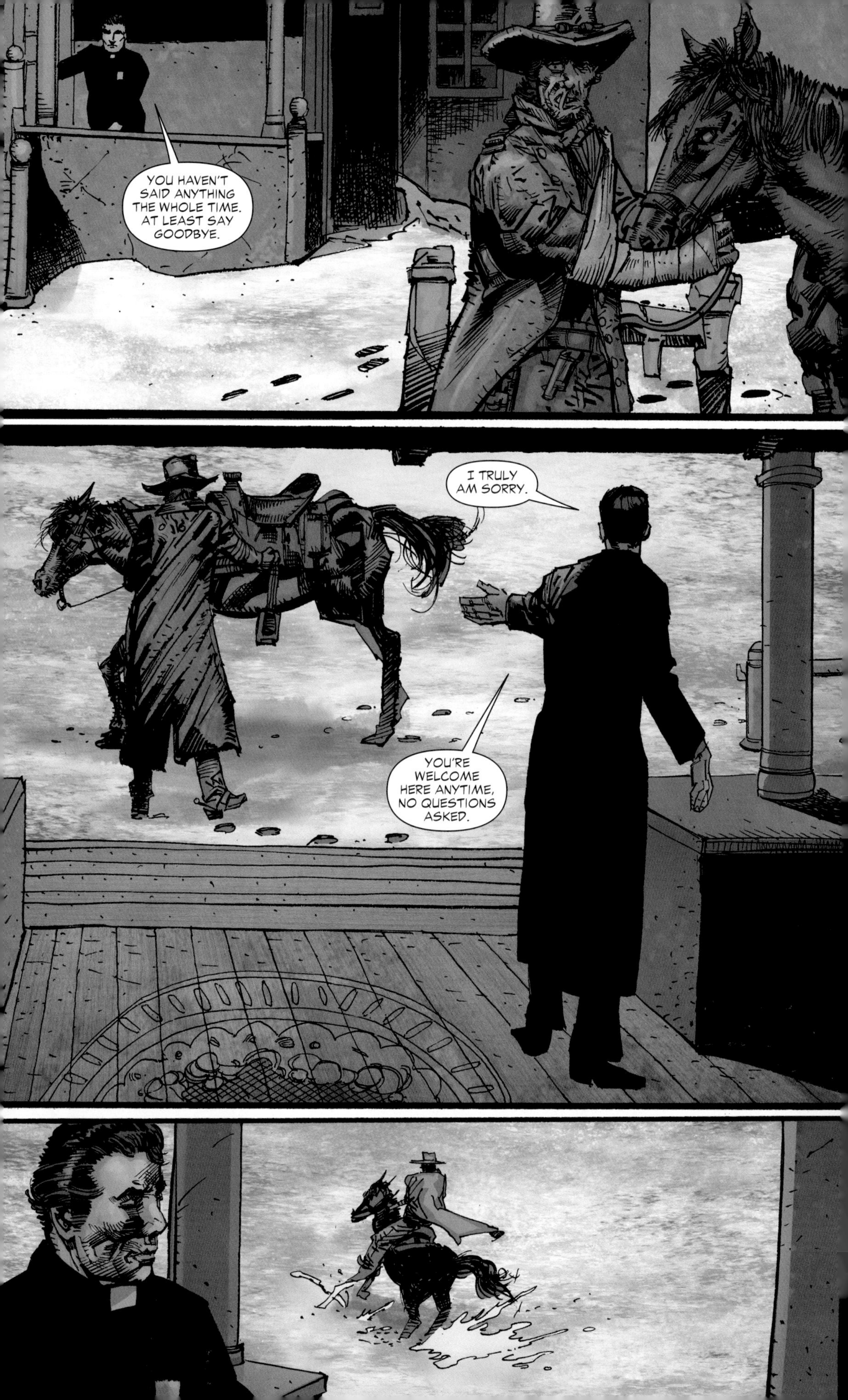
YOU HAVEN'T SAID ANYTHING THE WHOLE TIME. AT LEAST SAY GOODBYE.
I TRULY AM SORRY.
YOU'RE WELCOME HERE ANYTIME, NO QUESTIONS ASKED.

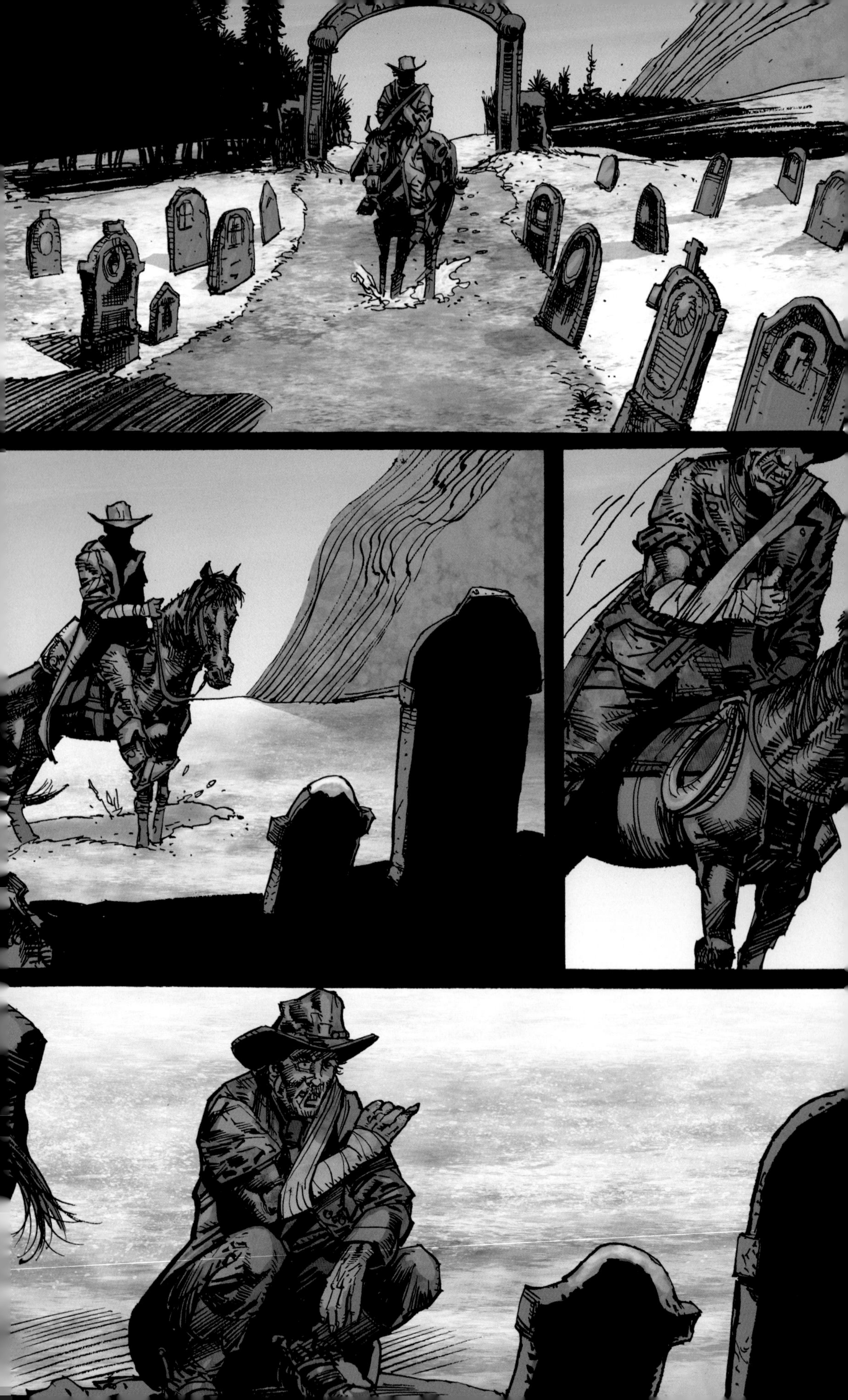

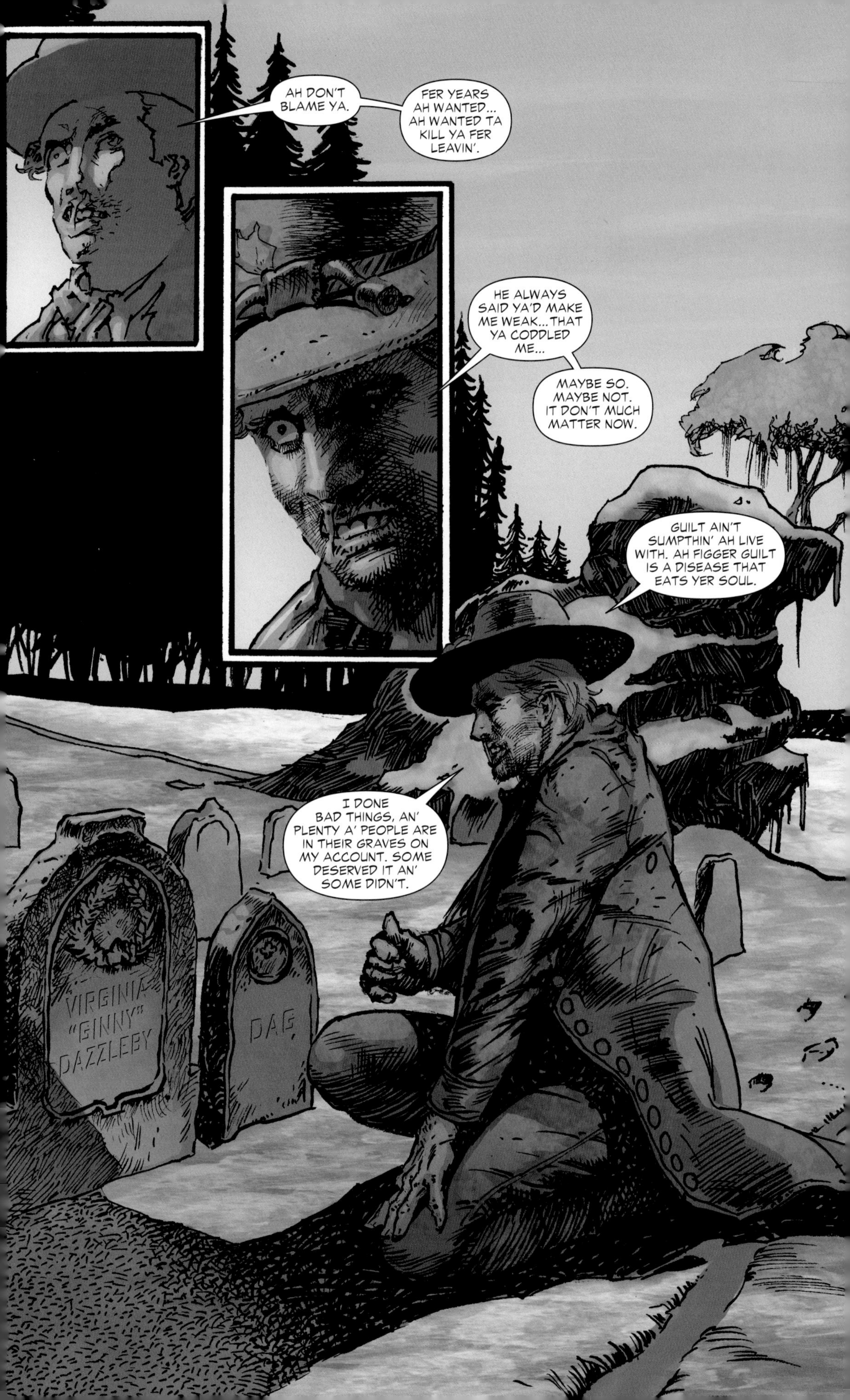
AH DON'T BLAME YA.
FER YEARS AH WANTED... AH WANTED TA KILL YA FER LEAVIN'.
HE ALWAYS SAID YA'D MAKE ME WEAK...THAT YA CODDLED ME...
MAYBE SO. MAYBE NOT. IT DON'T MUCH MATTER NOW.
GUILT AIN'T SUMPTHIN' AH LIVE WITH. AH FIGGER GUILT IS A DISEASE THAT EATS YER SOUL.
I DONE BAD THINGS, AN' PLENTY A' PEOPLE ARE IN THEIR GRAVES ON MY ACCOUNT. SOME DESERVED IT AN' SOME DIDN'T.
VIRGINIA "GINNY" DAZZLEBY
DAG

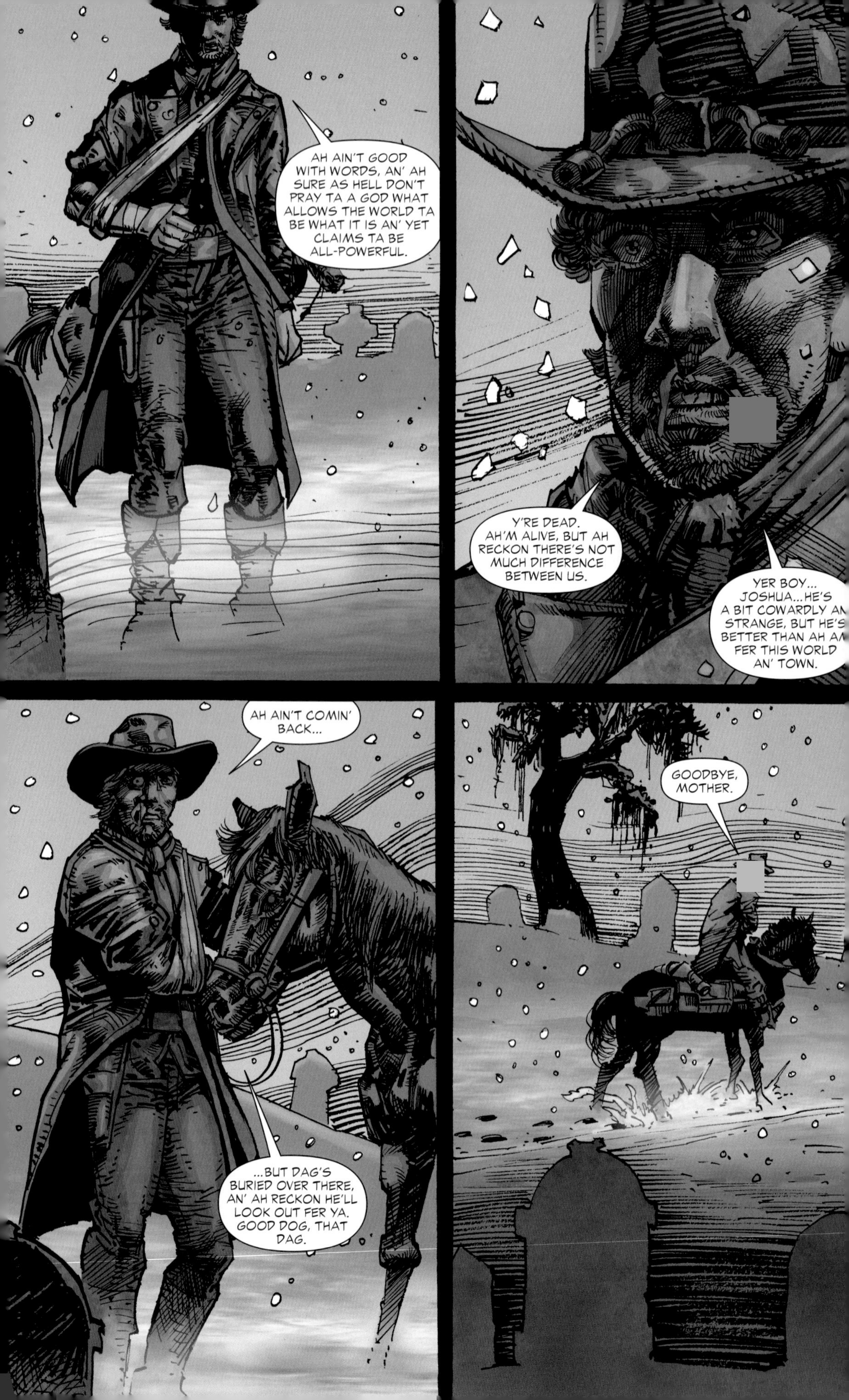
AH AIN'T GOOD WITH WORDS, AN' AH SURE AS HELL DON'T PRAY TA A GOD WHAT ALLOWS THE WORLD TA BE WHAT IT IS AN' YET CLAIMS TA BE ALL-POWERFUL.
Y'RE DEAD. AH'M ALIVE, BUT AH RECKON THERE'S NOT MUCH DIFFERENCE BETWEEN US.
YER BOY... JOSHUA...HE'S A BIT COWARDLY AN STRANGE, BUT HE'S BETTER THAN AH AM FER THIS WORLD AN' TOWN.
AH AIN'T COMIN' BACK...
...BUT DAG'S BURIED OVER THERE, AN' AH RECKON HE'LL LOOK OUT FER YA. GOOD DOG, THAT DAG.
GOODBYE, MOTHER.

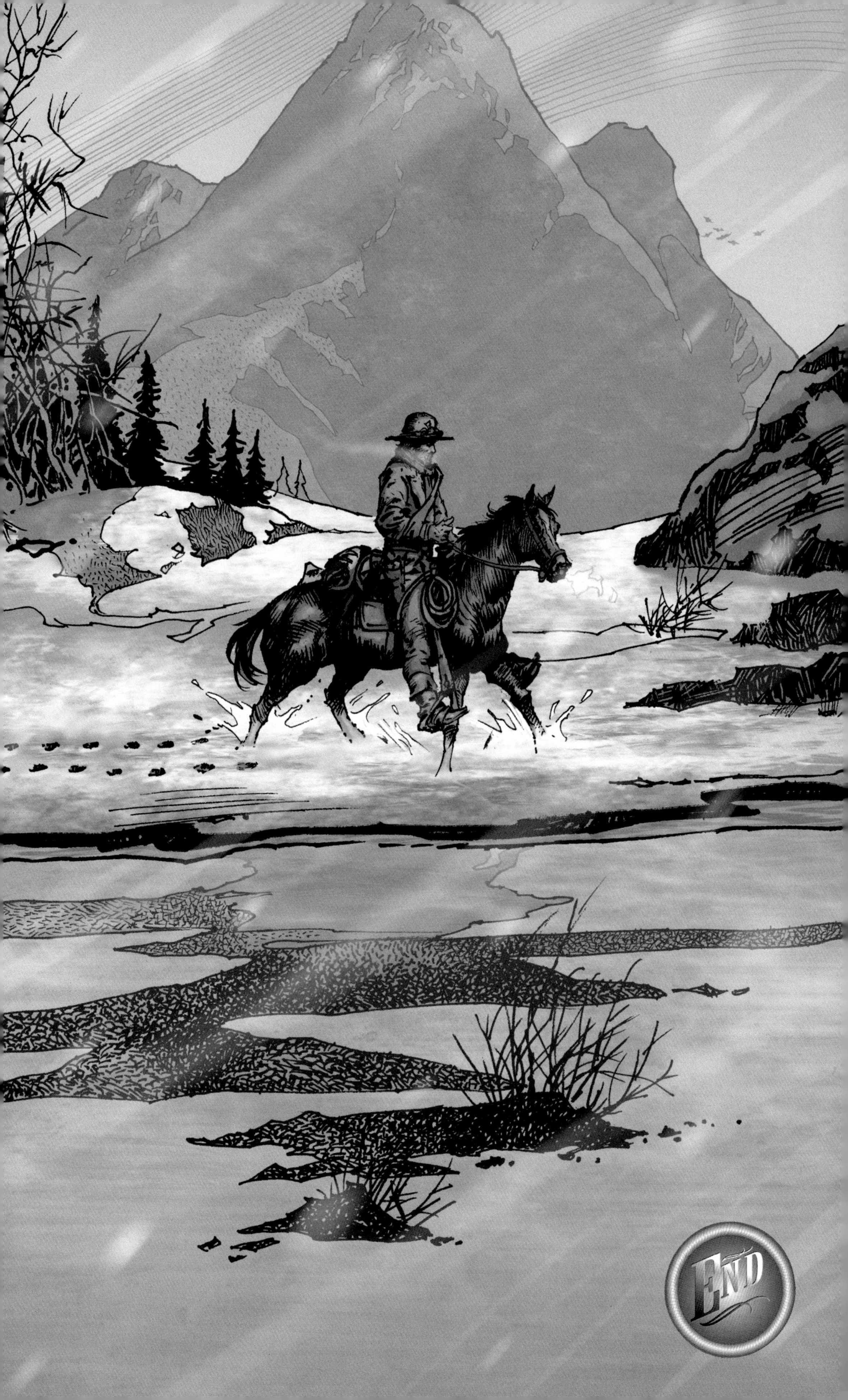
END

The End

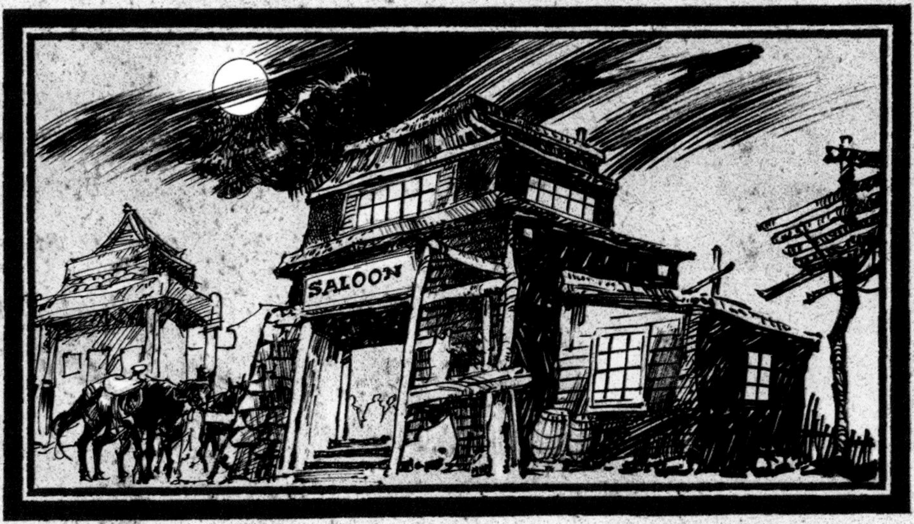
SALOON

Born in the Philippines, **Tony DeZuniga** was already an established artist in Filipino comics when he began drawing for DC Comics in the late 1960s. After working on DC romance and mystery titles, he illustrated the first adventure of Jonah Hex in 1972. He continued to bring his distinctive style to comics for both DC and Marvel, drawing the adventures of Conan the Barbarian, Spider-Man, The X-Men, The Hulk and many others, as well as providing art for projects from Scholastic, McGraw-Hill and Sega. JONAH HEX: NO WAY BACK marks DeZuniga's return to the Western anti-hero.

Justin Gray has collaborated with Jimmy Palmiotti on dozens of comics titles including THE MONOLITH, TERRA and POWER GIRL. He has also written for animation (*Speed Racer: The Next Generation*) and video games.

Jimmy Palmiotti has written a wide range of comics such as *Painkiller Jane* and *Back to Brooklyn*, including several collaborations with Justin Gray on such titles as POWER GIRL, UNCLE SAM AND THE FREEDOM FIGHTERS and JONAH HEX. In addition, Palmiotti has moved beyond the printed page, co-scripting the Midway video game Mortal Kombat vs. DC Universe.

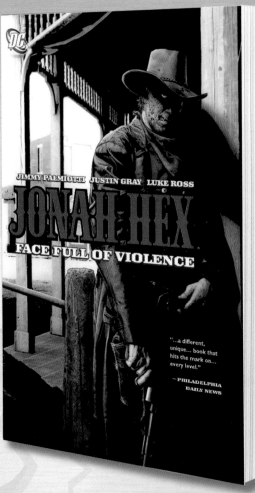
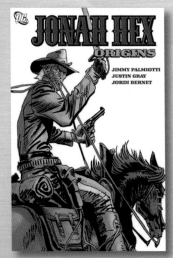
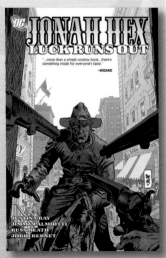
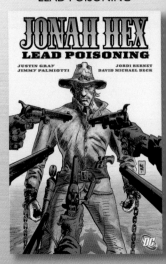